IMAGES of America

AROUND MORRISTOWN

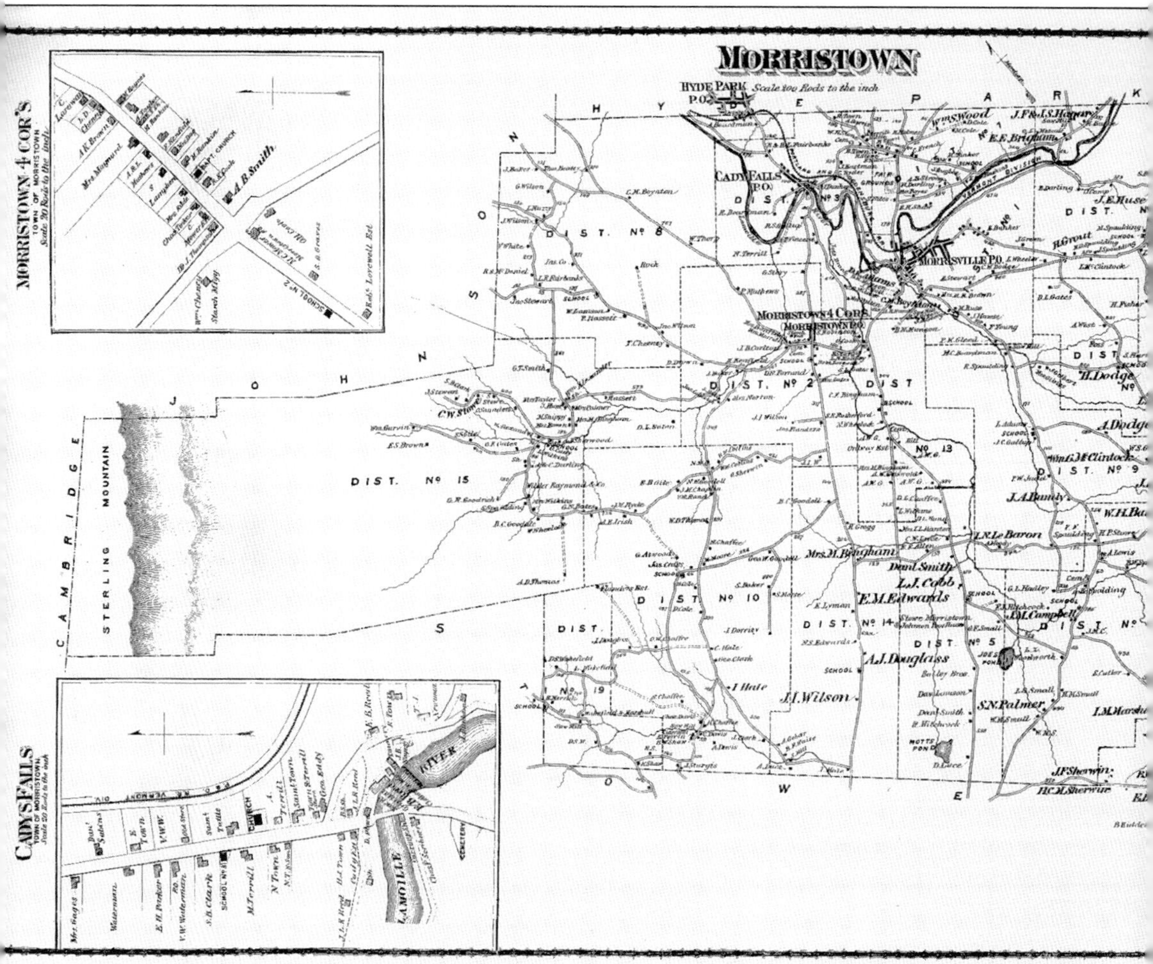

A Map of Morristown. This map shows the numbered districts of Morristown and the names of landowners. It has a scale of 200 rods to the inch. It is from the *1878 Atlas of Lamoille and Orleans Counties*, by F.W. Beers Company.

Dedicated to the fine photographers who recorded these images,

and by doing so, preserved the people, places, and ways of life

that would have otherwise been lost forever.

IMAGES
of America

AROUND MORRISTOWN

Shaun C. Bryer

ARCADIA
PUBLISHING

ISBN 978-0-7385-0923-5

Published by Arcadia Publishing
Charleston, South Carolina

Printed in the United States of America

Library of Congress Catalog Card Number: 2001092299

For all general information contact Arcadia Publishing at:
Telephone 843-853-2070
Fax 843-853-0044
E-Mail sales@arcadiapublishing.com
For customer service and orders:
Toll-Free 1-888-313-2665

Visit us on the Internet at www.arcadiapublishing.com

On the cover: **THE MORRISVILLE BOARD OF TRADE, 1906.** On September 28, 1906, members of the Morrisville Board of Trade met in front of the Randall Hotel with their automobiles. Their task was to examine the electric railway connection that ran from the Stowe terminal of the Mount Mansfield Electric Railroad to and through Morrisville and to follow the line north as far as Newport.

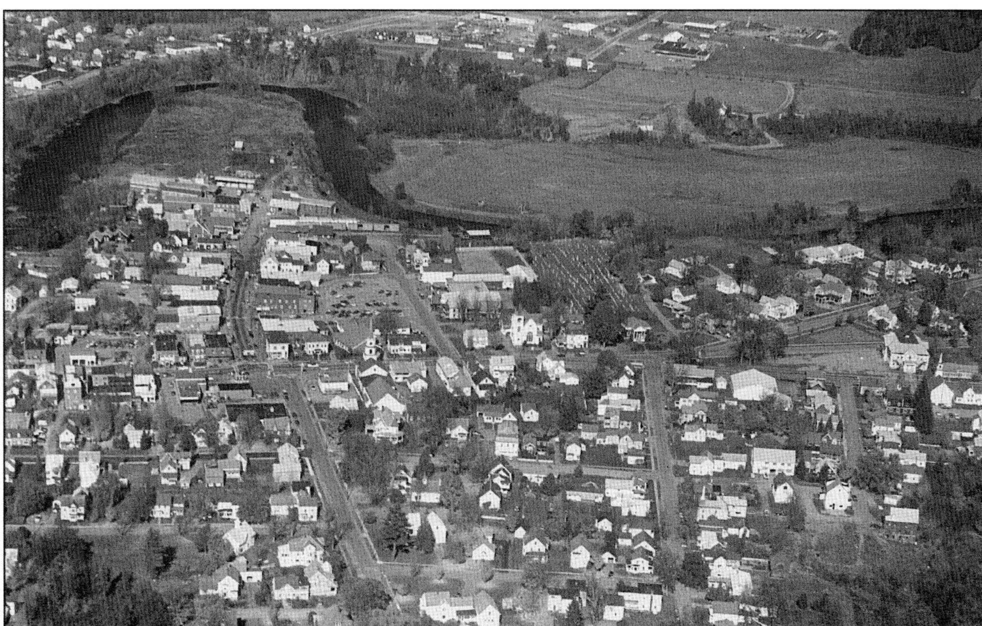

AN AERIAL VIEW. Morrisville, the central, most settled part of Morristown, is seen in this 20th-century aerial view, taken looking northward.

CONTENTS

ACKNOWLEDGMENTS

I wish to thank all who provided images, quotations, or historical information, and those who provided much encouragement and support during my months of work on this book. I truly could not have done it without you.

Andy Bourdeau
Douglas and Cynthia Bryer
Robert L. Hagerman
Ryan Haney
Phyllis Jewett
Ned Lang and the Stowe Historical Society
Mike Leonard
Bill Lizotte
Cathy Mander-Adams
Mary Sanders Mitchell
Ruth Reed
Cricket Smith and the Elmore Historical Society
Kevin P. Thomas
Village Photographer
Marguerite Woods

Most importantly, thanks to the Morristown Historical Society for allowing me to select the many fine images from their extensive collection at the Noyes House Museum.

I also wish to acknowledge the following sources from which information was taken for the writing of this book.

Willard K. Sander's *A Brief History of the Town of Morristown, Vermont* (1974)
Anna L. Mower's *History of Morristown, Vermont* (1935)
Robert L. Hagerman's *More About Morristown* (1982)
Robert L. Hagerman's *First Draft of More About Morristown* (1982)
Roberta F. Powers's *George M. Powers: A Biography* (1989)
Lamoille County Centennial Commission's *Lamoille County Centennial Celebration* (1936)
Green Mountain Yearbook Association's *Morrisville Vermont* (1931)
Lamoille County Weekly's May 17 edition (1976)
William P. Neal's *Molly: Squaw of Indian Joe* and *Indian Joe: The Friendly Indian Guide* (1976)
William H. Jeffrey's *Successful Vermonters of Lamoille, Franklin and Grand Isle Counties* (1907)
Oread Literary Club's *History of Johnson, Vermont* (1961)
Town of Hyde Park's *Hyde Park – Vermont: Shire Town of Lamoille County* (1976)
Edwin L. Bigelow's *Stowe Vermont: Ski Capital of the East 1763–1963* (1964)
Esther M. Swift's *Vermont Place-Names* (1977)
National Survey's *Gazetteer of Vermont Heritage (1966)*

INTRODUCTION

Let's start at the very beginning and, as all good stories begin . . .

Once upon a time . . . during Vermont's early tumultuous years, the General Assembly began granting land that was not occupied in an effort to raise an army and establish the funds to maintain it. This went directly against the resolutions that Congress had passed in 1779 and was considered a violation. The leaders of the Green Mountain Republic were asked to put an end to these actions. It was during these times that Dr. Moses Morse of Worthington, Massachusetts, prepared a printed form of petition to the General Assembly for a land grant. If the House made the grant, it then had to be accepted by the Governor and Council, who would name the grantees and the terms of the charter. On November 6, 1780, the General Assembly of the Independent Republic of Vermont gave Morristown its grant. Gov. Thomas Chittenden issued the town's charter on August 24, 1781.

Geographically, Morristown lies in 72°35' west longitude and 44°32' north latitude. At the time of its charter, Morristown contained 23,040 acres. In October 1788, Morristown's town lines were surveyed under the direction of Ira Allen. Morristown gained 6,252 acres of land after receiving a large portion of the former town of Sterling in 1855, as well as an exchange of land with the town of Hyde Park in 1896.

During the spring of 1790, Morristown gained its first settler. Jacob Walker, a surveyor from Bennington, was hired by Joseph Hinsdale, one of Morristown's Massachusetts proprietors, to survey lots. Walker took his payment in land and built a log cabin, at the age of 24, on what would later become the road from Waterbury to Hyde Park, which passed through Morristown's geographic center. He brought his brother and family, as well as two hired men who lived with him. In 1792, Comfort Olds arrived with his family. Many of Morristown's earliest residents came from Morse's hometown of Worthington, Massachusetts, and its surrounding towns. However, Morse died in 1783, prior to the town's settlement. In 1794, his son, Samuel Morse, arrived to inspect the township and deeded lots to his two grandsons, neither of whom ever moved to Morristown. The origin of the name Morristown has been heavily debated. It is possible that it is a modification of Morsestown.

By 1795, there were enough settlers to justify the creation of a town government. Olds was appointed the town clerk, and the first town meetings were held. It was during these early days in Morristown's center that a small, optimistic community began to spring up. A tavern that held the first school was built, a town house followed shortly thereafter, and a brick church that was shared by Congregationalists and Baptists was built *c.* 1800.

During the early years of the 19th century, there arose a movement in Morristown and the neighboring towns to form a new county. Morristown seemed to be in full support of this; however, there was some major opposition in the neighboring towns of Stowe and Elmore. A petition signed by 234 delegates was presented to the State Legislature in 1834. Fifty-nine of the delegates were from Morristown. The petition stated that a new county must be formed because of the distance to the various county seats, the natural situation of the territory to which the towns belonged, and the inconveniences involved in obtaining rights and immunities. After being fought through five sessions of the Legislature, the tiny county of Lamoille was formed and incorporated on October 26, 1835, thanks to a 108 to 80 vote. It was the smallest of the 14 counties and contained only 431 square miles. Morristown had originally been a part of Rutland County, and then Chittenden County, and later Orleans County. A committee was formed to choose the county seat, as the towns did not agree. The southern part of the county wanted Johnson to be the county seat, and the northern part wanted Morristown. As somewhat of a compromise, the town of Hyde Park was chosen. The county buildings were built and in December 1836, the court convened there. In 1828, part of the Lamoille County township of Sterling was annexed to Cambridge and later, in 1855, the Legislature abolished the town. Its remaining land was divided among Johnson, Stowe, and Morristown. Since then, Lamoille County has maintained 10 towns.

As early as 1798, a few people, including Dr. James Tinker, started settling on a "level plain to the south of the center." John Safford and his family settled there; he built Morristown's first sawmill and gristmill on the Lamoille River and a home for his family. After he died in 1813, his son, Jedediah Safford, took over the mill operations. Village meetings soon began at a newly constructed town house, and the bulbs that would bear Morrisville's roots had been planted. The early village settlement consisted mainly of High Street and Main Street; however, houses were also scattered in other areas. Morrisville was not Morristown's only outlying settlement. Cadys Falls was another. Morrisville, however, was by far Morristown's most successful and fastest growing outlying settlement. Morrisville soon became the center of a brisk lumber trade, which was fostered by mills that had sprung up and were now scattered throughout the town. In 1872, it emerged as a shipping point for agricultural products. Later, the arrival of the Portland & Ogdensburg Railroad helped solidify the growing predominance of the new village.

The mid-1800s spelled the eventual end of Morristown's bustling center at Morristown Corners and the incorporation of the village of Morrisville in 1888. Here, the story must be interrupted, as this is far from the end. In fact, it is just the very beginning.

When the idea of writing a photographic history book was planted in my mind several years ago, I never thought that it would become a reality so quickly. Thanks to the help of many who inspired me to "go for it" and not to give up, I was able to complete this book. I made the decision to organize the book in a chronological manner and to concentrate on the shift to the village, change, growth, prosperity, and new development that has helped Morristown become, as resident Lucy LeRiche once said, "the heartbeat of the county." I made the decision not simply to focus on Morristown's early days but to follow Morristown's growth up to the present day. I have also included historical accounts of Morristown's neighbors, which all in some way have helped influence what Morristown has become and have contributed to the betterment of life in Lamoille County.

This book is an invitation, an invitation for you to relax and explore the Morristown of yesterday. *Around Morristown* was written to be your guide, and I hope that it will spark discussions, stories, and will stir up previously forgotten memories in those of you who were young during those very times. It is also my hope that it will be used as a tool by parents and teachers to share Morristown's wonderful history with tomorrow's generation. It is quite a privilege to be able to take an ever-so-small glimpse into the past and see what it would have been like to live in Morristown throughout the 19th and 20th centuries. It is my dream that you and I and all Morristown residents will discover our roots, share with our children why Morristown is such a great place to live and, despite the constant pressures of our fast-paced society, sustain our spirited and unique family-oriented community throughout the 21st century. I hope that *Around Morristown* will earn a lasting place on the bookshelves of area homes, as well as in the hearts of those, young and old, who call Morristown, or any other Lamoille County town, home. Join me now as we turn back the pages of time and travel down memory lane to explore, through images, the growth and the changes that helped to shape Morristown.

—Shaun C. Bryer

One

THE EARLY DAYS 1790–1930

Long before the advent of photography, Morristown was settled by people of European descent. Much earlier than that, Native Americans inhabited the territory that became the Independent Republic of Vermont. Two of these Native Americans played significant roles during Morristown's earliest days.

Morristown's 1791 census recorded 10 inhabitants, two of whom were Indians by the name of Joe and Molly. Joe was born in Nova Scotia in 1739. After his tribe was almost completely annihilated by the English at the siege of Louisburg, he was brought up by the St. Francis Indians. His squaw, Molly, was a St. Francis Indian. Molly had two sons, Muxa-Wuxal and Toomalek, from a previous marriage. After being forced to leave the St. Francis Indians, Joe and Molly traveled throughout Vermont, fishing and hunting. Joe provided much help to Morristown's early settlers, and for a time he established his wigwam near Morristown on the Lamoille River island called Butternut. It was in Morristown that Molly's son Muxa-Wuxal drowned. Joe and Molly eventually left Morristown and continued their nomad life in Hyde Park, Derby, Danville, and eventually Newbury. Joe and Molly's assistance to the Walkers and other Lamoille County residents was invaluable. The two helped clear land and pointed out good water sources and hunting and fishing places. It is documented that Joe once killed a moose to feed a hungry Walker family.

A Native American proverb says, "Treat the Earth well for it was not given to you by your parents, it was loaned to you by your children. We do not inherit the Earth from our ancestors, we borrow it from our children." It is likely that Indian Joe would offer us those very words.

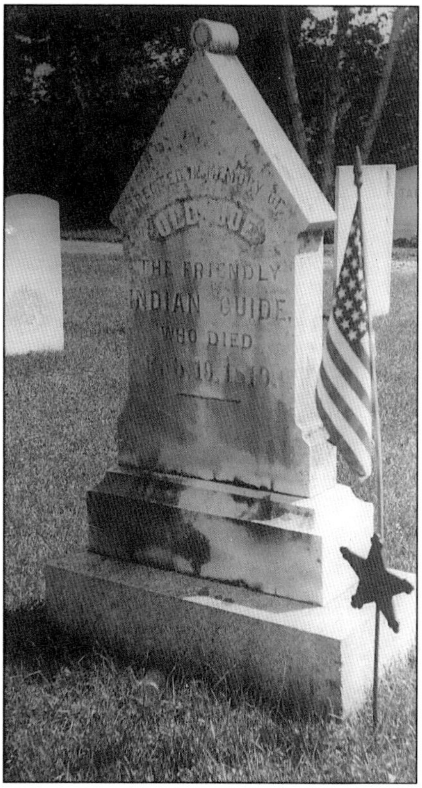

Old Joe, the Friendly Indian Guide, Died 1819. Joe and Molly left for Newbury shortly after John Safford built his sawmill and dam on the Lamoille River. They received state aid for several years. Molly died in 1800. "Old Joe, the Friendly Indian Guide," as his grave reads, died in 1819 at the age of 80. He was buried in the Oxbow Cemetery in Newbury.

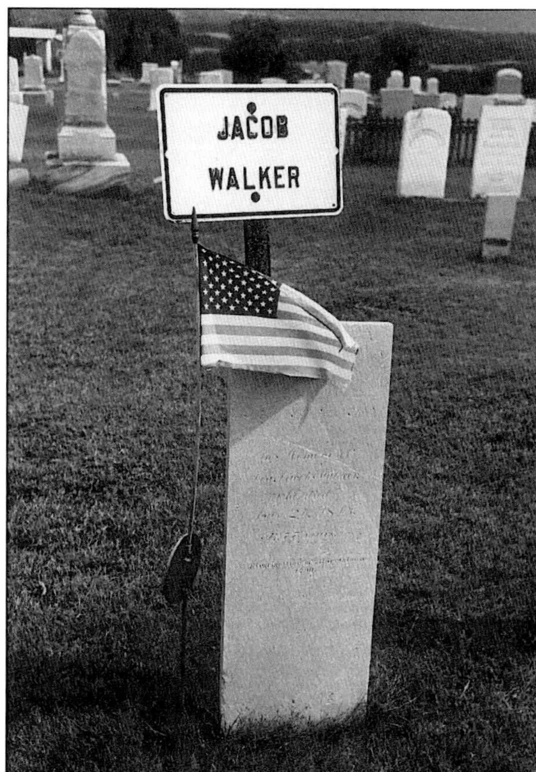

Jacob Walker, 1765–1843. Morristown's first settler, Jacob Walker was born in Brookfield, Massachusetts, on October 20, 1765. In an exchange for land, Walker surveyed the second division of the allotment of land for Morristown's proprietors in 1790. He married Phillipa Story on January 13, 1791. Known as a man of pure character, he is said to have had an incredible faith in God. His final residence was a house on the LaPorte Road. After his death in 1843, he was buried in Mountain View Cemetery.

BOARDMAN'S INN, 1796. Elisha Boardman founded and operated Boardman's Inn, a town house as well as Morristown's first tavern, just up the road from Jacob Walker's log cabin at the town center, Morristown Corners. Boardman, born in 1773 and originally from Canaan, Connecticut, served as Morristown's second town clerk, captain of the 1st Militia, and Morristown's first representative from 1804 to 1808.

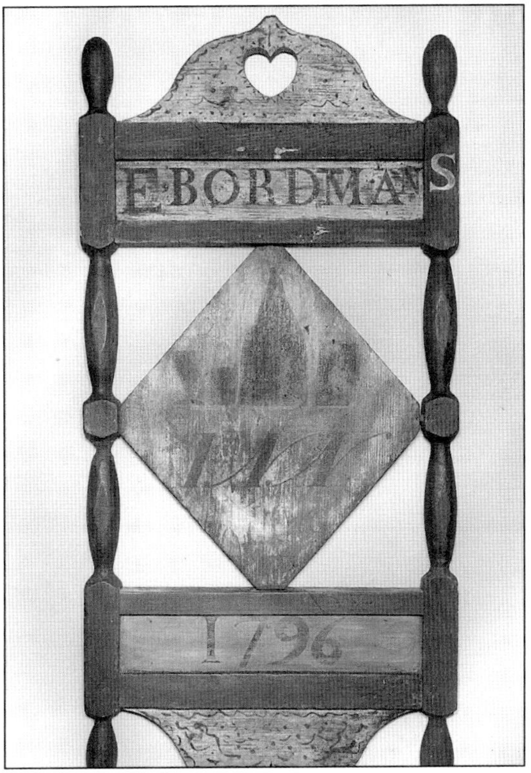

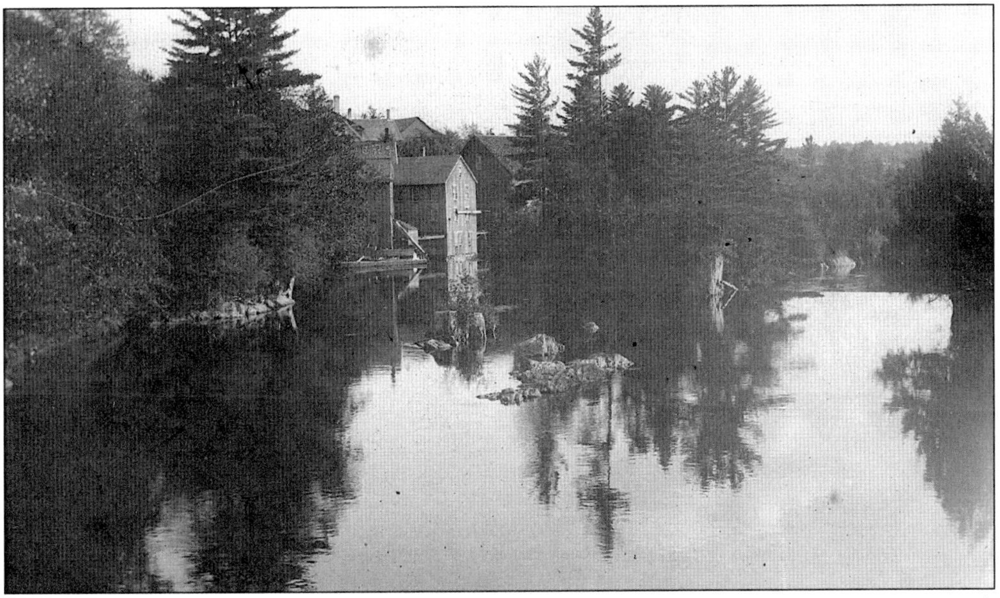

THE LAMOILLE RIVER AND SAFFORD MILLS, MID–1800S. In 1798, John Safford was very much interested in taking advantage of the waterpower that was produced by the Lamoille River. He built the first sawmill in town, along the banks of the Lamoille River in 1798 and, in 1812, built a gristmill. After he died in 1813, his son, Jedediah Safford, took over the mills. The Saffords were among the first settlers to call what later became the village, home. Seen here are the very tops of the mill buildings.

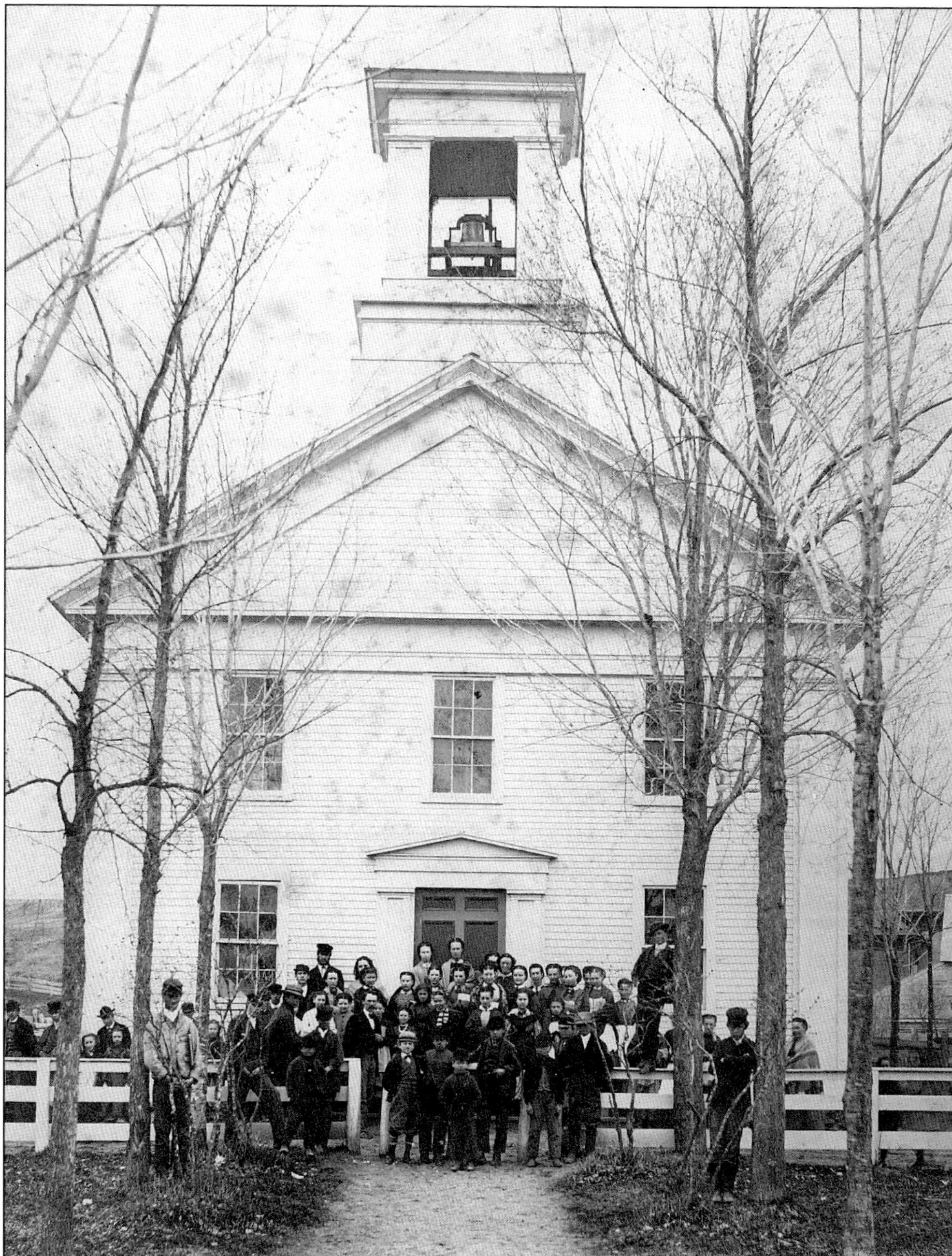

POOR PEOPLES ACADEMY AND MORRISTOWN GRADED BUILDING, 1847. The first Peoples Academy was built by Thomas Tracy in 1847, thanks to its many proprietors, the people of Morristown, many of whom contributed just $1. Ozias C. Pitkin was its first principal. Initially, 36 six men and 48 women came from 11 different towns to attend the institution established in part because of "the interest awakened by the late movements in the cause of education."

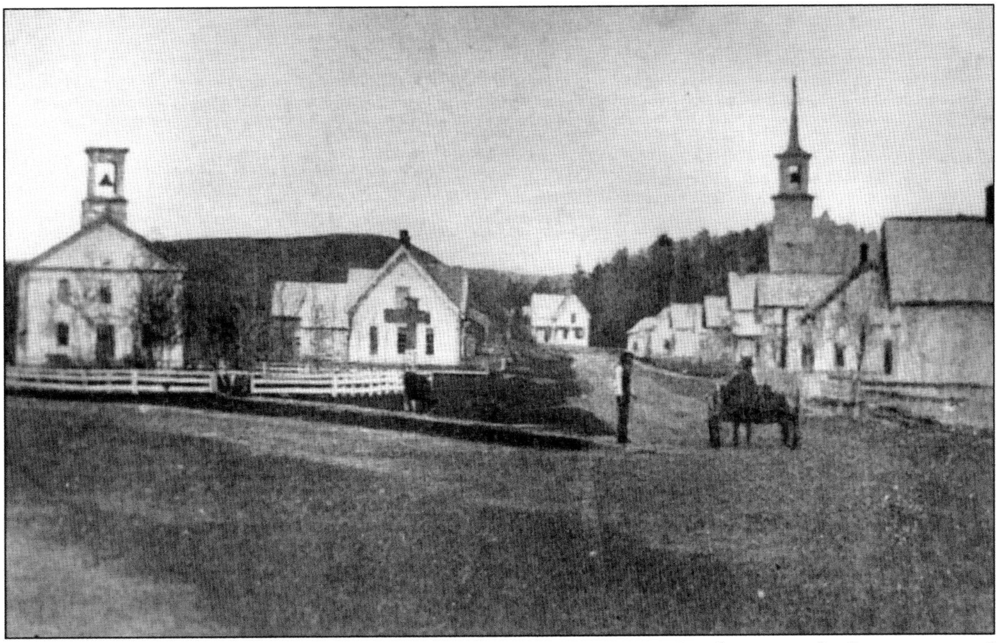

The Intersection of Main And Wolcott Streets, 1860. In this view looking eastward at the intersection of Main Street and Wolcott Street (later named Park Street), Peoples Academy is to the left, with Academy Park in front of the school and the Christian Church to the right.

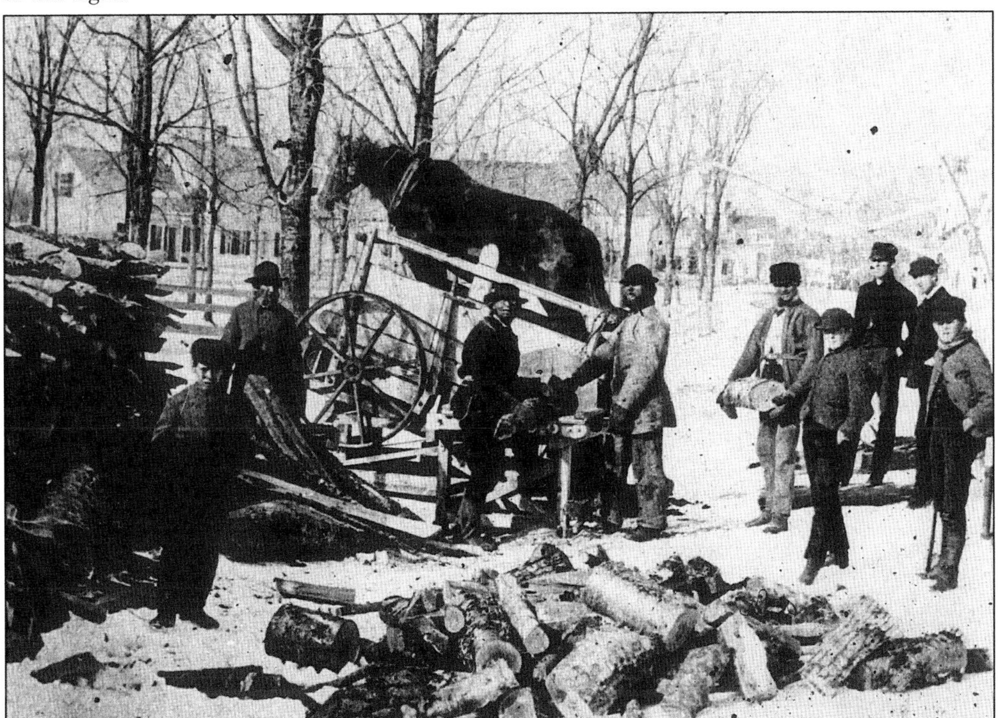

Academy Park, 1870. These unidentified men were photographed sawing wood with a horse treadmill in front of Academy Park in 1870.

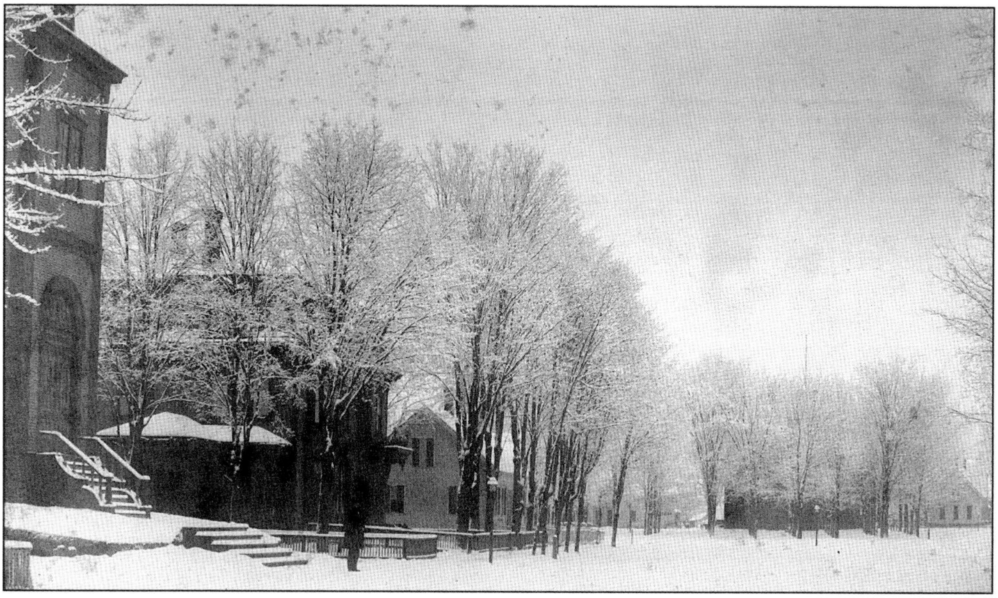

ACADEMY PARK, 1889. Given the name Academy Park thanks to the construction of Peoples Academy, this park had to its left the First Congregational Church, Gov. George W. Hendee's home, and the Hiram Kelsey house. To its right stood the Choate house, which was moved in 1899. The view of Peoples Academy is blocked by snow-covered trees.

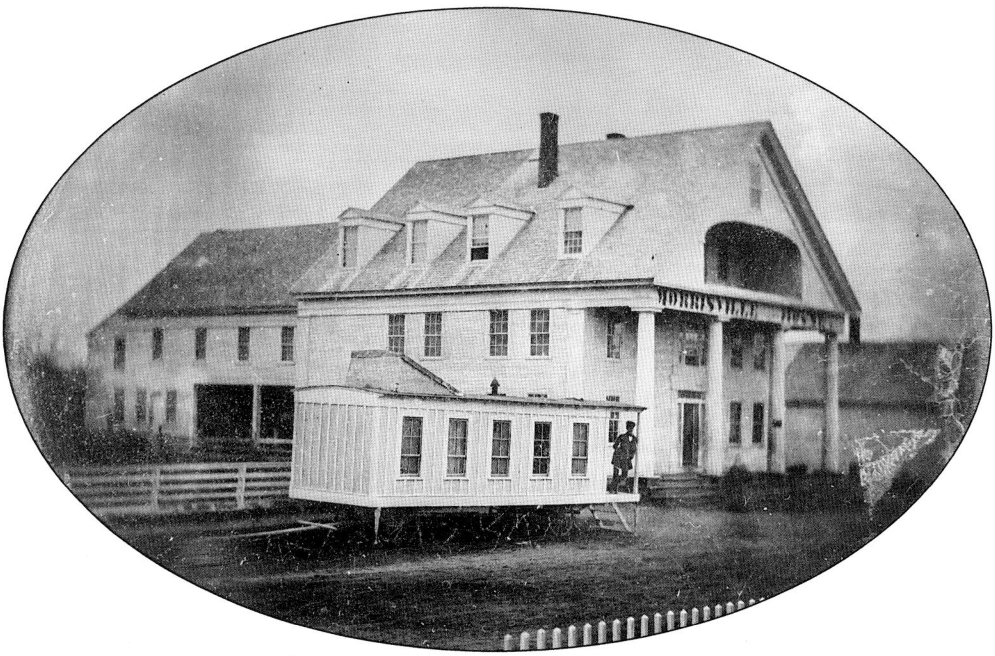

THE MORRISVILLE HOUSE, 1853. F.L. Matthews was proprietor of the Morrisville House and built the public house, owned and managed by Luther Bingham, on what was known as the Porter Block. Built in the new village settlement that was beginning to grow more popular, the Morrisville House was indicative of the new growth and settlement shift that was occurring in Morristown in the mid-1800s. The original Morrisville House burned to the ground in 1879 but was rebuilt shortly afterward, with L.B. Boynton as the new owner.

THE MASONIC LODGE, 1860. Built in 1860 through an appropriation of $150, the Masonic Lodge was built on the grounds of Mr. Gleed's office, located at the intersection of Main and Portland Streets. The Morrisville Post Office was located in this building from 1861 to 1869, when a devastating fire destroyed the lodge. The Masons continued to meet on the second floor of the town hall after the fire.

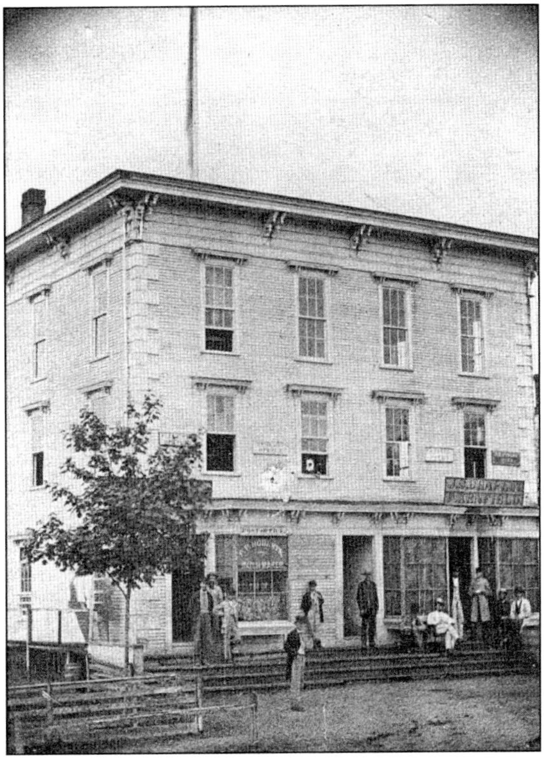

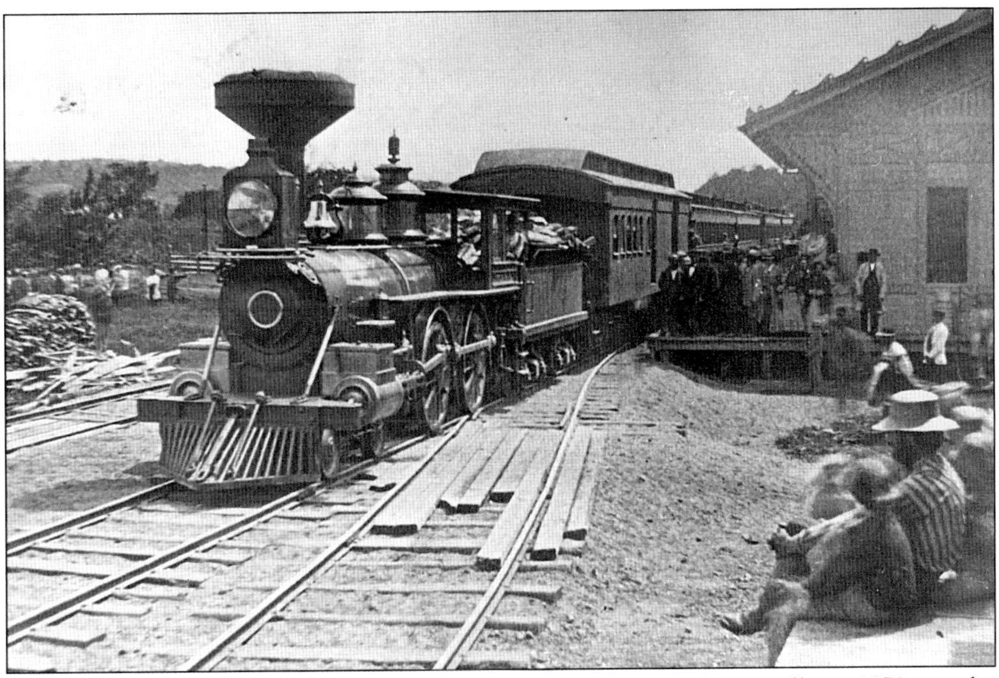

THE LAMOILLE VALLEY RAILROAD COMPANY, 1874. Arriving in Morrisville in 1872 was the Portland & Ogdensburg Railroad. The line was not totally completed until 1877. The arrival of the railroad brought Morrisville yet another modern advancement not present at the original settlement, located at the town center.

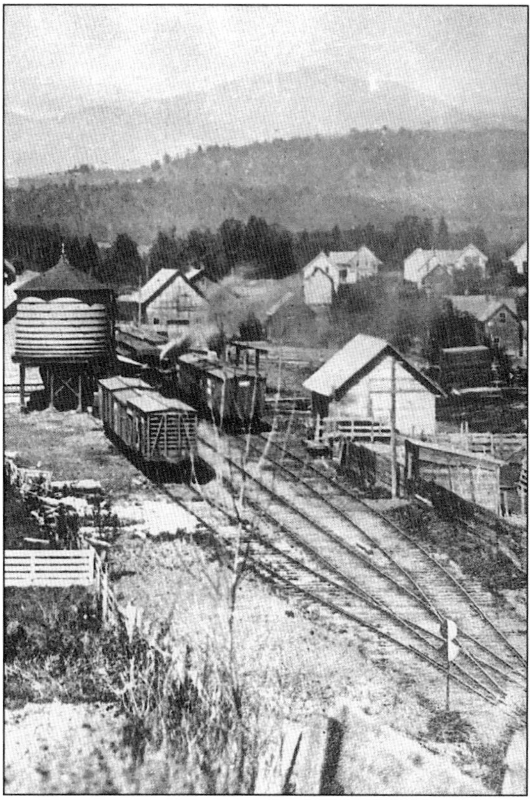

THE ST. JOHNSBURY & LAKE CHAMPLAIN RAILROAD YARD, 1880. This view from Riverside Cemetery shows Morrisville's railroad yard three years after the completion of the line. The railroad brought to Morrisville growth in industry, business, population, and gave Morristown residents easy accessibility to other towns along the line. The newer village had been the trend since before 1840, and with the arrival of the railroad, still more people chose to settle in Morrisville.

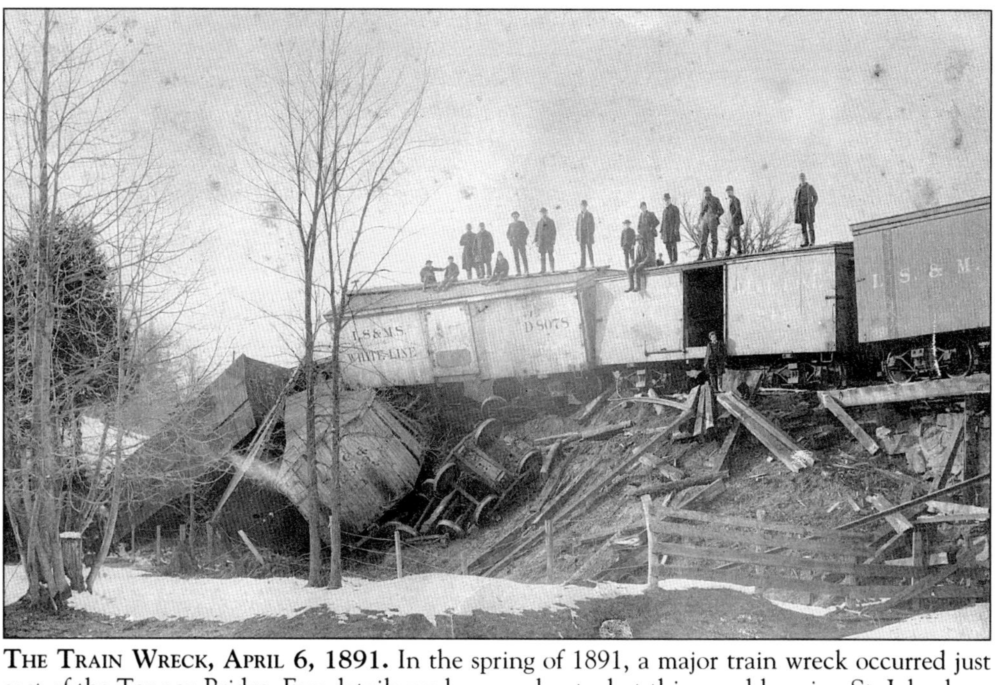

THE TRAIN WRECK, APRIL 6, 1891. In the spring of 1891, a major train wreck occurred just east of the Tenney Bridge. Few details are known about what this wood-burning St. Johnsbury & Lake Champlain Railroad train was carrying on that fateful day.

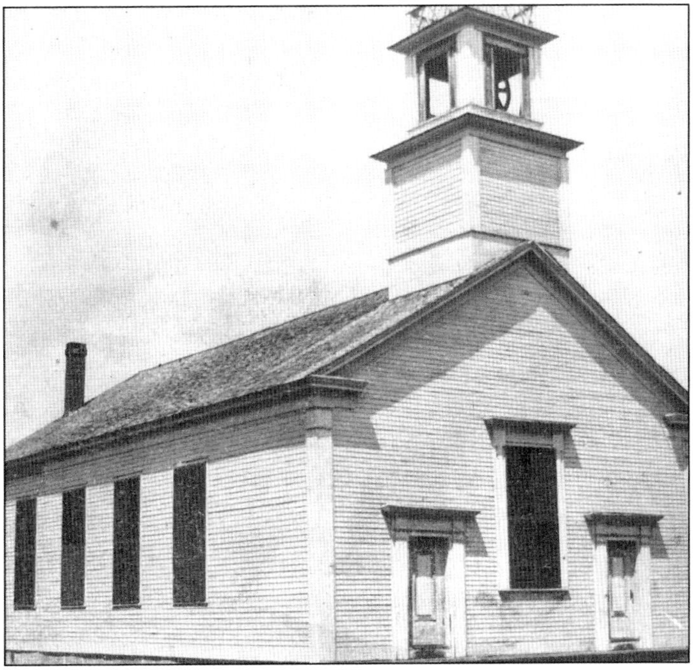

The First Congregational Church, 1873. In 1806, a committee subscribed to the Congregational Society. After sharing a church building at the town center with the Baptists for some 10 years, the Congregational Church shifted its focus to the newly formed village northeast of the center. This church was erected in Morrisville in the 1830s under the leadership of Rev. Septimius Robinson.

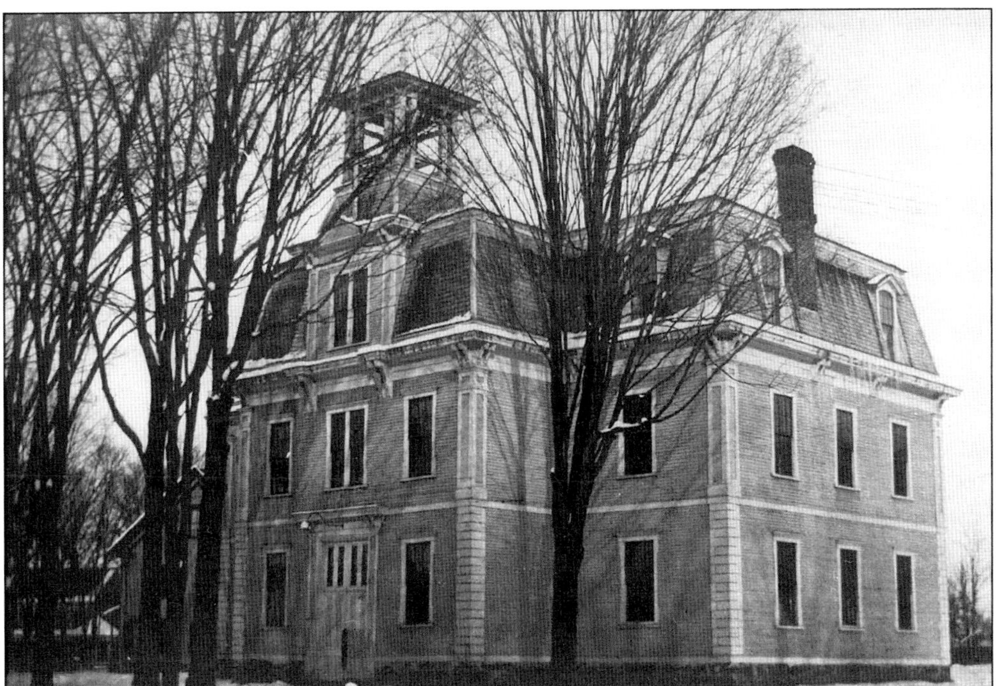

The Second Peoples Academy, 1874. The first Peoples Academy building was moved to Pleasant Street in 1874 to make way for the construction of another, larger Peoples Academy. The three-story building held grade school and the academy in the same structure. Its third floor was used for public exercises and special presentations. A.J. Blanchard was the first principal to serve in the new building.

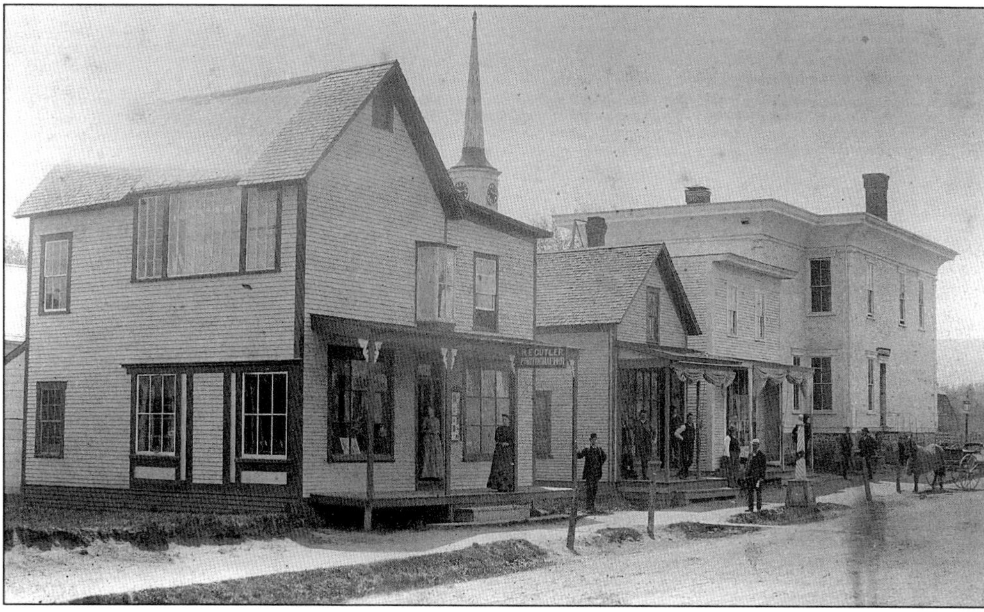

Portland Street, 1890. The east side of Portland Street was home to several businesses, including H.E. Cutler's Photography, a shoe and barbershop, and a small grocery store. The Powers-Gleed Block, later called the Fleetwood Building because of attorney Frederick G. Fleetwood, can be seen at the far right. The building was rebuilt after the devastating fire of 1869. The bottom floor was home to the post office and Amasa O. Gates's drugstore.

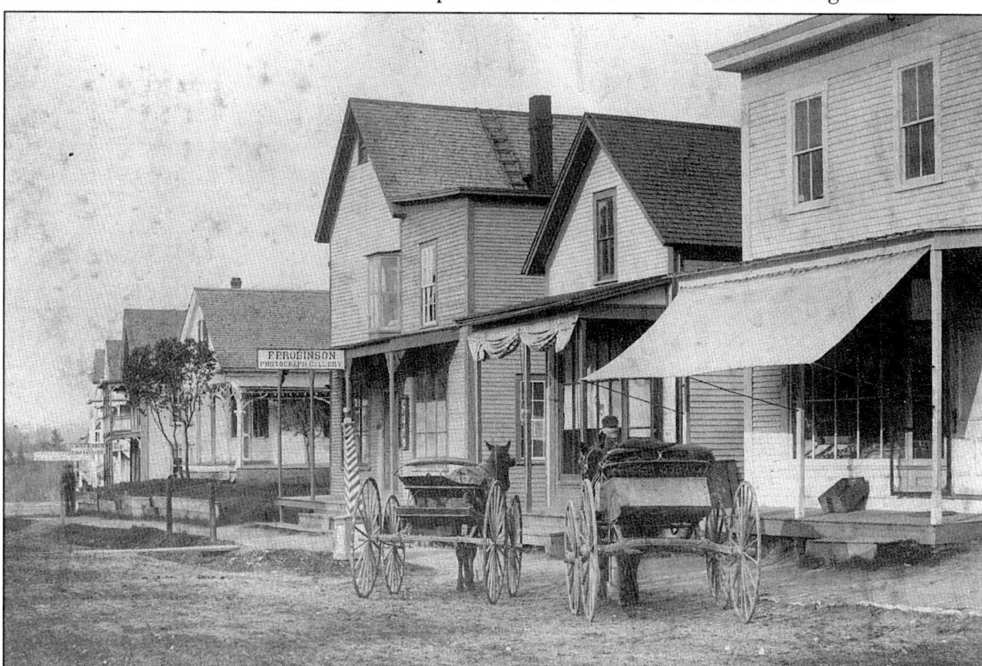

Portland Street, 1890. This view of the east side of Portland Street looking north shows the grocery store, the barbershop-shoe store, Cutler's Photography, which also housed F.P. Robinson's photograph gallery, and the home of O.D. Matthews.

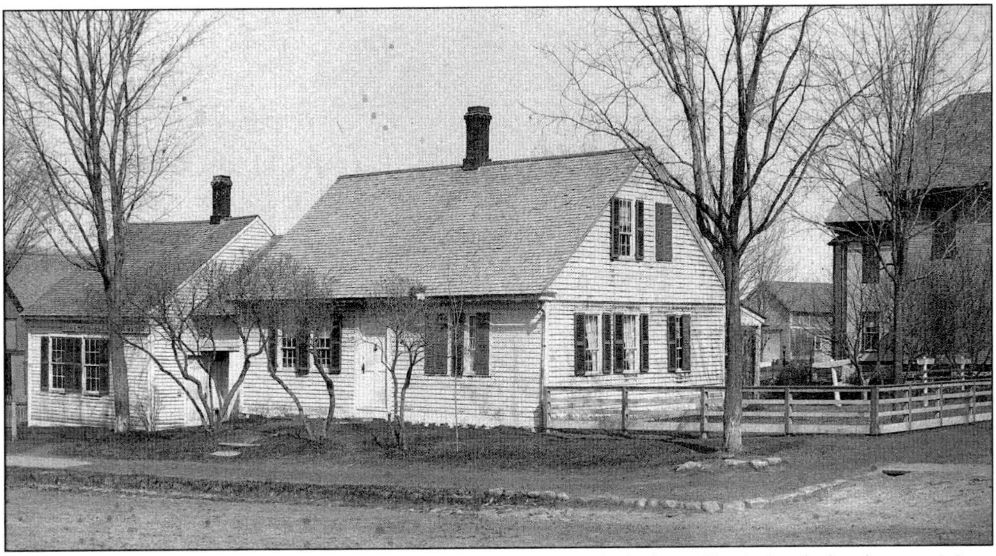

The Home of Squire John Miles, 1889. In 1827, Jedediah Safford deeded a lot on Main Street to Robert Gleason and, in 1828, he deeded the lot to John Miles Sr., who built a home. The house was constructed south of what would become the intersection of Main and Portland Streets prior to the opening of Portland Street in 1872.

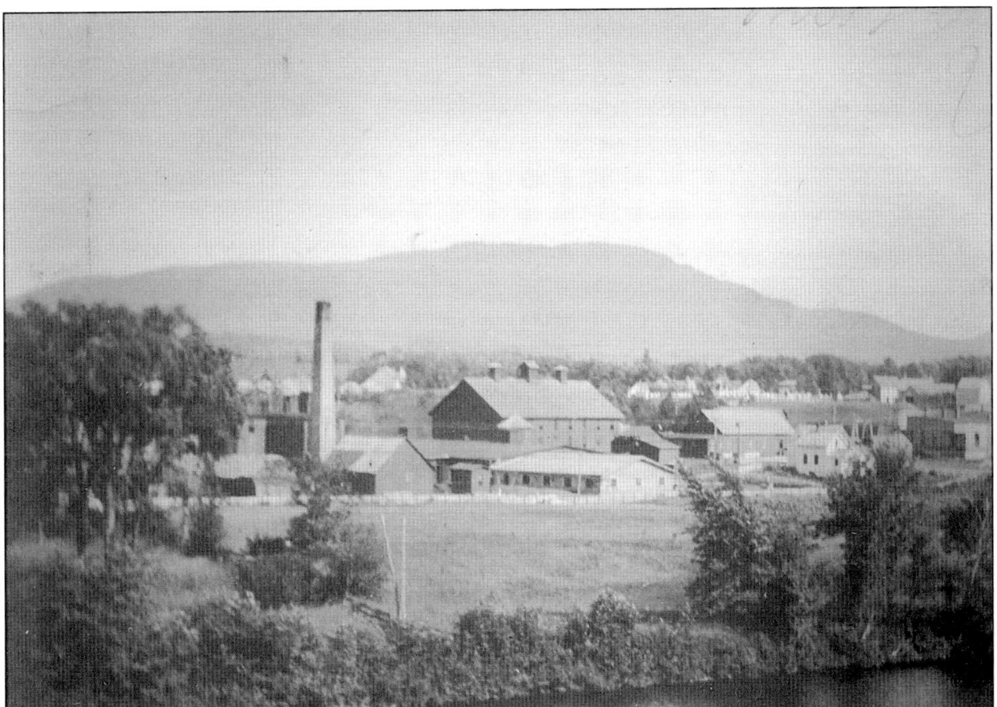

The Morrisville Tannery, 1889. The Morrisville Tannery was built by Edward Webster and C.H.A. Stafford of Stowe near the bend in the Lamoille River at the bottom of Portland Street in 1889. The tannery soon became one of Morrisville's most stable industries.

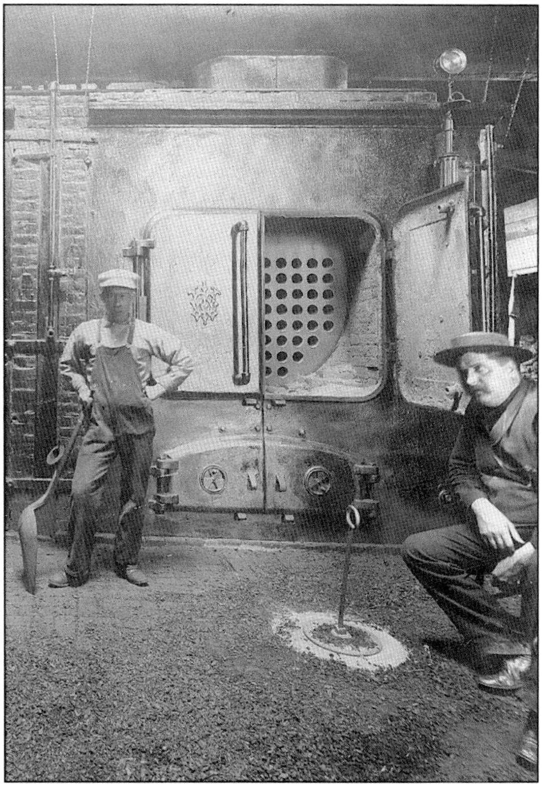

THE BOILER ROOM, 1890. E.H. Webster (right), co-owner of the Morrisville Tannery Company, is seen here seated in the tannery's boiler room with a worker. In 1900, the tannery was sold to Charles Warren of Waterbury, and it then became known as the Warren Leather Company.

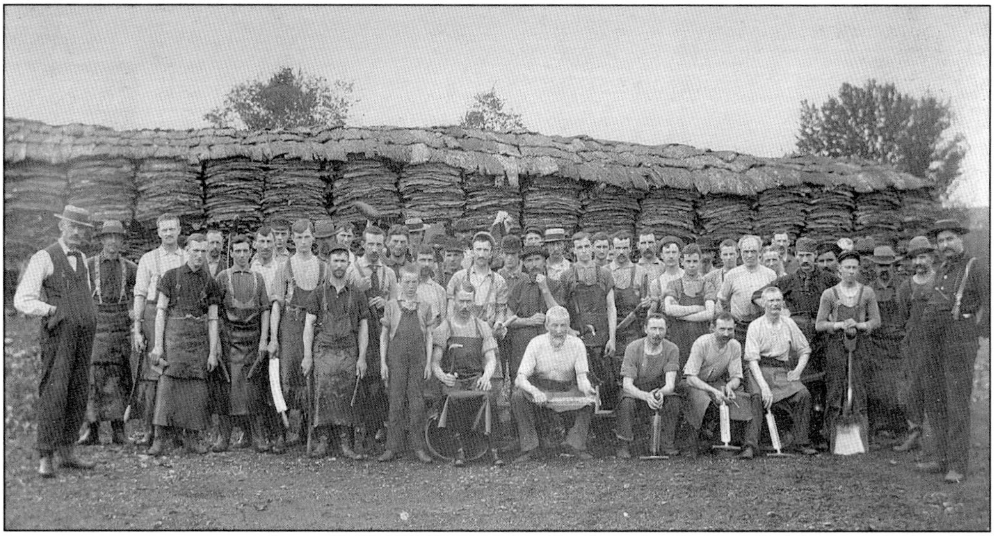

MORRISVILLE TANNERY COMPANY EMPLOYEES, 1890. Among the tannery's large work force were Henry Slicer, Mr. Tifft, H.J. Sears, Frank Blair, Frank Smith, Harry McCombre, George Stewart, Joseph Bassett, Frank Bassett, Arin Russell, Rob Sparks, Dennis Cleveland, Ernest Gates, Fred Boardman, Frank Churchill, Elmer Wade, Frank Boyce, Harrison Smith, Charles Muzzy, and Russell Barrows. Here, they are joined by owners C.H.A. Stafford (far left) and E.W. Webster (far right).

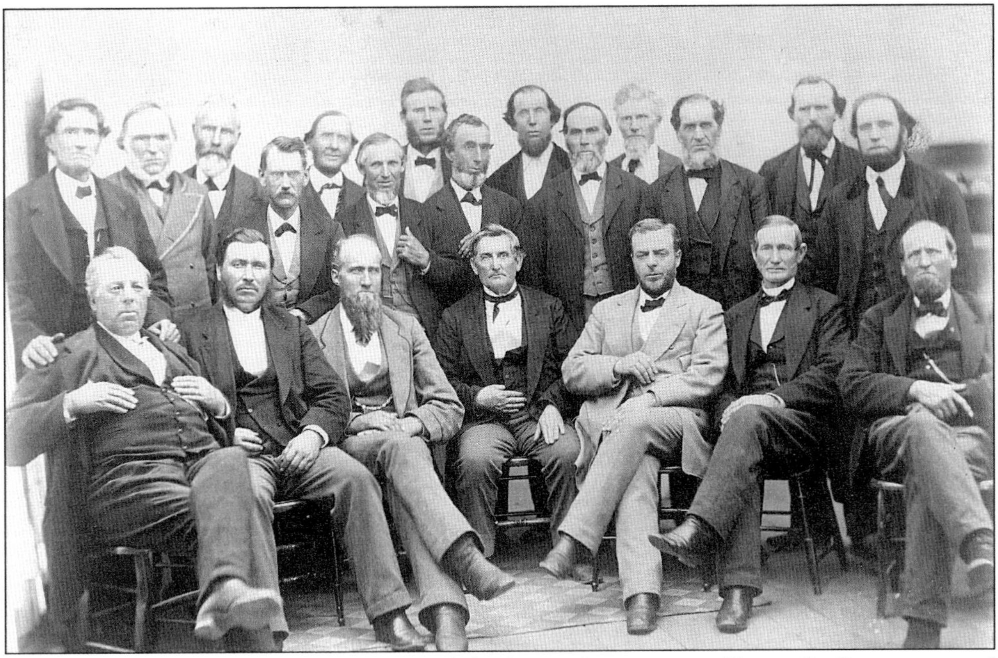

The Lamoille County Court, 1875. While the southern towns of Lamoille County wanted Johnson to become the county seat, the northern towns favored Morristown. A committee chose Hyde Park, and county buildings were constructed. Court convened for the first time in December 1836. Several Morristown men are included in this photograph of the May 1875 term of the Lamoille County Court.

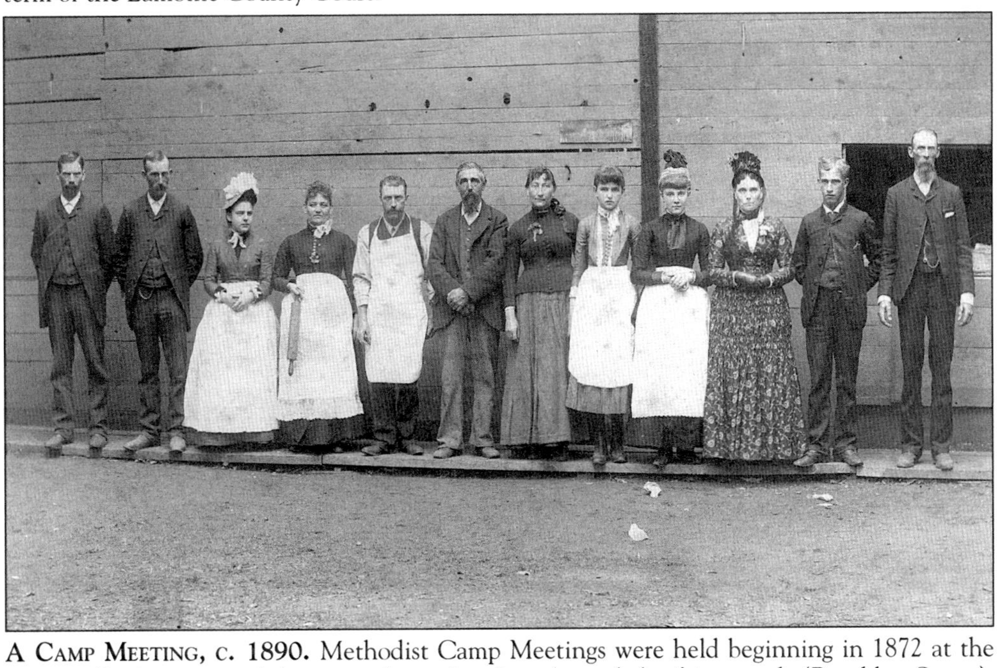

A Camp Meeting, c. 1890. Methodist Camp Meetings were held beginning in 1872 at the Morrisville Campground, between the railroad tracks and the fairgrounds (Brooklyn Street). Before 1872, the meetings were held by the Lamoille River in Cadys Falls. Thousands who attended the meetings would stay in tents, listen to Methodist preachers, and sing hymns.

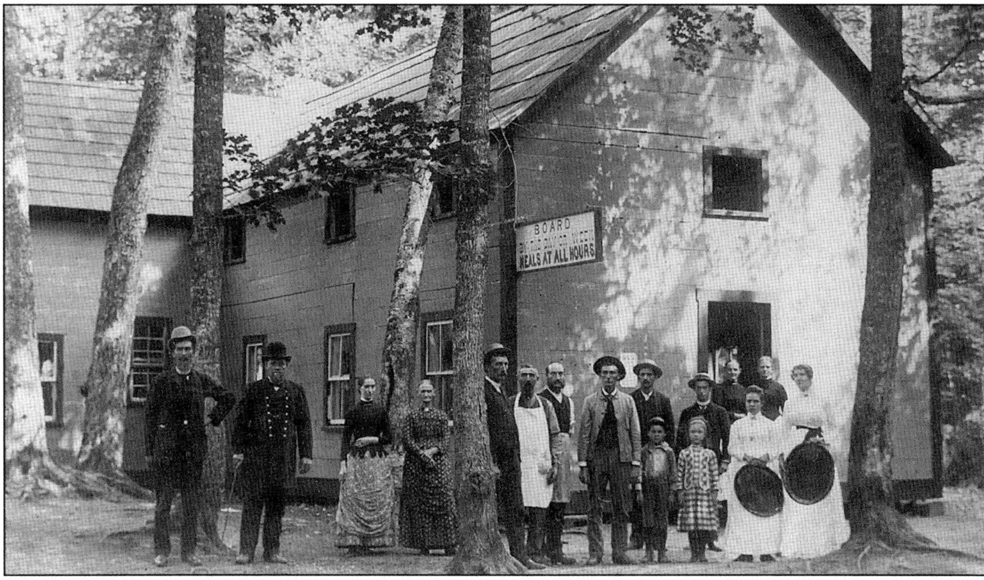

THE CAMPGROUND BOARDINGHOUSE, 1890. The boardinghouse was built in 1873 and was run by H.H. Elmore. Campers could "Board by the Day or Week" with "Meals at All Hours." Cottages were also built by neighboring towns to house their residents. In addition to having the Methodist Camp Meetings, which ended in August 1902, the Morrisville Campground was used for Republican political rallies.

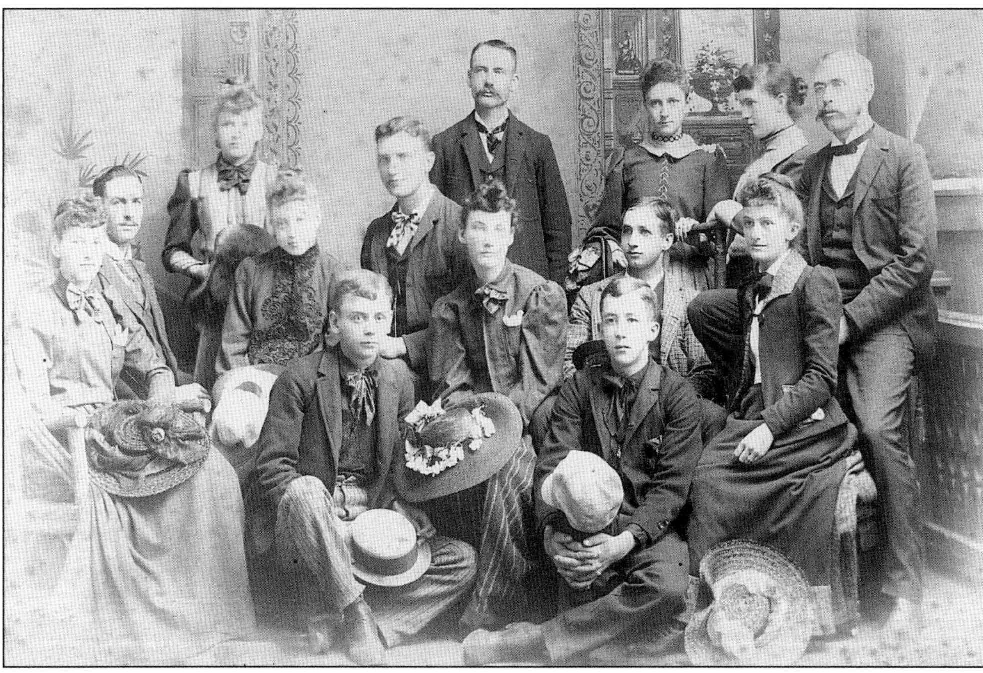

THE MORRISVILLE CAMPING GROUP, 1890. The Morrisville Camping Group camped in Milton and at Lake Champlain in 1890. Pictured, from left to right, are the following: (front row) Will Whipple and Harry Hardy; (middle row) Mira Rogers, Ed Heath, Alice Doty, Ernest Gates, Ella Barrows, Will Slayton, and Mrs. and Mr. Will Robinson; (back row) Anna Doty, Lyman Jones, Lillian Leach, and Sarah Rublee.

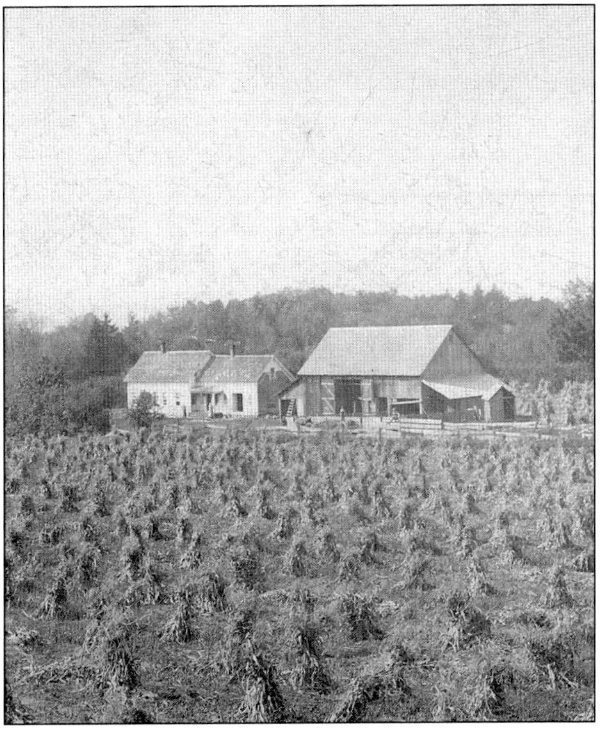

THE SPAULDING HILL SCHOOL, 1880. The Spaulding Hill School (later Sand Hill School) was constructed on the Elmore Road in 1883 by H.R. Burke. The house beside the school belonged to Myron Spaulding. Built in 1812, it is perhaps Morristown's oldest two-story house.

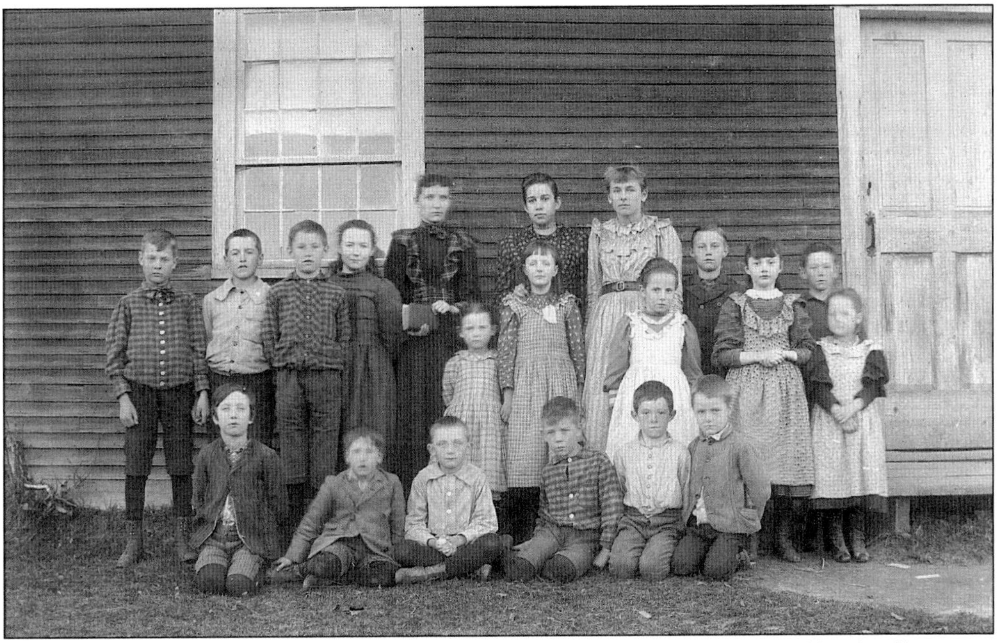

THE OLD CORNERS SCHOOLHOUSE, 1892. This photograph shows the old schoolhouse at Morristown Corners prior to an 1895 relocation. Pictured, from left to right, are the following: (front row) Cleon Wilkins, Lee Wilkins, Roy Macamber, Erwin Hoyt, Erwin Terrill, and Walter Tinker; (middle row) Myrtie Macamber, Sadie Sturger, Nina Merrill, and Ruth Stary; (back row) Ray Leach, Chauncey Stary, Charles Tinker, Arpha Stary, Laura Irish, Kate Carleton, Florence Sherwin, Fay Tinker, Blanch Leach, and Leon Terrill.

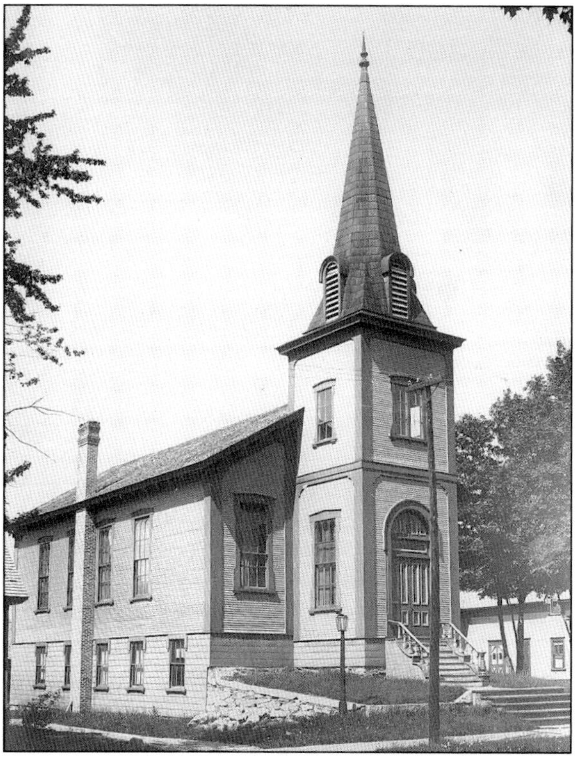

The First Congregational Church, c. 1875. The First Congregational Church built in Morrisville was enlarged in 1856 to accommodate the growing number of members. This photograph shows the church after the major remodeling of 1875. The church was raised up and a furnace was added, as well as a kitchen, a ladies' parlor, and a vestry. In 1885, a pipe organ was installed; it was the first one in town.

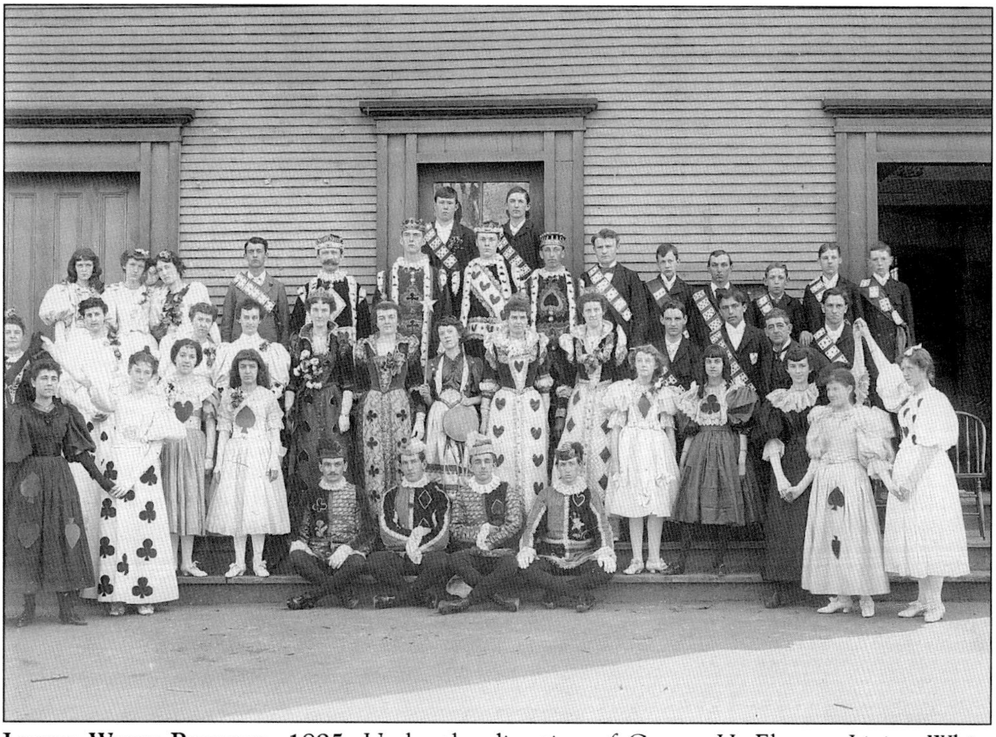

Living Whist Pictures, 1895. Under the direction of George H. Elmore, Living Whist Pictures gave a show in Morrisville on April 19 and 20, 1895.

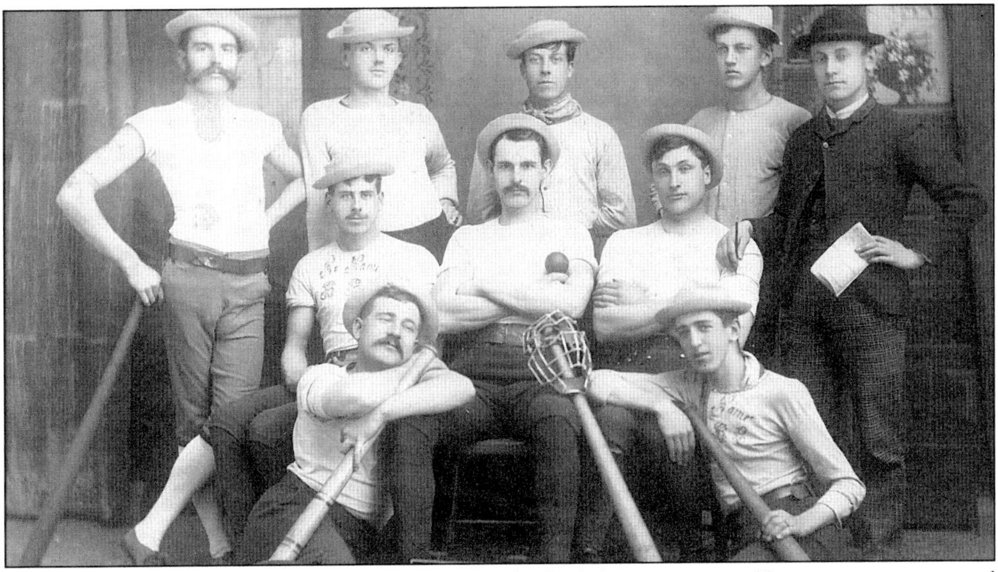

The No Names, 1885. This baseball club, which did not give itself a name, was started in 1885. It soon became known as Morrisville's No Name Baseball Club. This photograph includes the original members, who played barehanded, without any gloves. Shown, from left to right, are the following: (front row) Walter Jackson and Thomas C. Cheney; (middle row) Andy Daniels, Carl A. Gile, and Napoleon St. Louis; (back row) George M. Powers, Fred C. Page, Harvey B. Daniels, Frank Healy, and Clifford Tift.

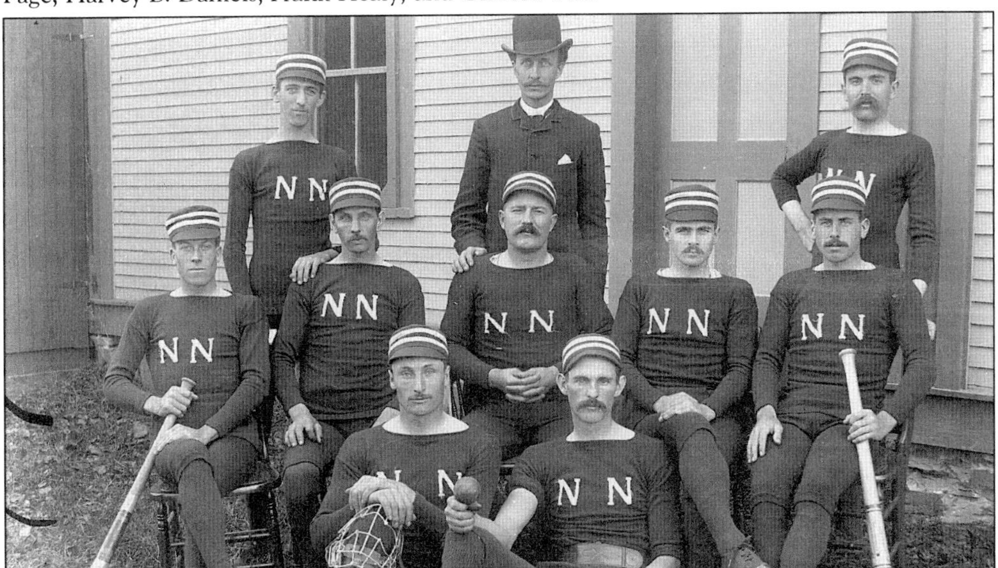

The No Names, 1887. Seen here are the No Names shortly after the acquisition of new uniforms in 1887. The baseball team had built quite a reputation and had won the championship among the towns of northern Vermont. Only several team members had changed in the two years since their formation. Seen here, from left to right, are the following: (front row) Napoleon St. Louis and Carl A. Gile; (middle row) Harvey B. Daniels, Fred Gauthier, Walter K. Jackson, George Foss, and Andy Daniels; (back row) Thomas C. Cheney, manager Fred Livingston, and George M. Powers.

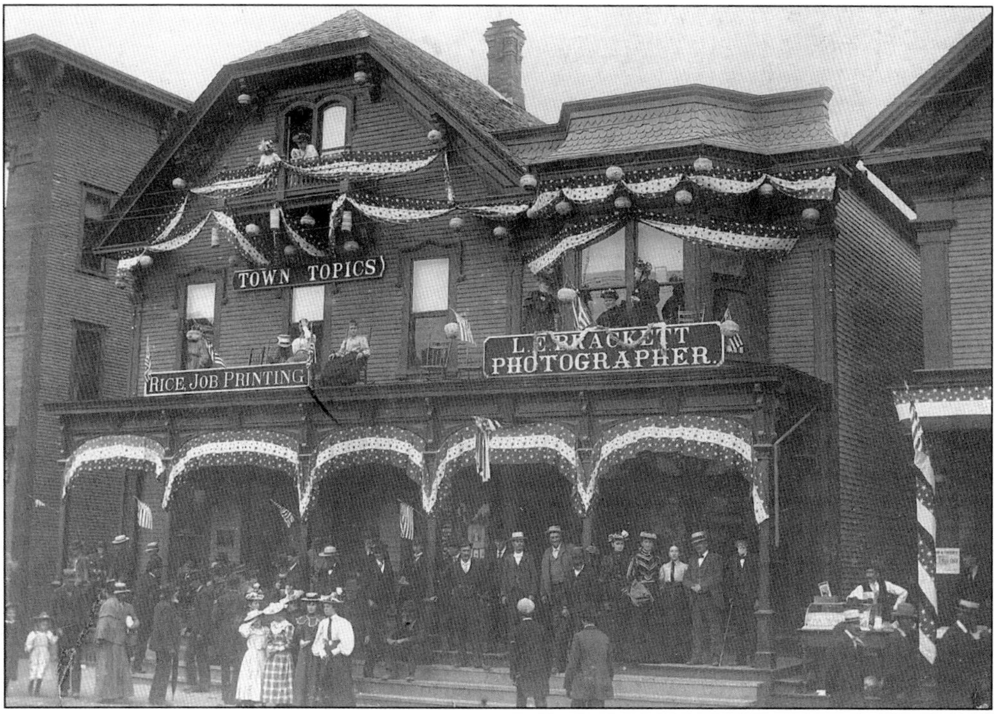

PORTLAND STREET, 1900. This photograph of the Warren Block shows photographer L.E. Brackett's store on Portland Street. Although the occasion is unknown, it is most likely taken during or near Independence Day in 1900.

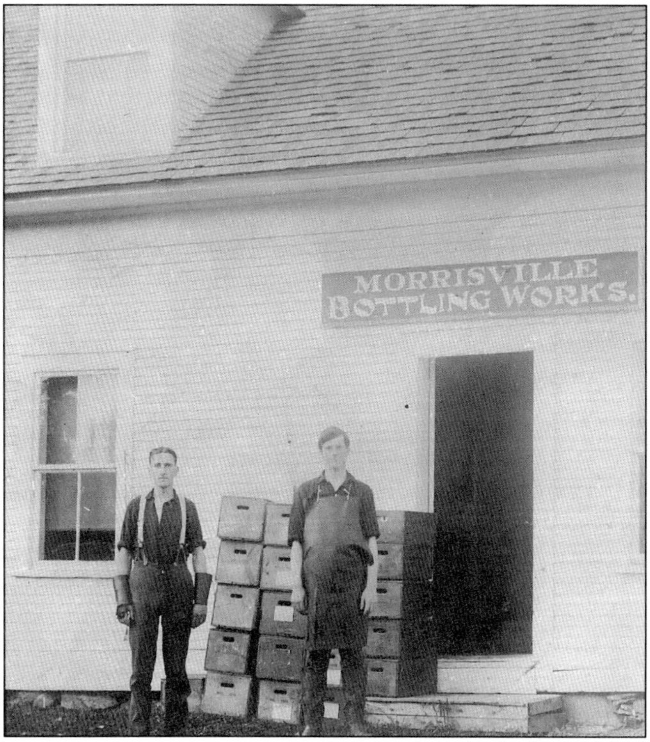

MORRISVILLE BOTTLING WORKS, 1900. Sam B. Doty began manufacturing homemade beer in 1890. His plant, later known as Morrisville Bottling Works, was located on Elmore Street. It produced sodas and tonics, including birch beer, cream soda, banana soda, pineapple soda, and more than 30 other flavors. Seen here are employees William G. Goodrich (left) and Earl Harris.

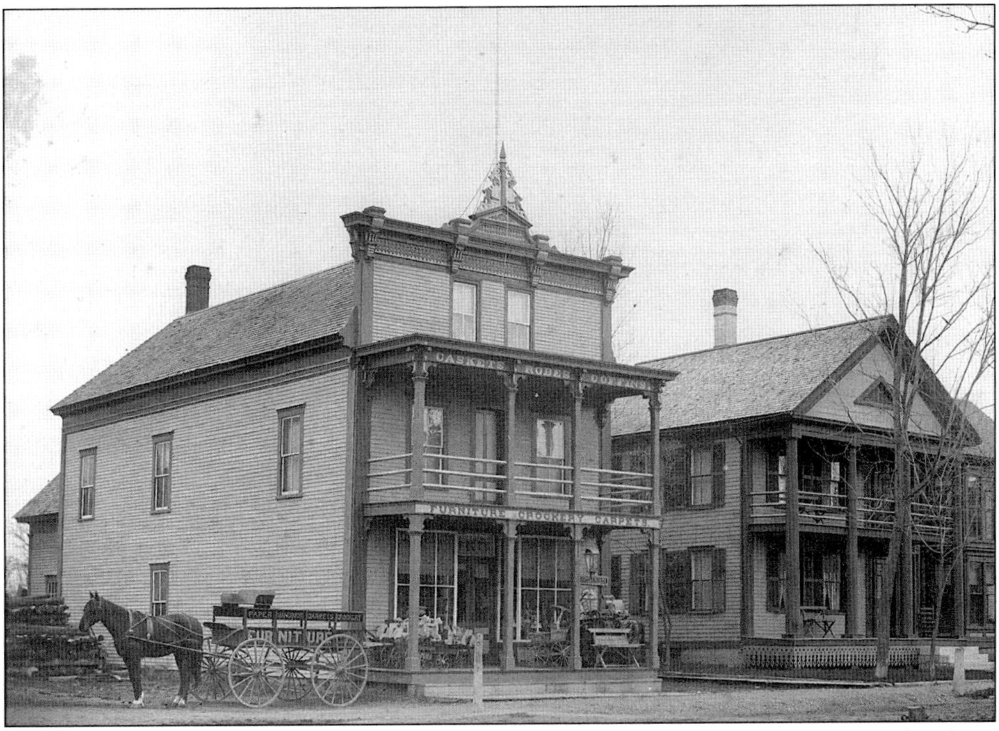

THE GEORGE W. DOTY STORE, 1889. This photograph shows the furniture and undertaking establishment of Civil War veteran George W. Doty. Doty's business was the leading furniture, undertaking, and crockery establishment in Lamoille County. The G.W. Doty Store was located on Main Street.

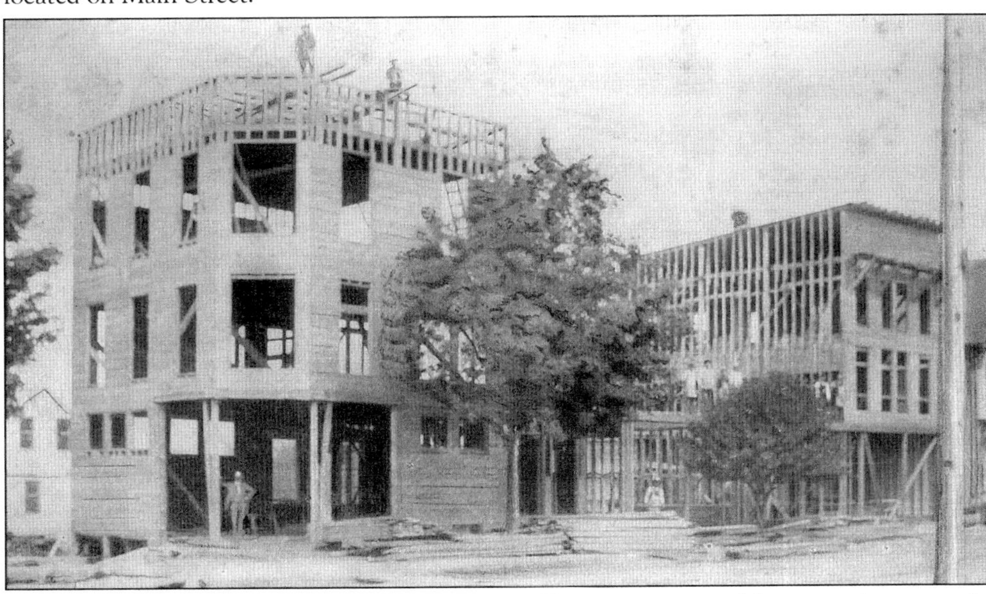

THE CENTENNIAL BLOCK CONSTRUCTION, 1890. To commemorate Morristown's centennial year and to keep up with the pace of growth and development of Morrisville and the general spirit of progress, the Centennial Block was built on the corner of Main and Portland Streets. Construction began in 1890.

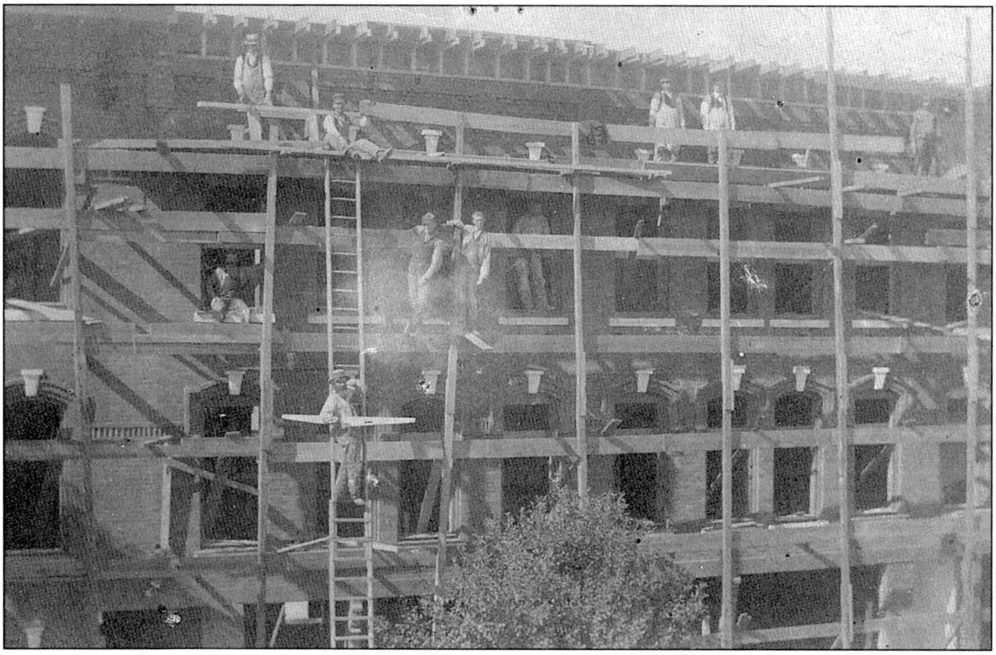

THE CENTENNIAL BLOCK CONSTRUCTION, 1890. The Centennial Block was built thanks to the initiative of Dr. E.J. Hall. The architect and builder, C.W. Fitch, completed the project in 1891. It became home to A.L. Cheney's drugstore shortly after completion.

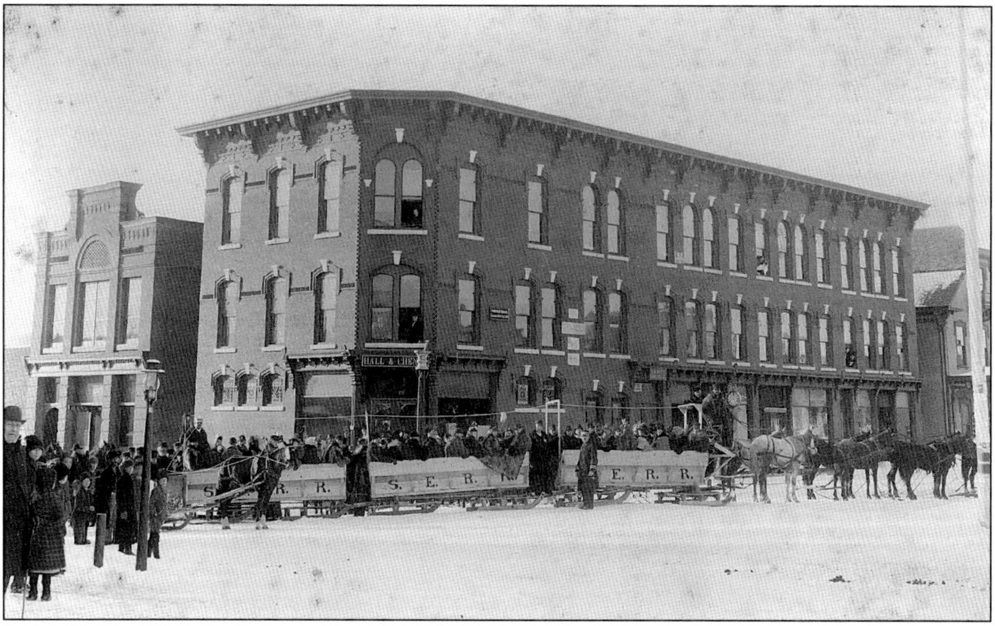

THE CENTENNIAL BLOCK, 1894. This photograph, taken on February 22, 1894, shows the completed Centennial Block. The large sleigh is filled with people attending a promotional event for a proposed electric railroad between Waterbury and Newport.

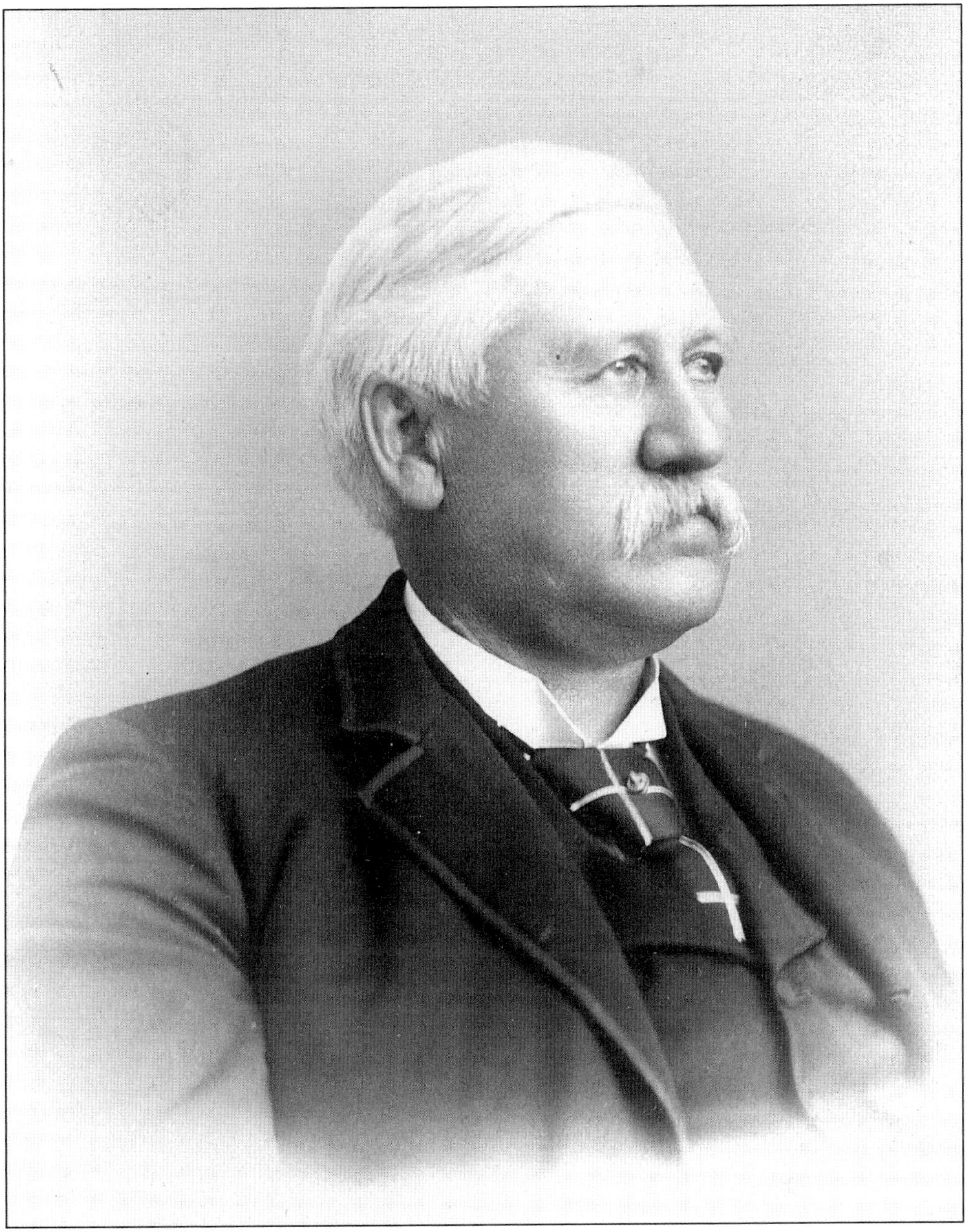

GEORGE W. HENDEE, 1869. George Hendee was born to poor parents in Stowe on November 30, 1832, and was educated at Peoples Academy. At the age of 20, he commenced the study of law in the office of W.G. Ferrin, in Johnson. In 1855, Hendee was admitted to the Lamoille County Bar. He was one of the pioneers in the construction of the railroad, president of the Union Savings Bank & Trust Company, superintendent of schools at the age of 21, and president of the Lamoille Valley Fair.

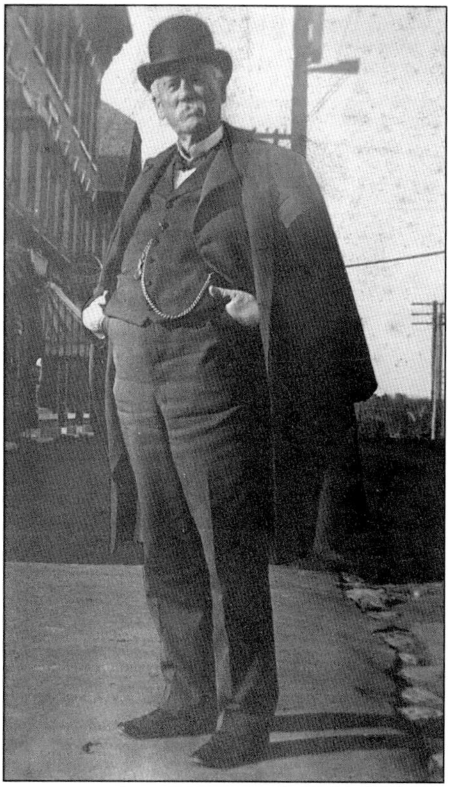

GOV. GEORGE W. HENDEE, 1832. From 1861 to 1862, George Hendee served in the Vermont House of Representatives and then as lieutenant governor in 1869. The death of Gov. Peter T. Washburn gave Hendee the opportunity to serve as governor for the remainder of Washburn's term. Hendee also served three terms as president of the village trustees in Morrisville and six years as president and treasurer of the Morrisville Foundry Company.

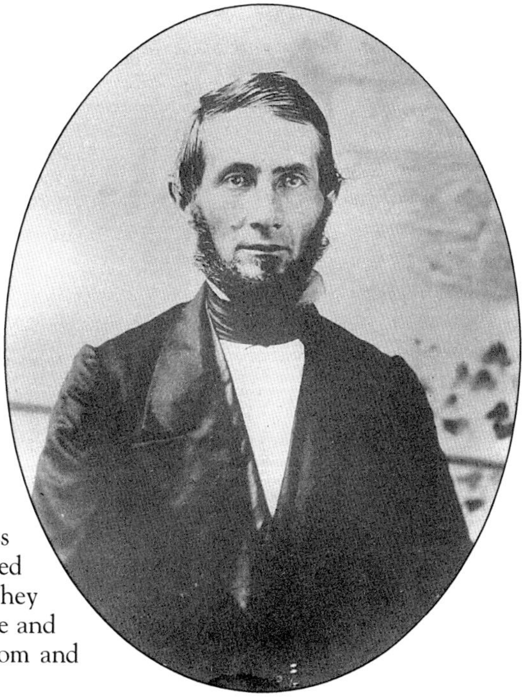

DR. DAVID RANDALL, 1891. David Randall, the first doctor in the town of Eden, and his son Carroll F. Randall built the Randall Hotel on the corner of Main and Congress Streets in 1891. The Randalls had purchased the Morrisville House property in 1891. They decided to make use of the Morrisville House and moved it back to be used for the dining room and kitchen of the new Randall.

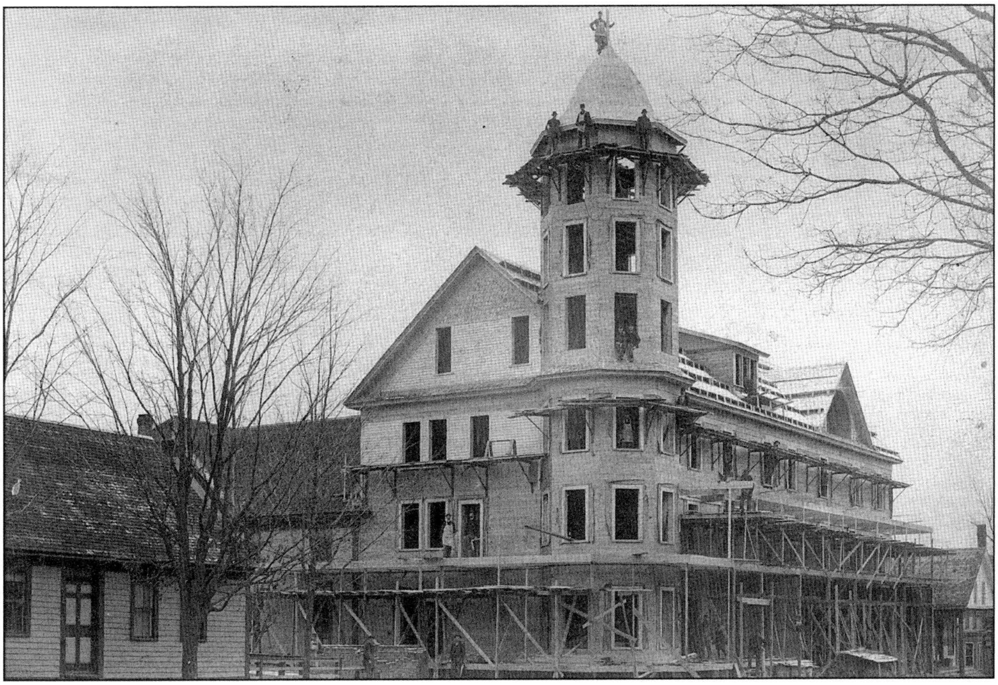

THE CONSTRUCTION OF THE RANDALL HOTEL, 1891. When this photograph was taken, David and Carroll Randall were in the process of constructing the three-story hotel. Once the hotel was completed, they advertised famous cooking and comfortable accommodations. A later brochure advertised electric call bells, steam heat, 50 rooms, reasonable rates, good sewage, pleasant parlors, bathrooms, hairdressing rooms, and modern conveniences. One brochure called the Randall "one of the most popular hotels in Vermont."

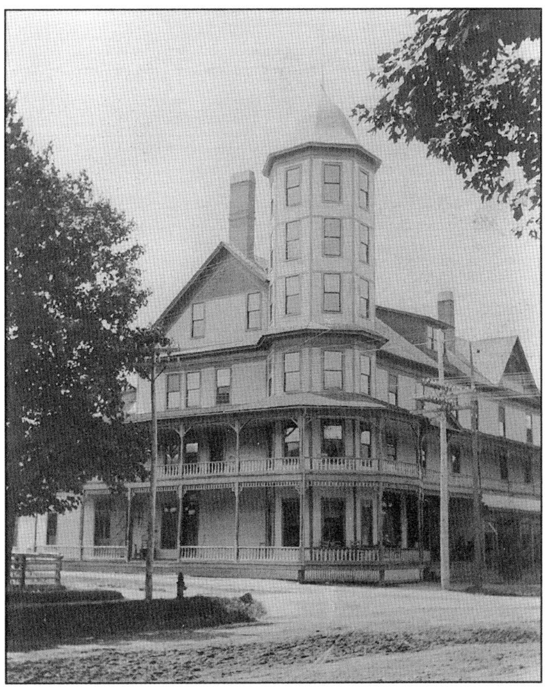

THE RANDALL HOTEL, LATE 1890S. Although not completed in time for Morristown's centennial, both the Randall Hotel and the Centennial Block are indicative of the changes that were occurring rapidly in Morrisville. Churches, schools, businesses, industries, and families were establishing themselves in Morrisville, thanks to the opening of the LaPorte Road and the arrival of the railroad. The days of the town center at the Four Corners were over, and Morrisville's flourishing was only just beginning.

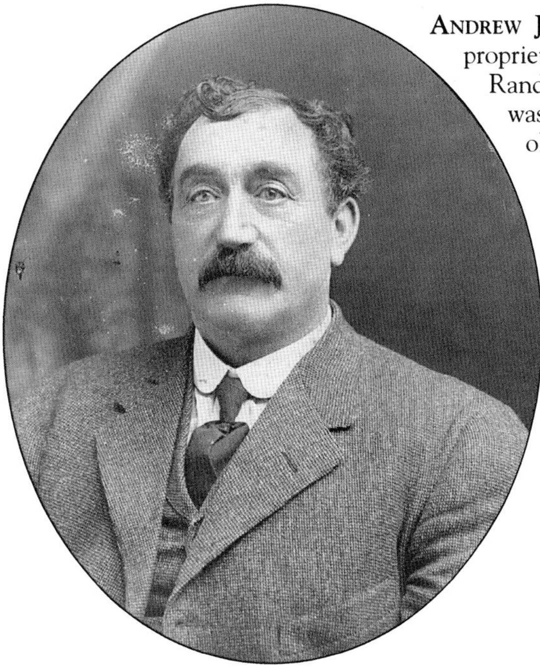

ANDREW J. SMITH, 1890S. Andrew Smith was the proprietor of the livery stable to the rear of the Randall Hotel. A famous horse handler, he was in charge of the six-horse teams on the old stagecoach.

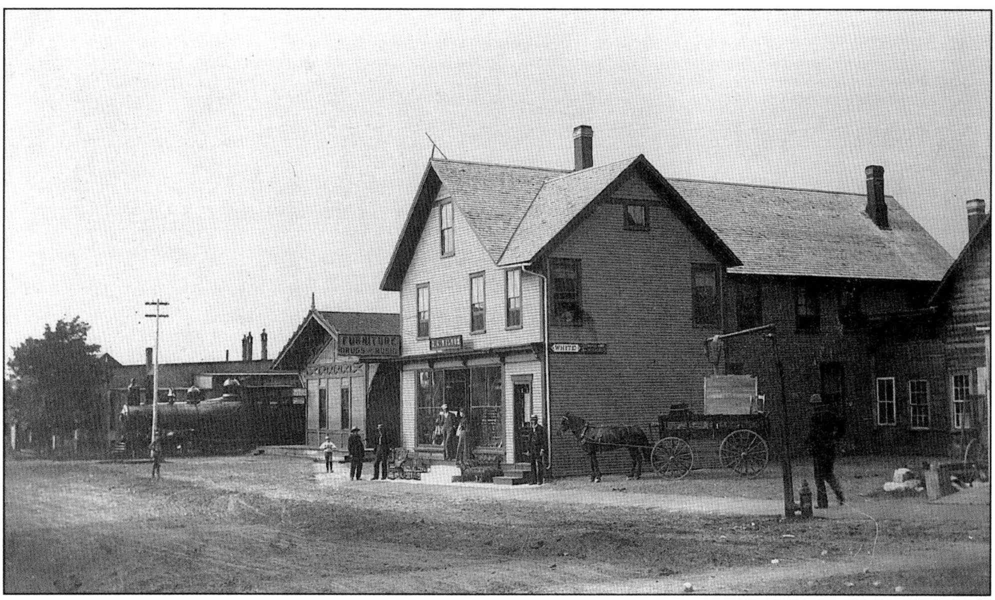

THE E.G. WILSON STORE, 1899. Edward Wilson operated this store on the north end of Portland Street in 1899. To the left are the Morrisville Railroad Depot and the steam engine train, and to the right is the village washtub. Wilson sold furniture, drugs, music, and sewing machines. By 1899, more and more businesses were opening in Morrisville, especially on Main Street and Portland Street. Some, including Wilson's, were very short-lived.

Henry A. Slayton, 1900. Henry Albert Slayton was born on July 23, 1851, in Calais. He came to Morrisville and was educated at Morrisville Graded School and Peoples Academy. After his first wife, Edna Hathaway, died in 1879 he married Lillia Noyes. Lillia Noyes was the daughter of the Honorable Carlos S. Noyes, who was known as the father of Lamoille County banking and who came to Morrisville from Hyde Park and bought the Main Street Safford house in 1820.

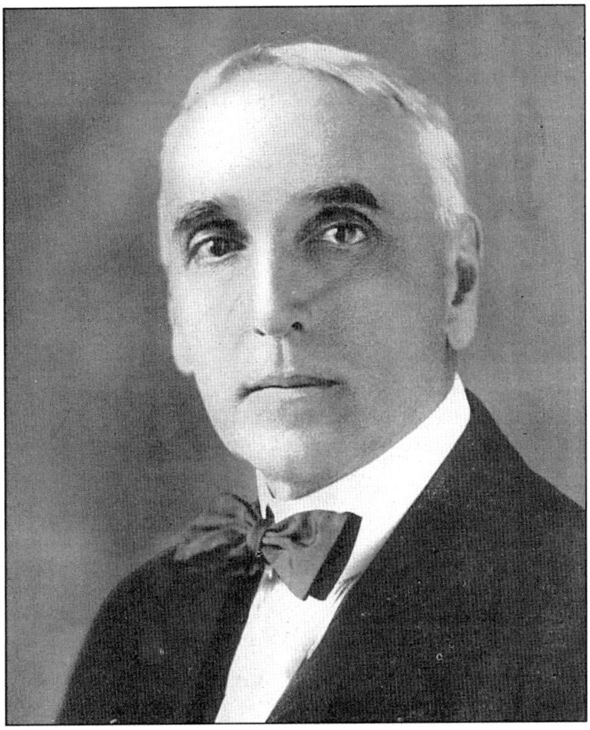

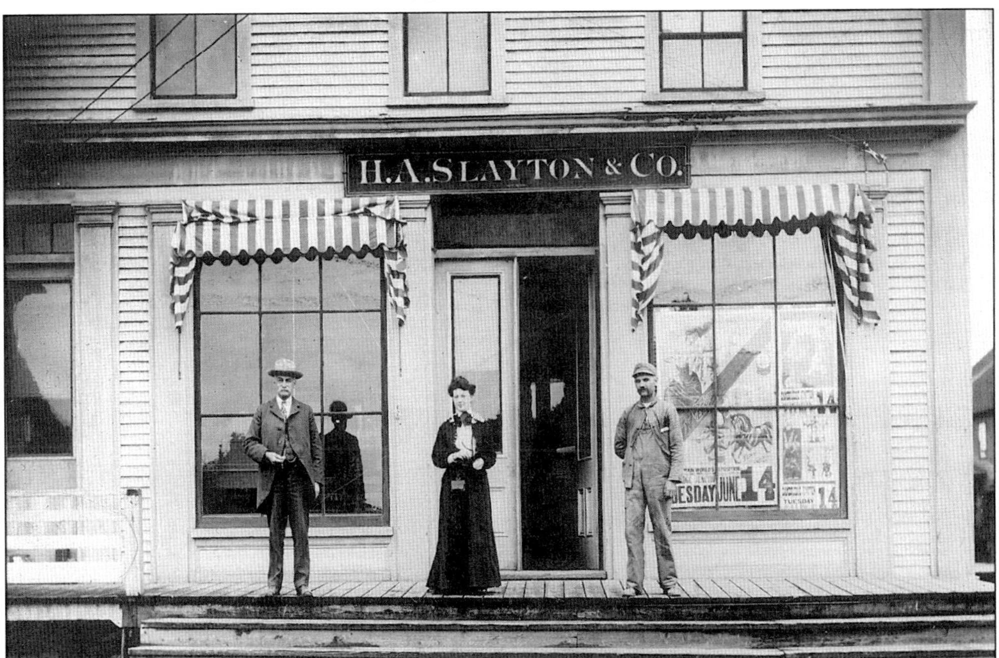

H.A. Slayton & Company, 1904. H.A. Slayton began selling flour and feed in 1878. His Portland Street building was repeatedly enlarged to accommodate the demands of increasing business. At the time of this photograph, he also offered sugar, oil, lime, and cement at both retail and wholesale prices. Seen here, from left to right, are Henry Slayton, Blanche Foss, and Will Fairbanks.

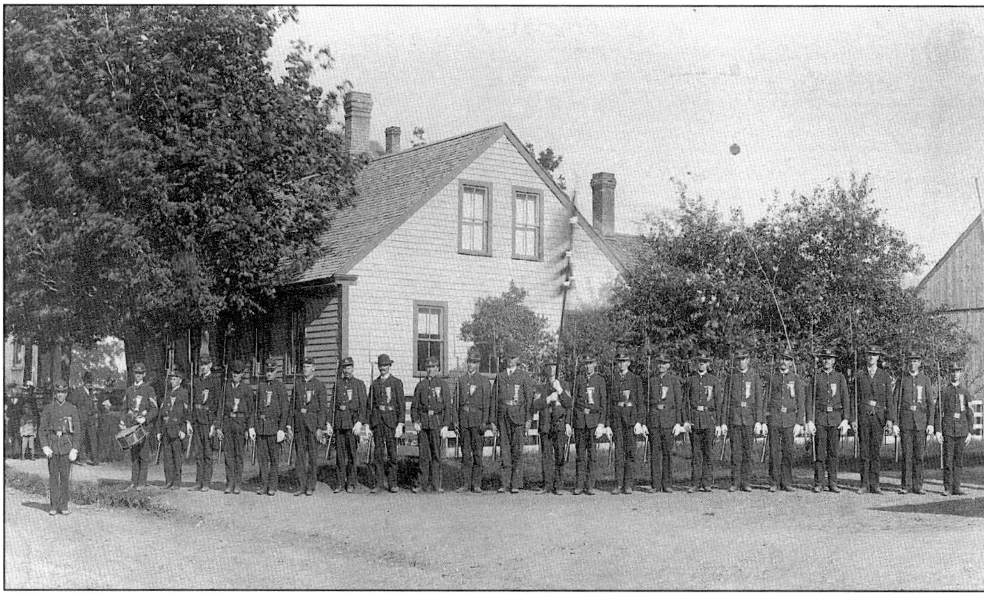

SONS OF VETERANS, 1890. Memorial Day of 1890 brought together a gathering of the G.W. Doty Camp Sons of Veterans. Included among them are Don Sanders, Charles Bridge, Vernon Fisher, Harvey Daniels, Rache Richardson, Frank Churchill, Charles Scriber, Andy Daniels, Merritt Spaulding, Guy Addams, Fred Shippy, and Elmer Camp. All were sons of Civil War veterans and were gathered at the corner of Congress and Main Streets.

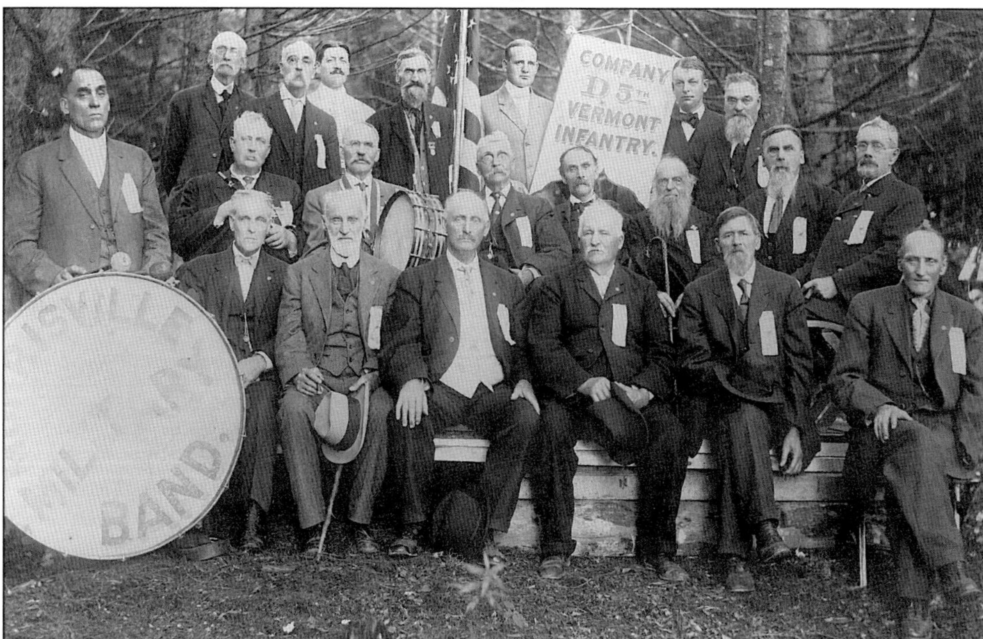

COMPANY D 5TH VERMONT INFANTRY, ESTABLISHED 1861. When the Civil War began in 1860, Morristown had a population of 1,751, of which 168 went to the front. Shown here is a reunion of members of those who fought in Company D 5th Vermont Infantry unit. The original role consisted of 84 volunteers, and 9 were from Morristown. The 5th Vermont was composed of 10 companies. It left for the front on September 17, 1861.

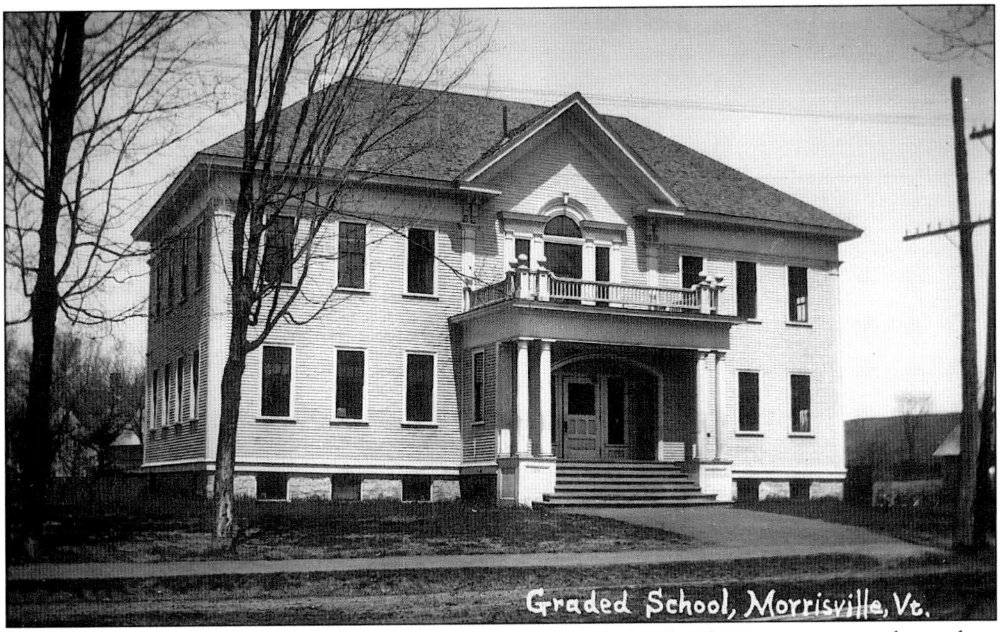

The Morrisville Graded School, c. 1900. A graded school was constructed in close proximity to Peoples Academy in 1899, leaving its original quarters strictly for academy use. The graded building soon was outgrown, and a $25,000 addition was added in 1917.

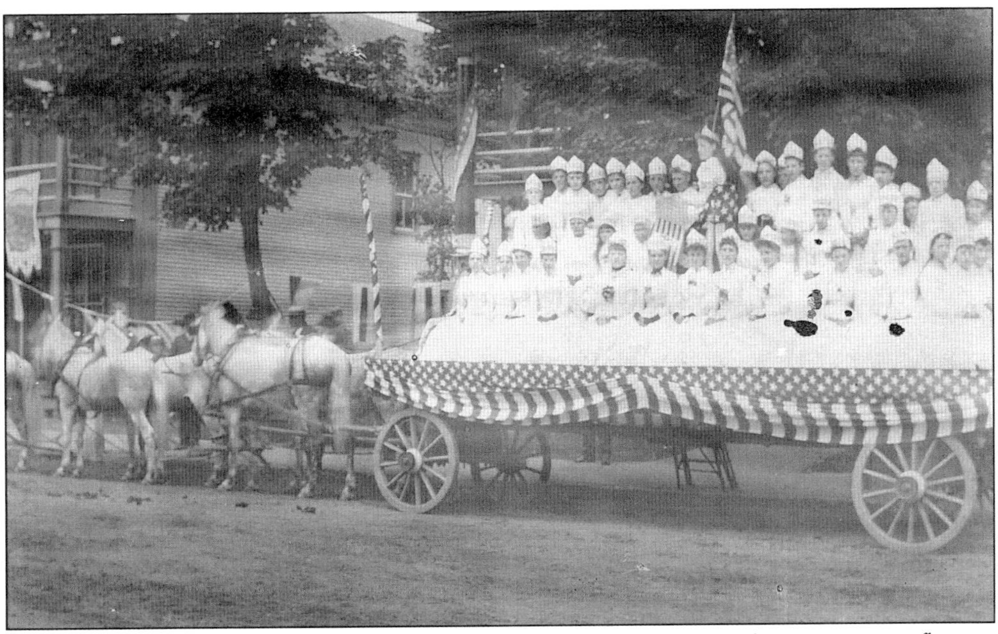

Morristown's Centennial, 1890. This photograph shows a group of women atop a float in Morristown's Centennial Parade on July 4, 1890. The 44 women were each representing a state in the union.

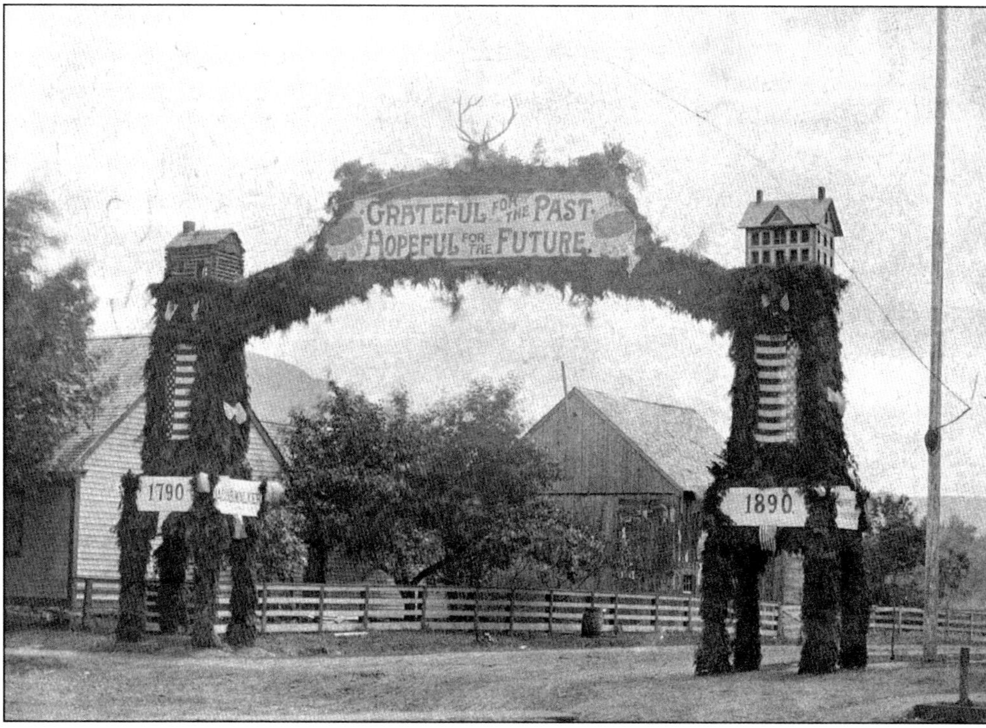

MORRISTOWN'S CENTENNIAL, 1890. Morristown celebrated its 100th birthday on July 4, 1890. Flags and 20,000 yards of bunting decorated the streets. Spanning Congress Street was a giant arch, which read "Grateful for the Past—Hopeful for the Future" on one side and "One Hundredth Anniversary of Settlement" on the other. Activities included a large parade, speeches and other events under a tent built near Harrison Avenue to hold 2,000 people, a No Name baseball game, and fireworks. The events were tremendously successful, and records indicate that at least 10,000 people attended the centennial.

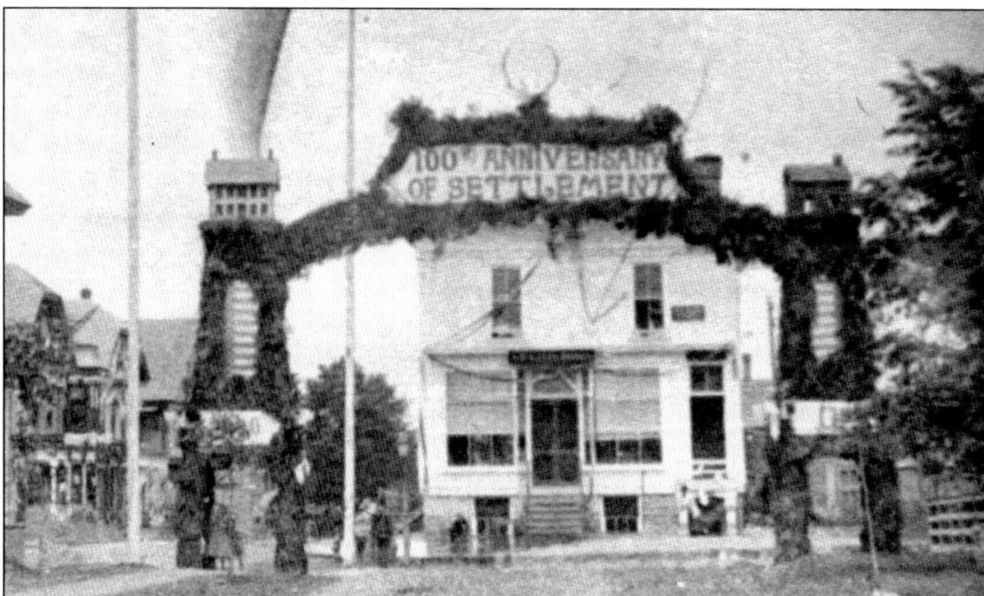

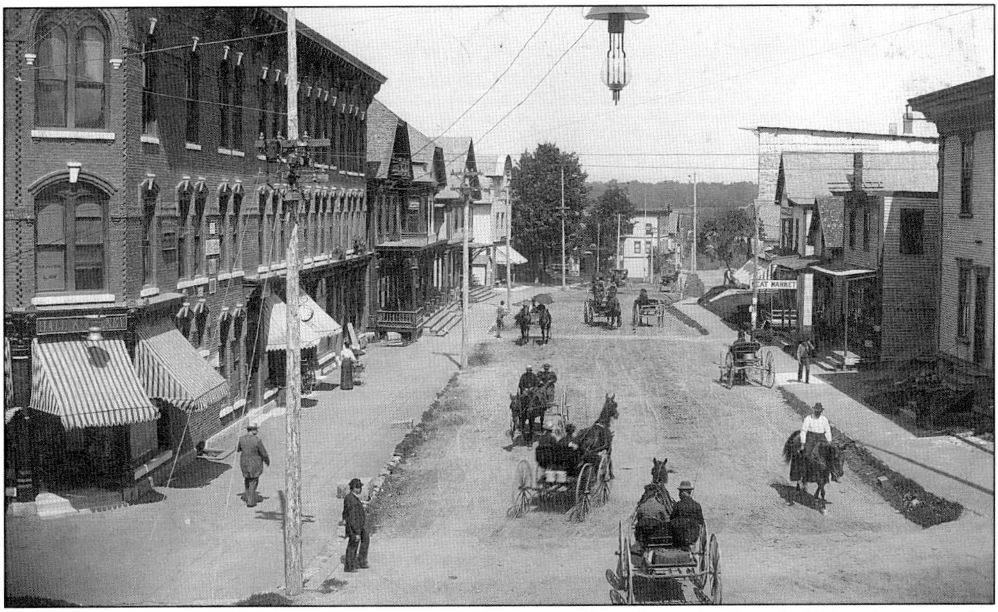

PORTLAND STREET, 1900. This Portland Street view, taken from the Randall Hotel, shows the Centennial Block occupied by Hall & Cheney Druggists on the left. The arc light seen in the center was hung in 1895.

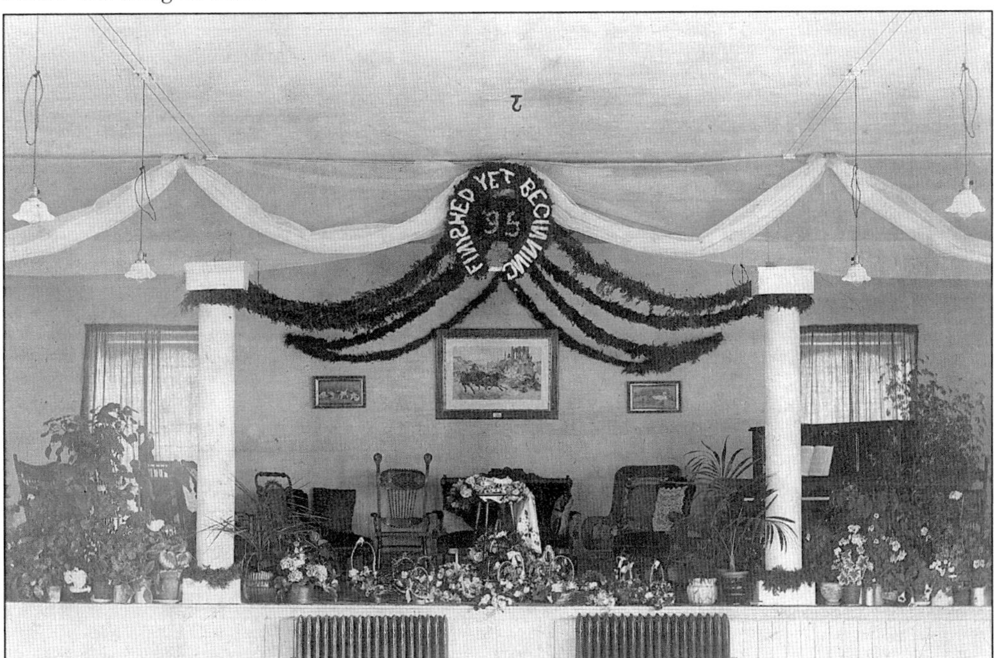

FINISHED YET BEGINNING, 1895. The stage of the second Peoples Academy building is shown in 1895, decorated for the commencement ceremonies of the 47th graduating class. For Lamoille County the 19th century had brought major advancements, new growth, the arrival of the railroad, and the beginning of a new way of life. The century was quickly coming to a close; yet, the prosperity was just beginning. The 20th century was about to arrive like a steam locomotive on the St. Johnsbury & Lake Champlain Railroad.

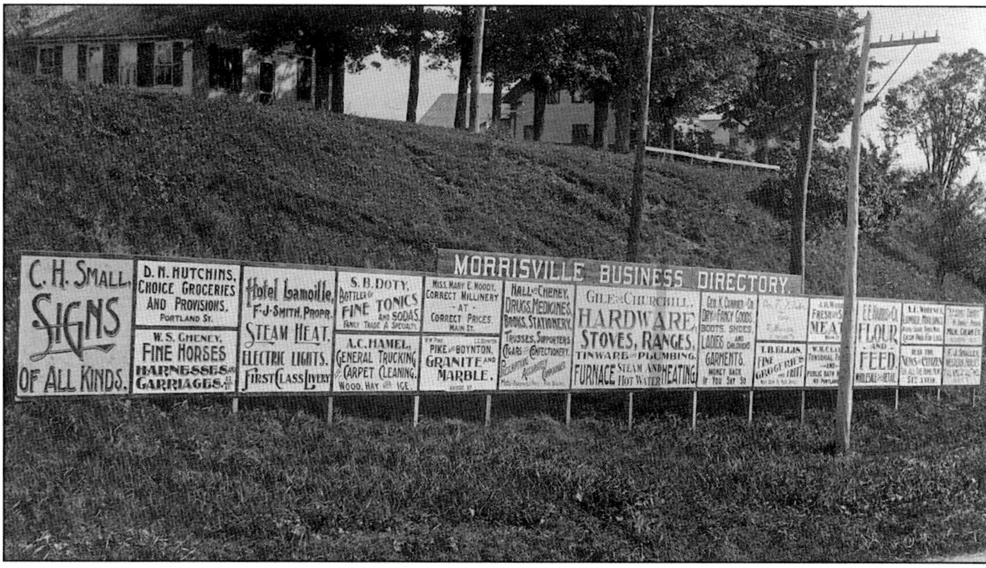

The Morrisville Business Directory, c. 1900. Morrisville's downtown businesses had grown tenfold since the village's 1888 incorporation. This business directory, advertising 20 businesses, was situated in a prime location on the bank below East High Street, so that is could be easily seen by travelers from Stowe as they entered the village of Morrisville.

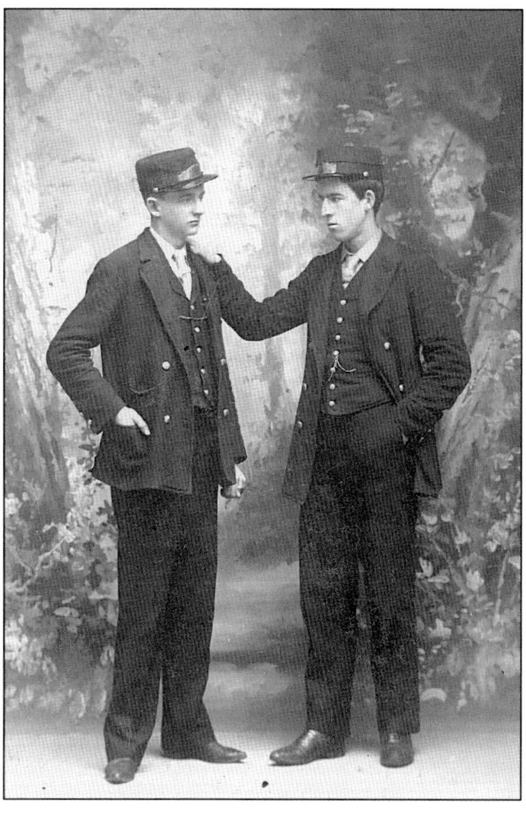

St. Johnsbury & Lake Champlain Conductors, 1900. The arrival of the Portland & Ogdensburg Railroad in 1872 brought a sense of flourishing to Morrisville and other Lamoille County towns. The beginning of the 20th century was marked with rapid growth and change. Morrisville was in its heyday. Here are "Bloom" Palmer (left) and Fred Peck, conductors on the St. Johnsbury & Lake Champlain Railroad.

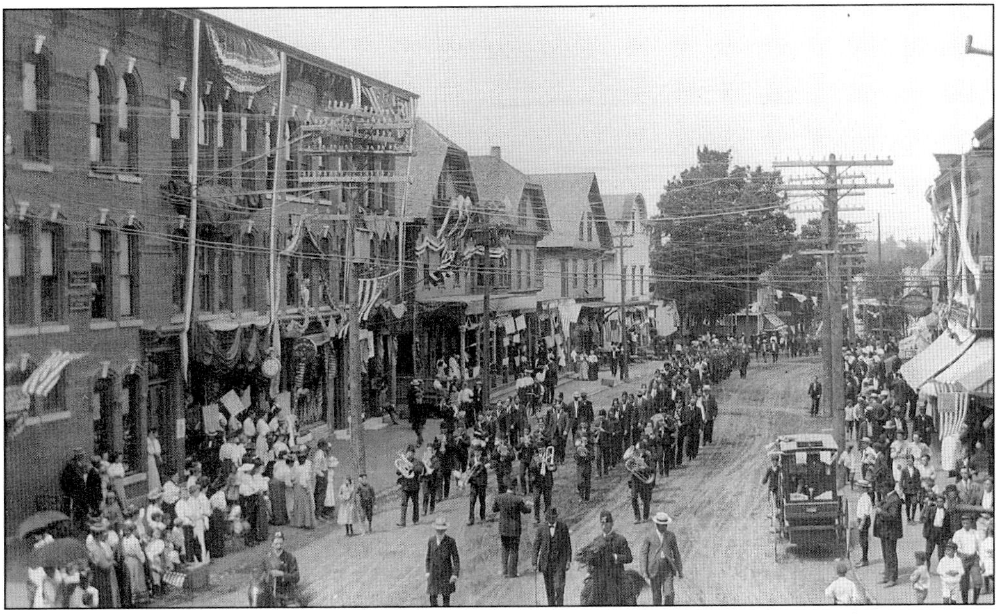

A Parade, 1900. Morristown's centennial in 1890 had given Morristown residents a reason to celebrate in a big way. The celebrations continued into the 1900s, and large parades became customary each year on several occasions. This unidentified parade is probably celebrating the Fourth of July or a Shriners Day.

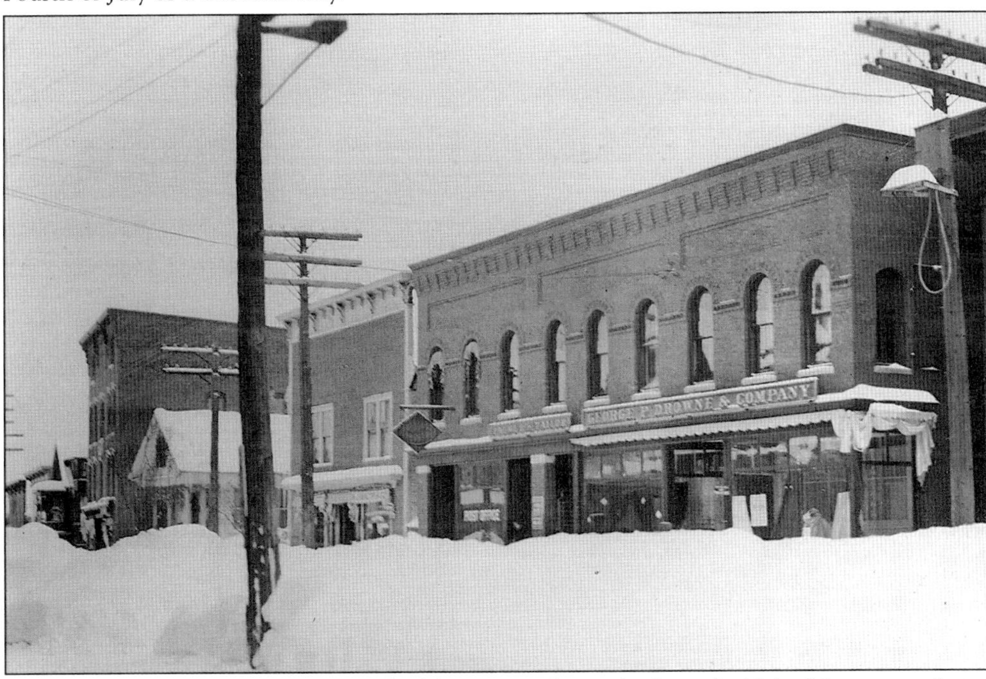

The Drowne Block, 1901. New buildings were being built and old buildings were being moved in Morrisville in the early 1900s. This 1901 photograph shows the newly built Drowne block on Portland Street. Two other buildings were moved to make way for the large brick Drowne Block. Part of the building became the new home of the post office, under the direction of H.J. Fisher, postmaster.

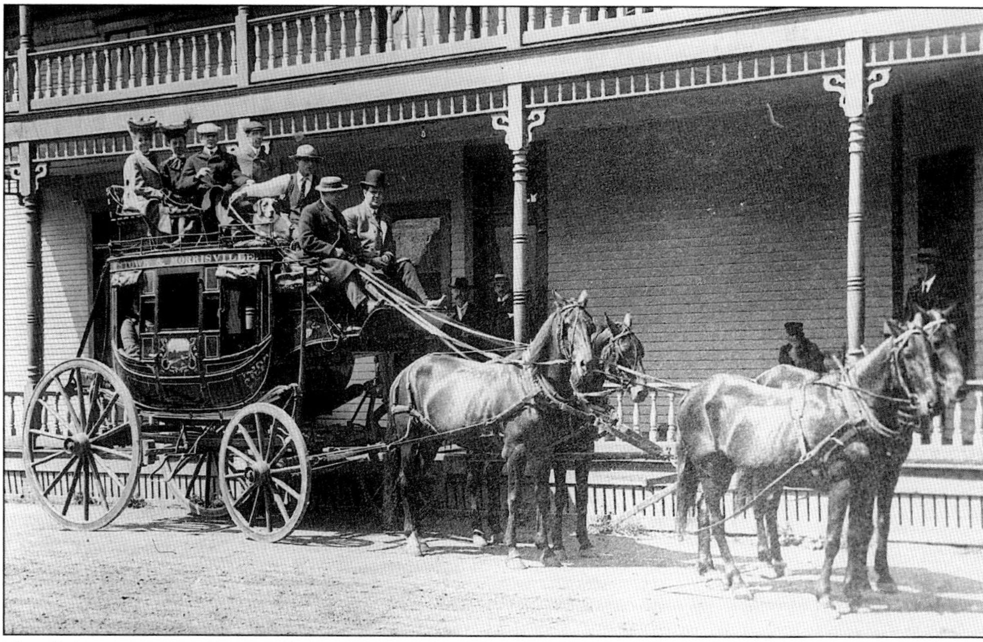

THE MORRISVILLE–STOWE STAGECOACH, 1900. Traveling was now easier for Lamoille County residents with the arrival of the train, but many still relied on the stagecoaches to get from town to town—at least until the automobile arrived some years later. Stowe and Morrisville's Concord Stagecoach was built in 1831 and was used well into the 20th century. It was later moved to the Museum of Science and Industry in Chicago, Illinois.

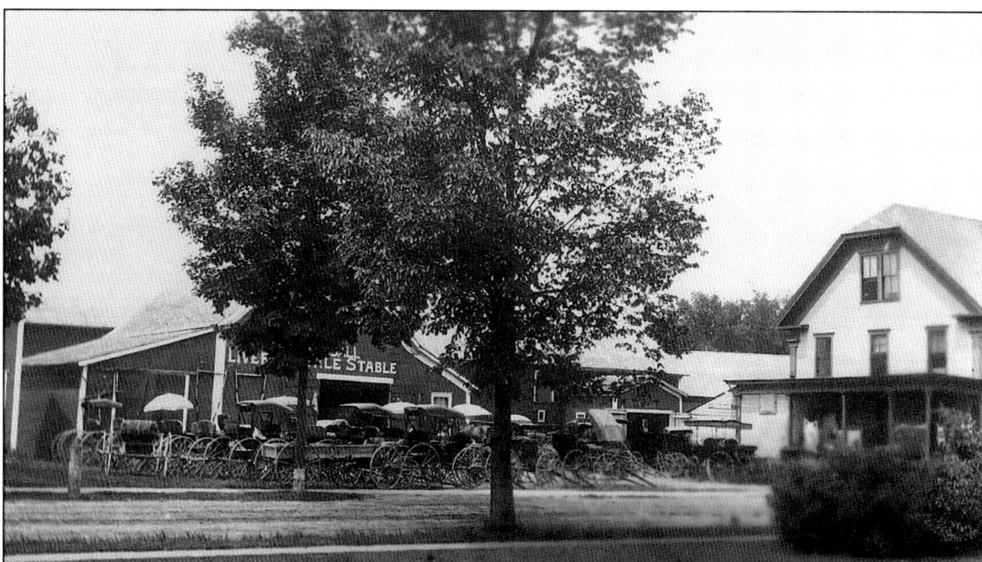

THE RANDALL HOTEL AND LIVERY STABLE, 1900. People from as far away as Detroit stayed at the Randall Hotel on their way through Lamoille County. Their presence increased business at A.J. Smith's Livery and Sale Stable, located behind the Randall. On the right is the back of the Randall, which had been converted from the Morrisville House.

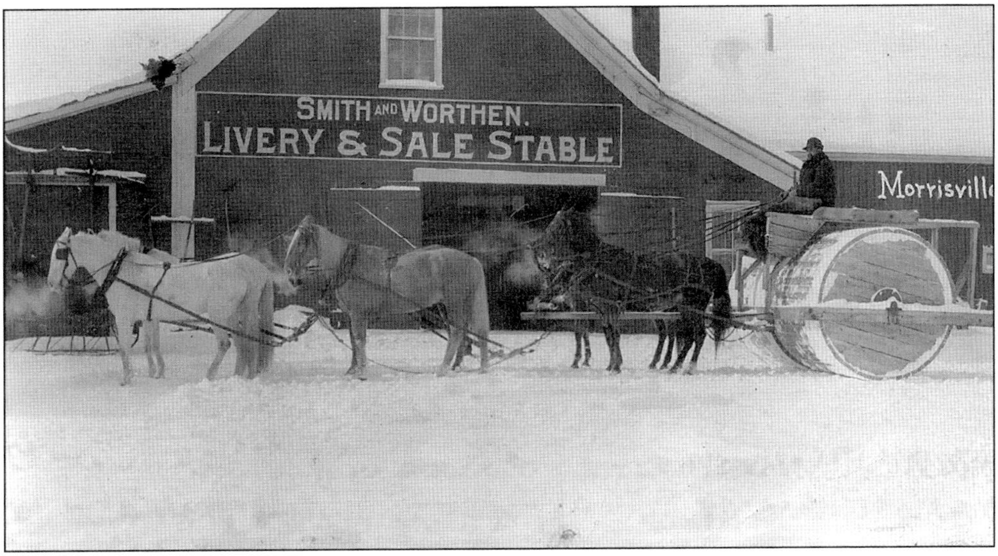

A SNOW ROLLER, 1900. During the cold and snowy Vermont winters, Andrew Smith used this snow roller drawn by three pairs of horses to help pack down the record snowfalls of the early 1900s.

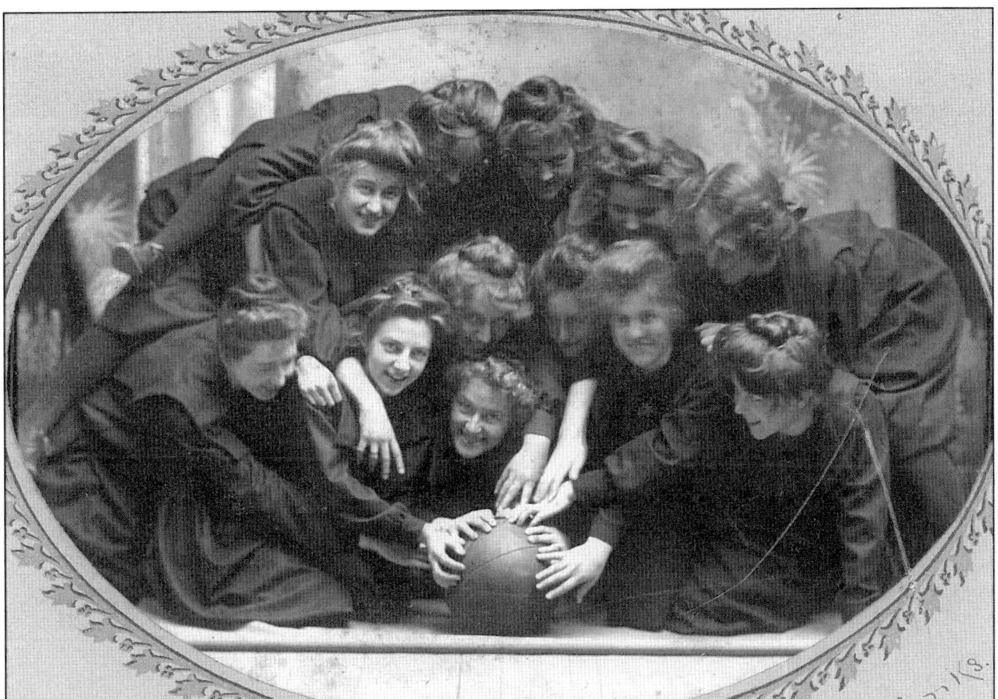

THE GIRLS' BASKETBALL TEAM, 1903. Another example of the changes occurring in Morrisville that were indicative of the changes occurring all over the United States was the increase in team sports available to girls at Peoples Academy. This photograph shows the first girls' basketball team at Peoples Academy, in 1903.

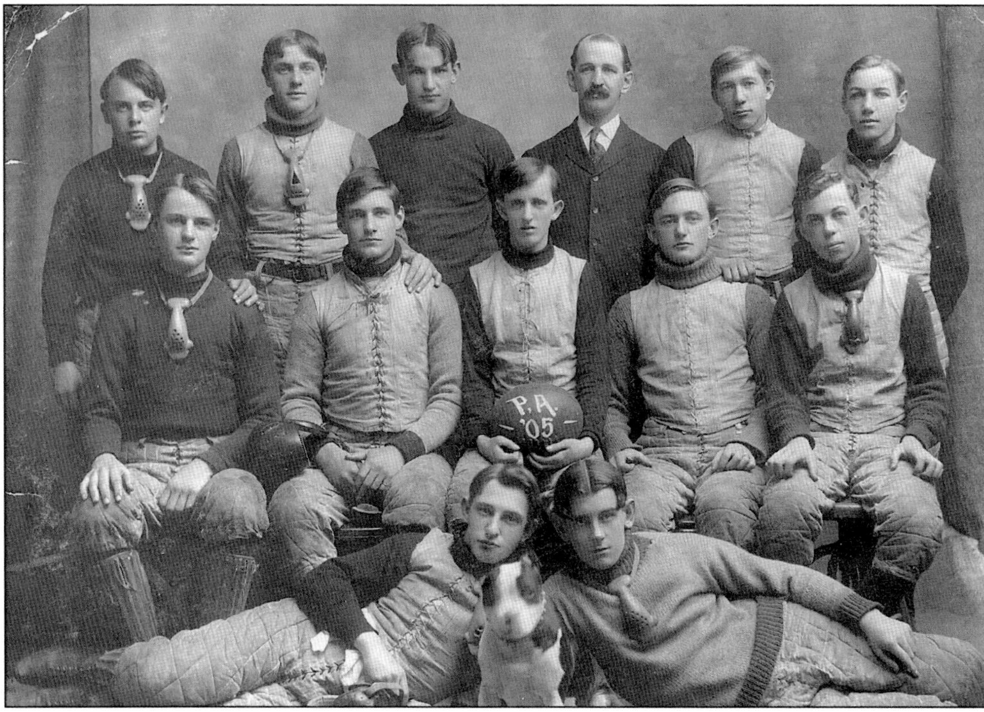

The Football Team, 1905. For some people, the fact that Peoples Academy had a football team is almost unbelievable. These boys played on the academy's 1905–1906 team. Their record is unknown.

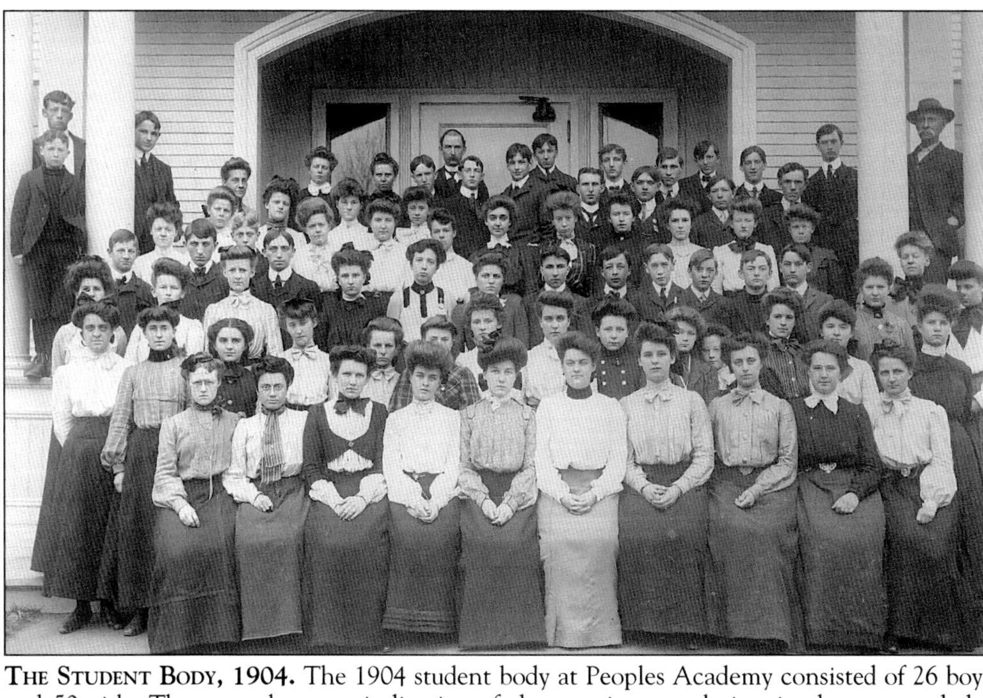

The Student Body, 1904. The 1904 student body at Peoples Academy consisted of 26 boys and 50 girls. These numbers are indicative of the growing population in the area and the increased need to be educated.

THE MIKADO, 1903. In 1903, these women, from left to right, Agnes Dooley, Mrs. G.M. Powers, and Ella Brownell, took part in a Burlington production of *The Mikado*.

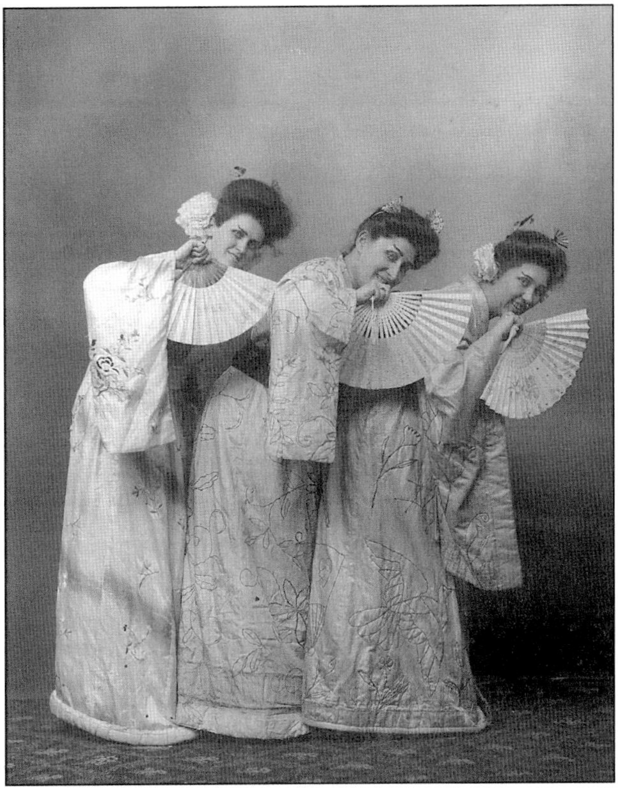

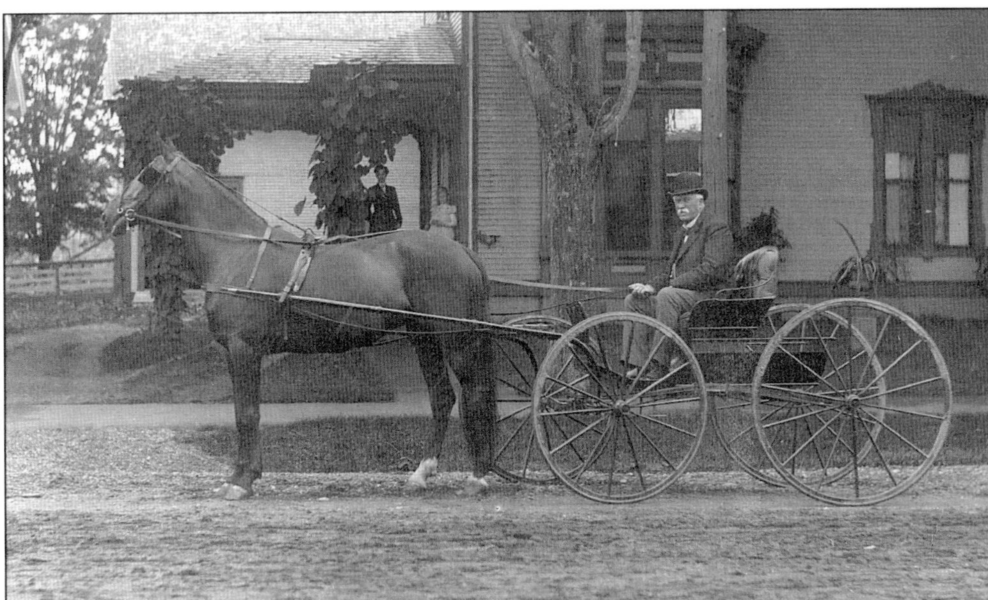

GEORGE W. HENDEE, 1906. A short time before his death in 1906, Gov. Emeritus George W. Hendee married his third wife, Mary Watts of Stowe. To the end, Hendee remained a proud and active man, turning his back on the scrutiny he received for marrying a girl young enough to be his granddaughter. Seen on the porch of his Main Street home is Lottie Vreeland, who kept house for him for some years.

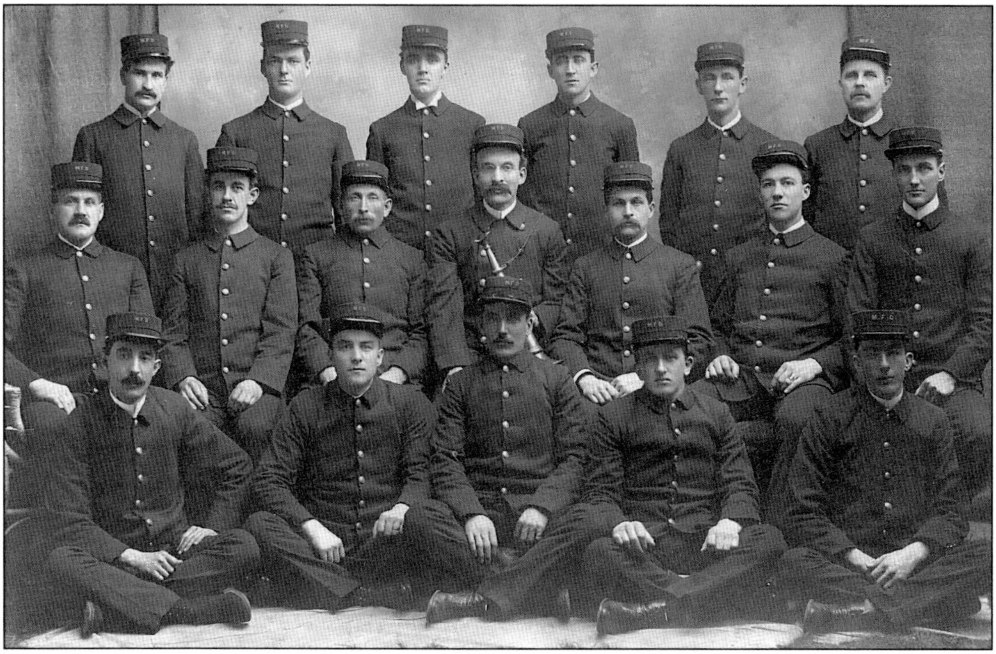

THE MORRISVILLE FIRE DEPARTMENT, 1906. This photograph shows the Morrisville Fire Department in 1906. Just six years earlier, under the direction of G.W. Doty, the fire department had gone through a major reorganization. Union Street had been picked for the location of the firehouse in 1897, following the department's establishment in 1890. E.M. Davis led the department as fire chief from 1906 to 1907.

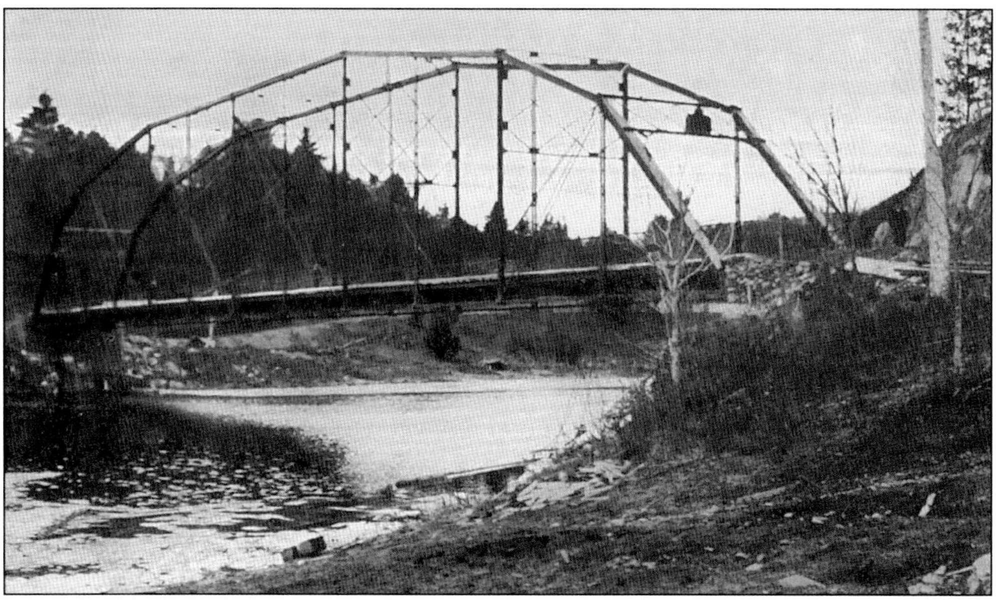

THE LONG BRIDGE, 1907. Due to the damming of the Lamoille River to create Lake Lamoille, or Lake Morrisville as many called it, a new road needed to be created between Morrisville and Cadys Falls. The Long Bridge was built in 1907 and, at 264 feet, it was Vermont's largest single-span bridge north of Brattleboro at the time. Its 37-foot-high trusses and concrete abutments sat on solid rock at both ends of the bridge.

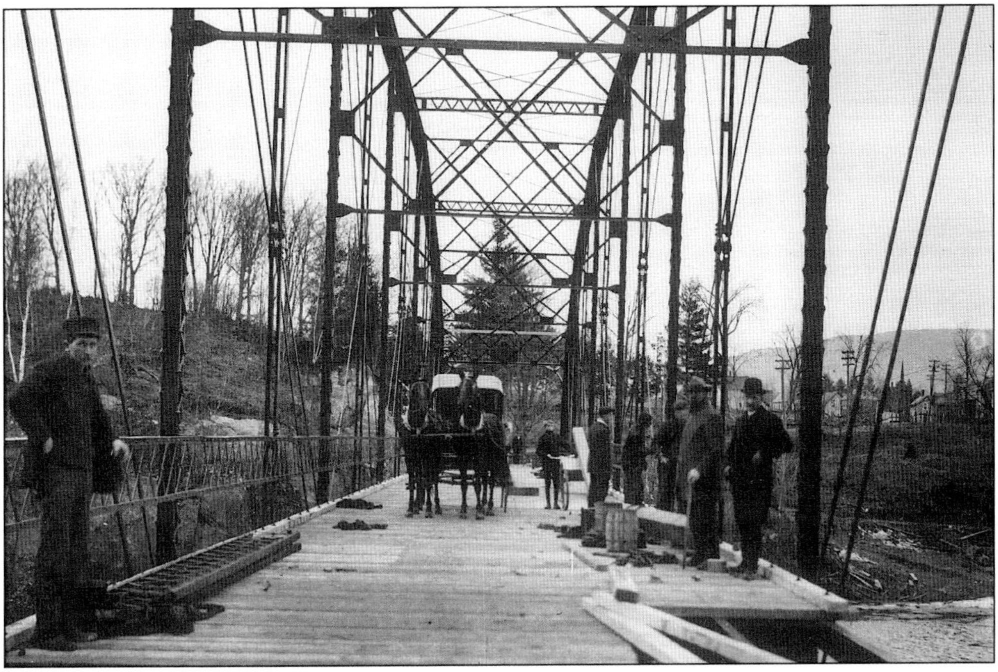

THE DEDICATION OF LONG BRIDGE, 1907. On November 23, 1907, Selectmen G.W. Doty and C.L. Gates, along with their wives, brought the first team across the newly constructed Long Bridge.

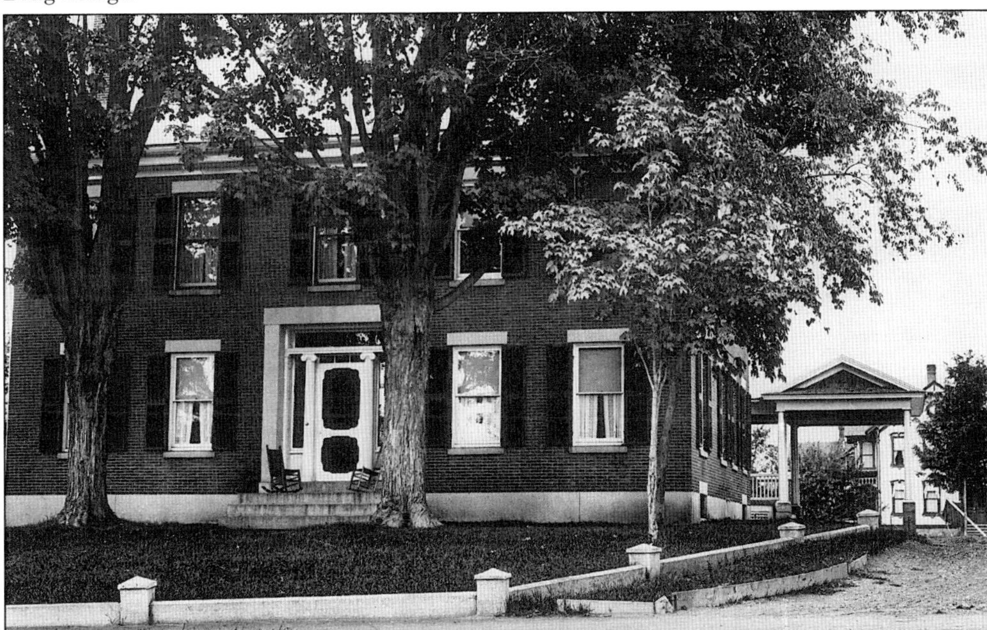

THE NOYES-SLAYTON HOUSE, 1907. On the north side of lower Main Street stood the brick house of Carlos Noyes. In 1866, Carlos Noyes sold the house and surrounding land to George J. Slayton and Charles M. Peck. Peck sold his share to Slayton in 1873. This photograph shows the house prior to major changes and improvements by George Slayton's son, Henry Slayton, in 1910.

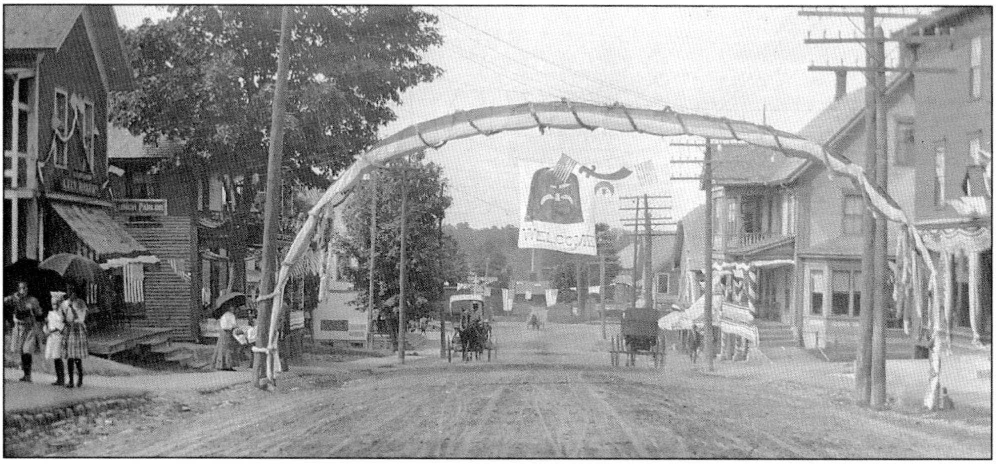

SINAI SHRINERS DAY, 1908. Seen here is the Sinai Shriners Day parade held on July 2, 1908. Little is known about this event, which brought together Shriners from far and wide. This Portland Street view also shows the Kelley Block on the right.

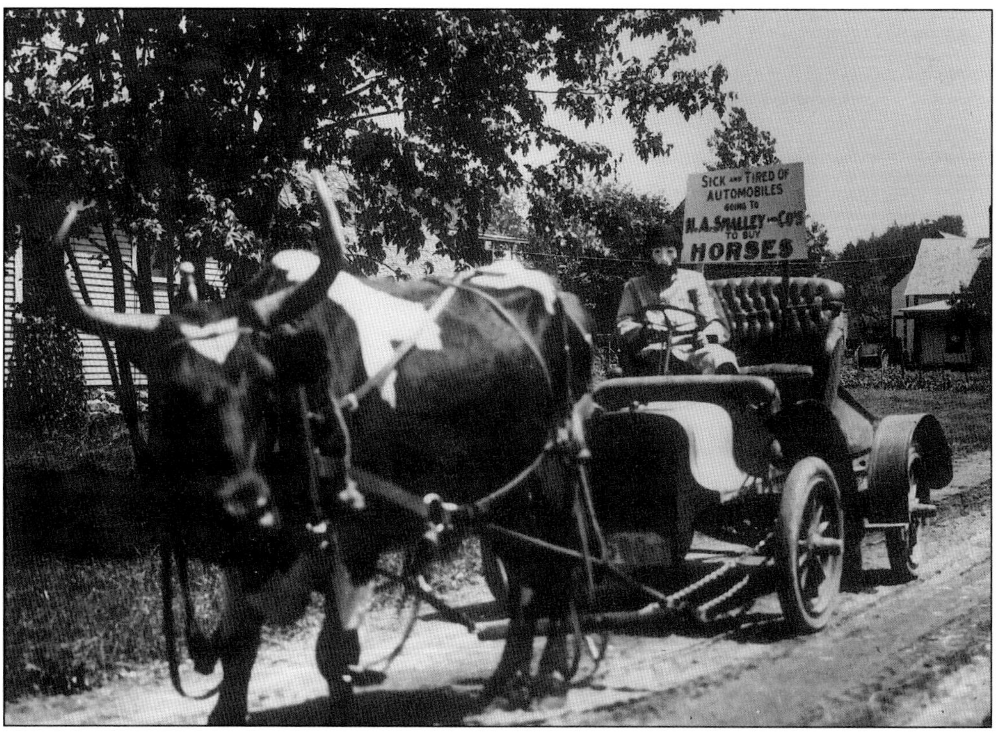

H.A. SMALLEY & COMPANY, 1908. A.R. Campbell had brought the first automobile to the county in 1903. The advent and arrival of the automobile was another major change that those in the horse business failed to appreciate. H.A. Smalley & Company, a horse-dealing firm, created this spoof of the automobile to make it clear that the car was more trouble than it was worth and if people were sick and tired of automobiles they could still buy horses at Smalley's.

THE MORRISVILLE FENCING TEAM, 1902. Little information is available about the only known fencing team organized in Morrisville. Members shown here are Frank Harris (left) and Hugh Cushman. It is possible that they were associated with Peoples Academy, and it appears that they also boxed.

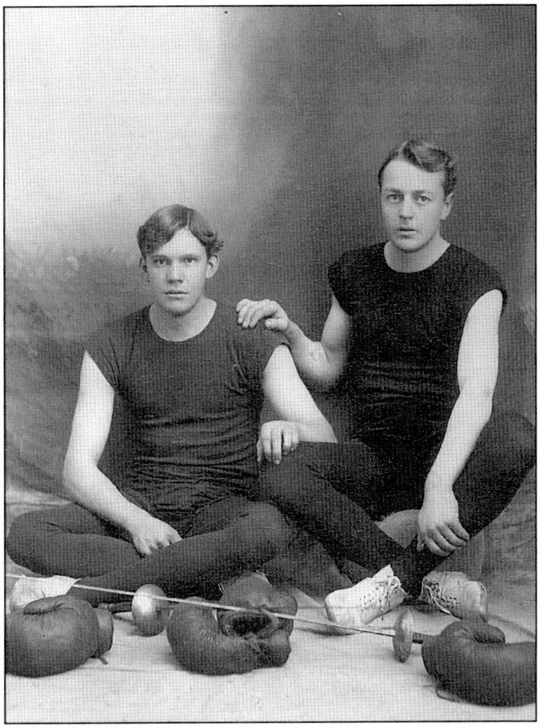

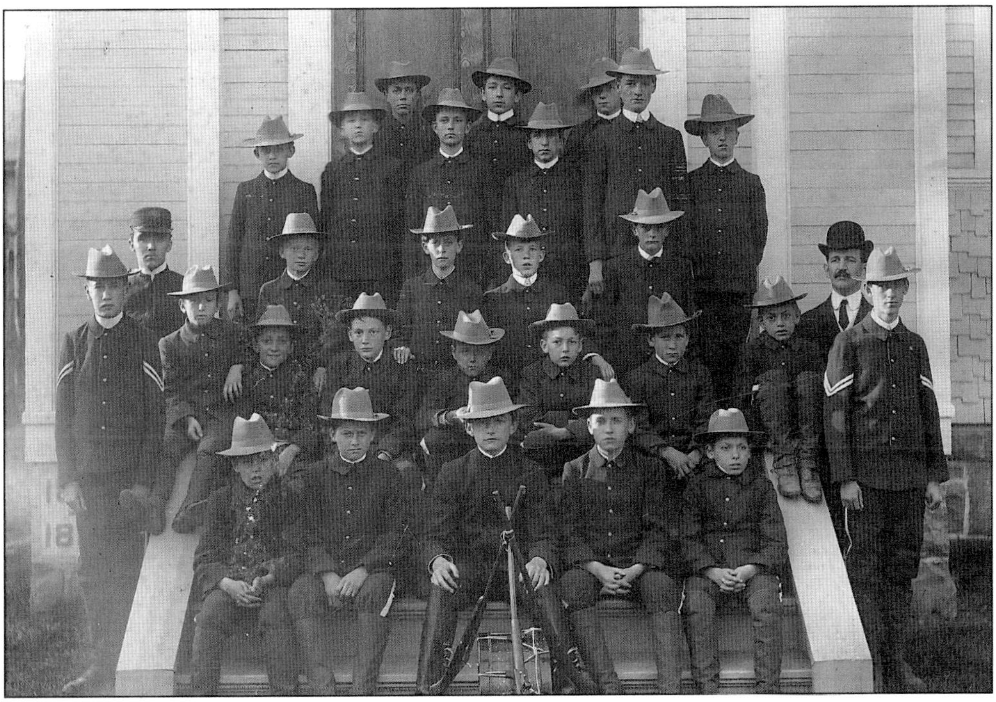

THE CADETS, 1906. This boys' club was sponsored by the First Congregational Church in 1906 and 1907. Under the direction of Rev. Christopher C. St. Clare, the cadets practiced drilling and gave benefit marching performances at the town hall to raise money. The boys were grouped in squads according to age.

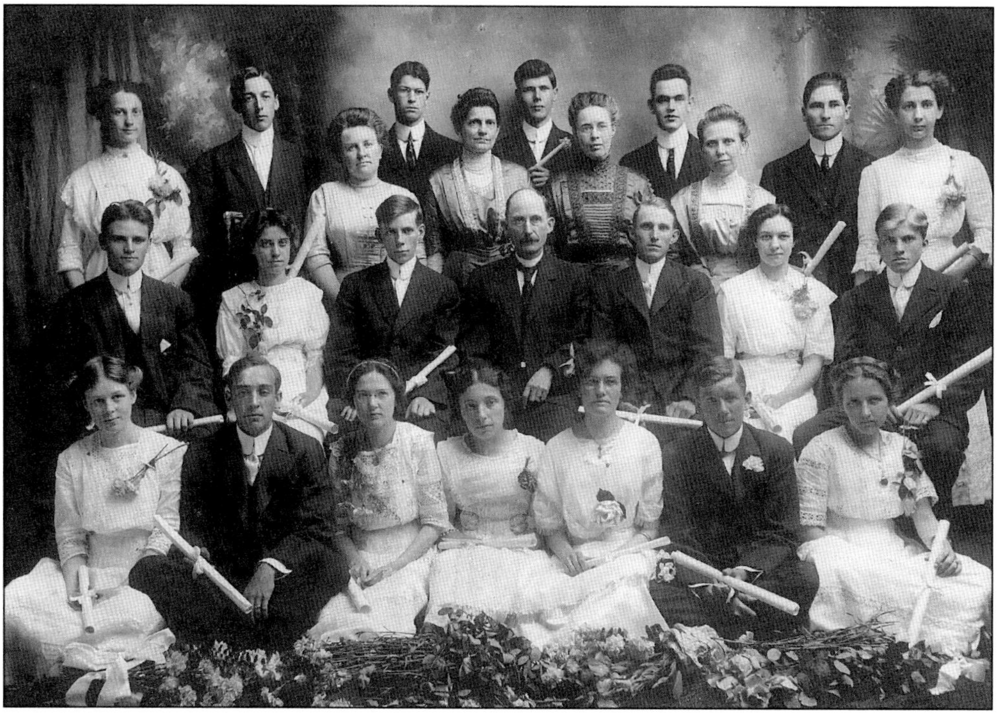

The Graduating Class of 1912. The 20 graduates of Peoples Academy's Class of 1912 are pictured here with four teachers and Principal William A. Beebe (center). Beebe's final year as principal of Peoples Academy was 1912.

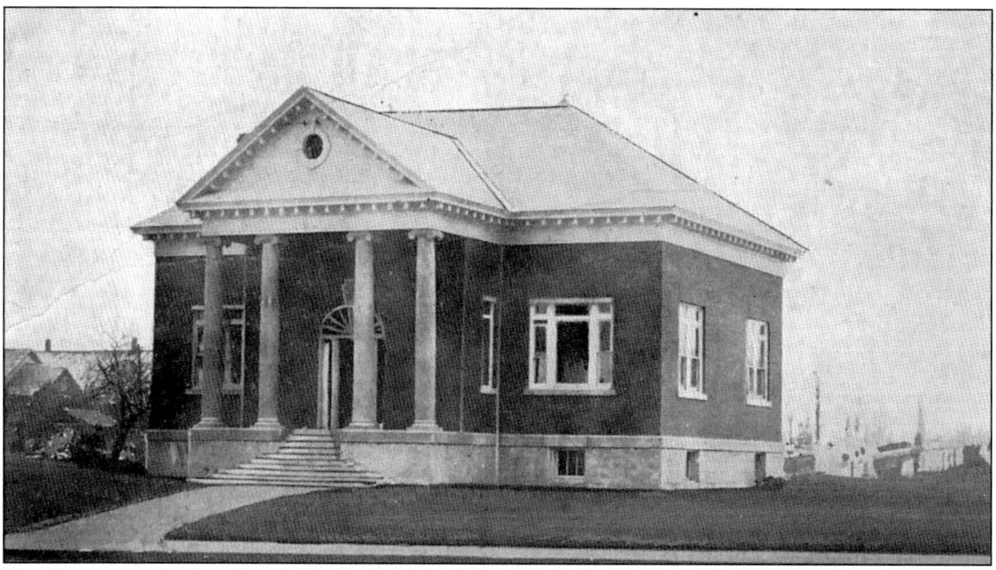

The Morristown Centennial Library, 1913. Laura Gleed began a small public library in Morrisville shortly after 1885. The library was housed in several different places until a grant was obtained from the Carnegie Library Foundation. In 1912, the Kelsey Block on Main Street was purchased. The house was moved, and the Morristown Centennial Library's new home was under construction. The new library opened for use in July 1913, just a year after Laura Gleed died without seeing its completion.

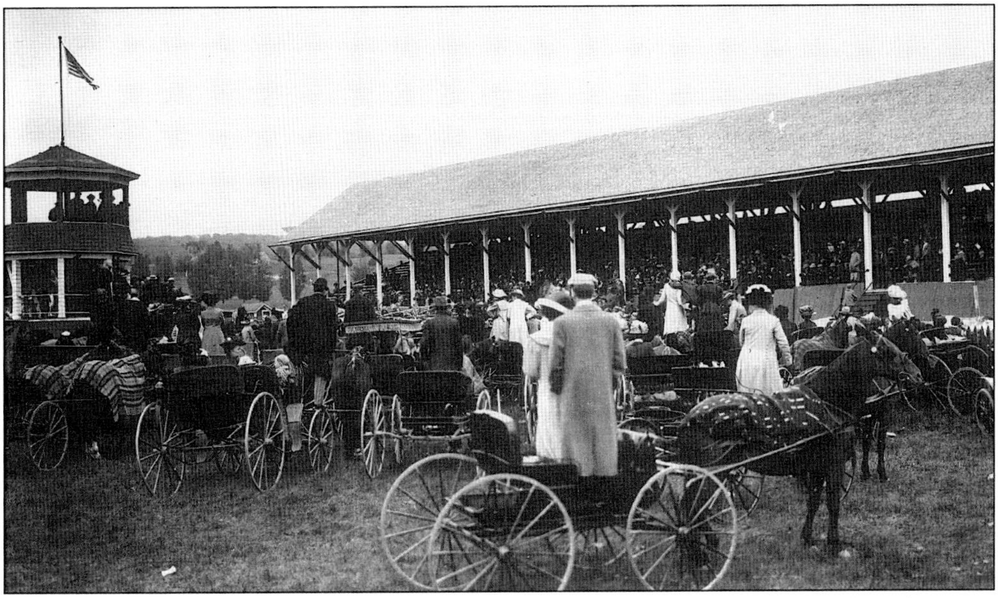

The Lamoille Valley Fair, c. 1910. Beginning in 1866, a fair was held east of Maple Street in Morrisville. Fairgoers enjoyed a racetrack and exhibit hall. In 1872, amid bitter opposition, the Lamoille Valley Fairground Company was formed and 17 acres of land on the west side of Brooklyn Street was acquired for new fairgrounds. The majority of the opposition to the move came from village merchants who felt that they would lose out when the fair moved north of the railroad tracks.

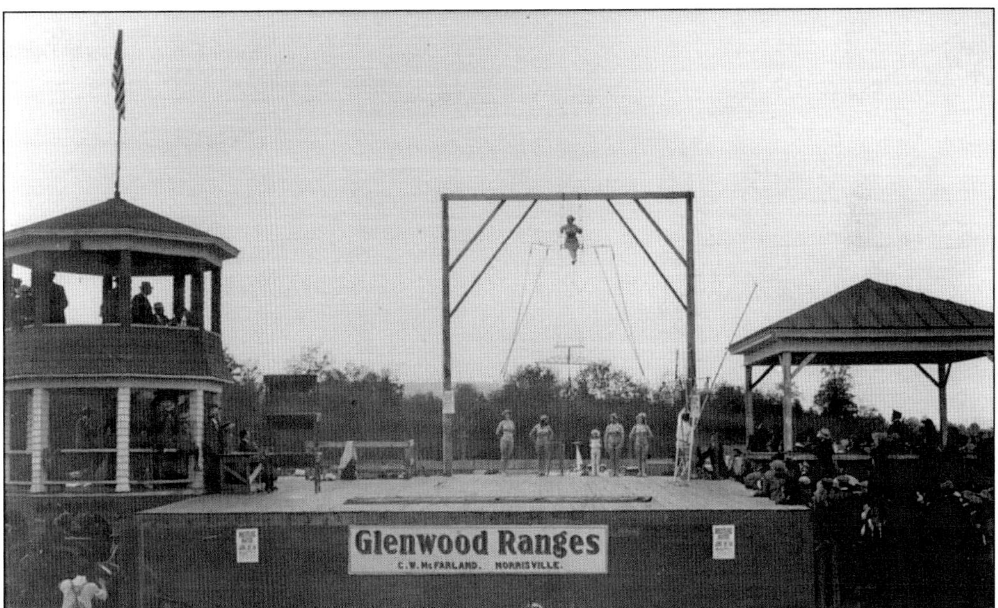

The Lamoille Valley Fair, c. 1910. The new fairgrounds turned out to be easier for many to access because of the close proximity of the railroad. The fair was extended from two to three days, a racetrack was laid, and a floral hall was built. Other buildings were soon added.

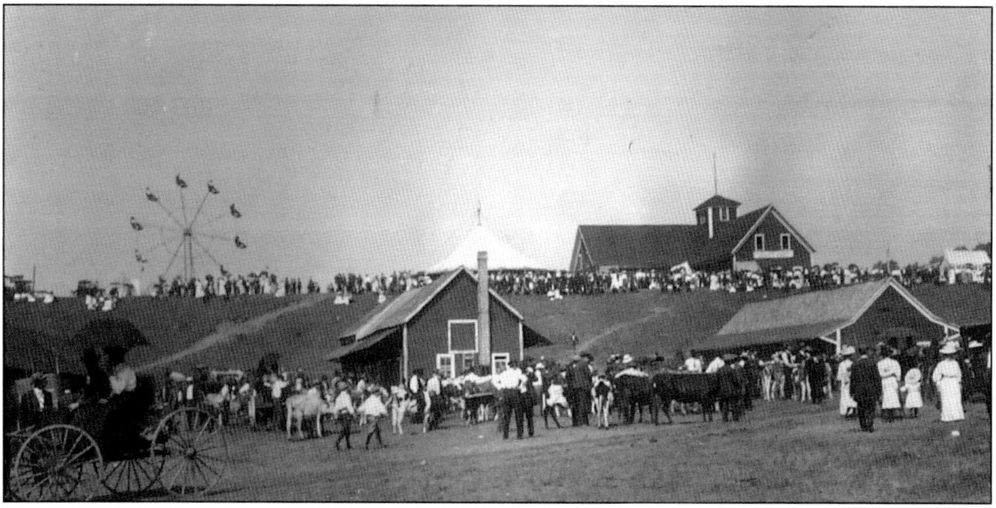

The Lamoille Valley Fair, c. 1910. The Lamoille Valley Fair was originally agriculturally focused, and while it retained that focus into the 20th century, it also became more carnival-like after the move to Brooklyn Street. A balloon ascension was added, as well as Fakir's Row, a merry-go-round, and a large midway.

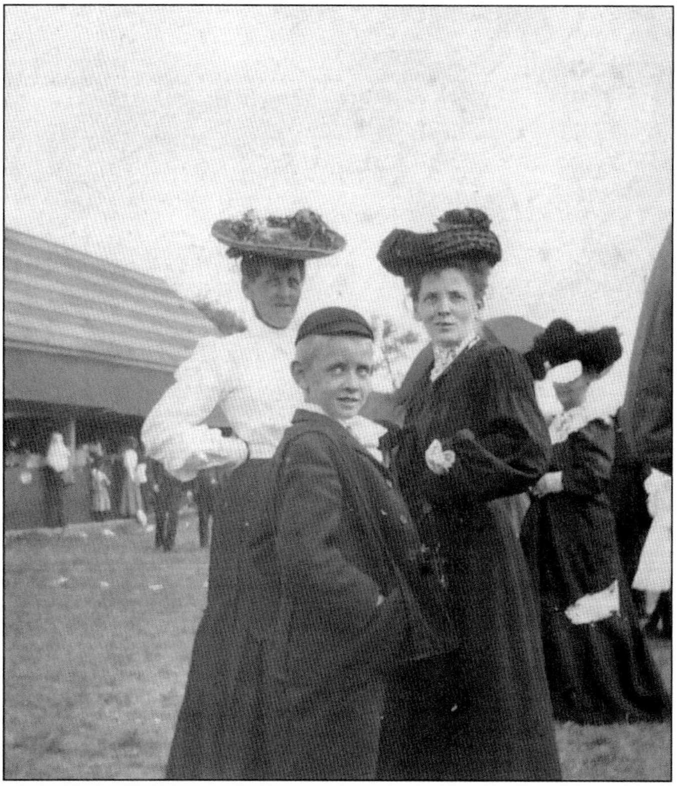

The Lamoille Valley Fair, 1910. Enjoying the Lamoille Valley Fair in 1910 are, from left to right, Anna Doty Jones, Walter Jones, and Emma Spearzat.

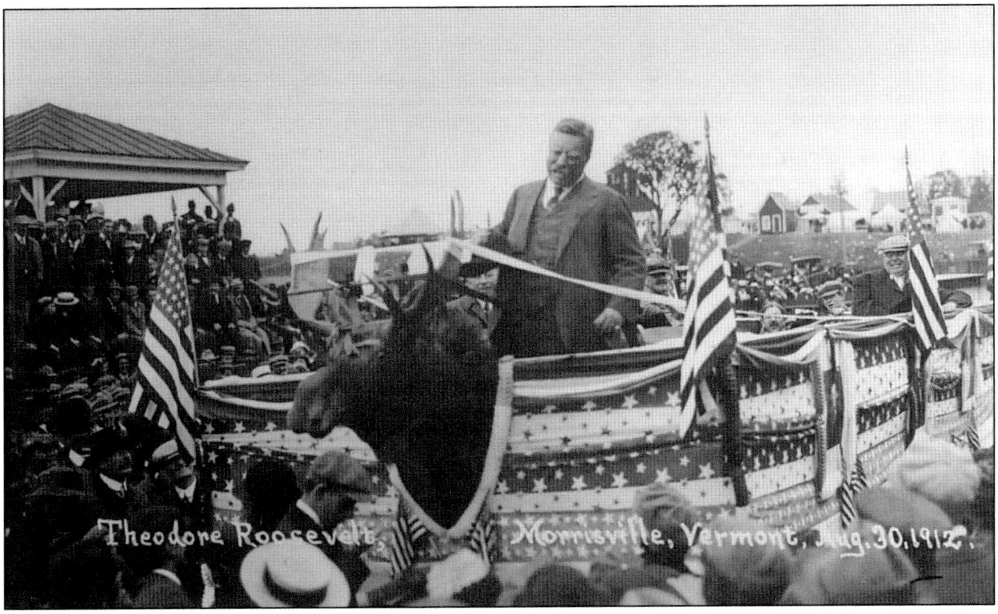

THE LAMOILLE VALLEY FAIR, 1912. On August 30, 1912, presidential candidate Theodore Roosevelt arrived in Morrisville during his tour of New England as part of his famous Bull Moose campaign. The Lamoille Valley Fair was continued another day to accommodate his arrival.

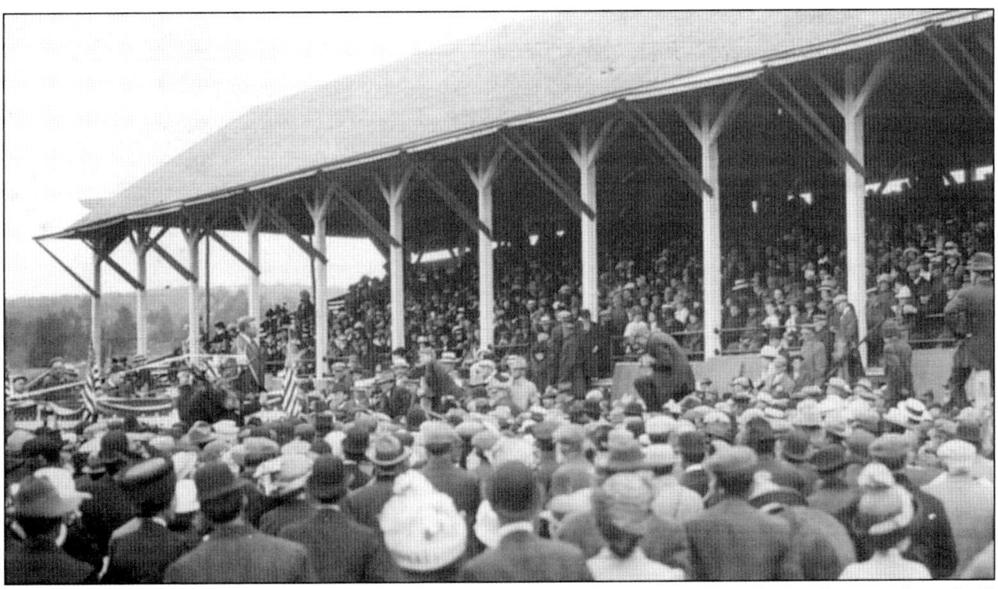

THE LAMOILLE VALLEY FAIR, 1912. Theodore Roosevelt sits atop a large float with a Bull Moose head on the front pulled by 14 yoke of oxen. Capt. S.B. Waite of Hyde Park led the procession, followed by the Morrisville Military Band.

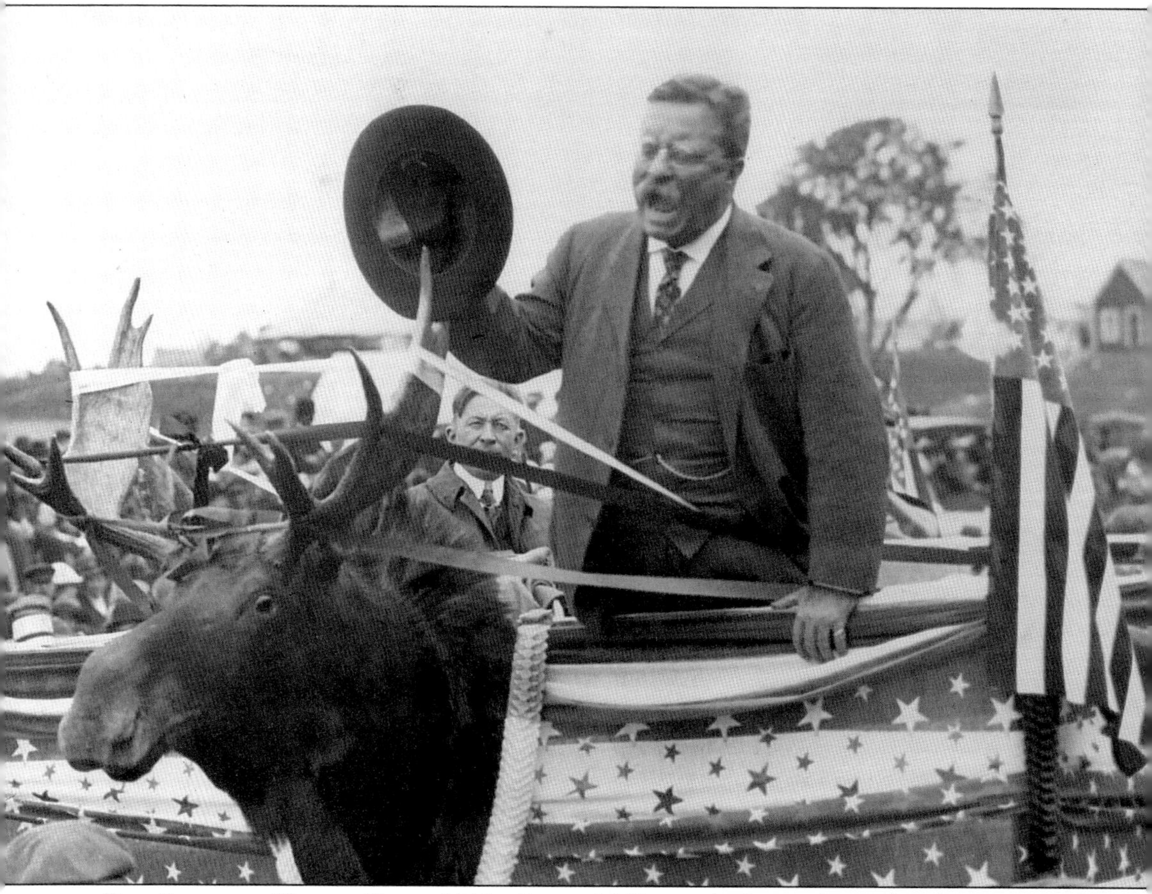

The Lamoille Valley Fair, 1912. Some 6,000 people listened to Theodore Roosevelt speak for 30 minutes, as he defined his ideas on progressive principles. Despite his visit, when the November elections came around, Lamoille County voted Republican once again. Sorry, Mr. Roosevelt.

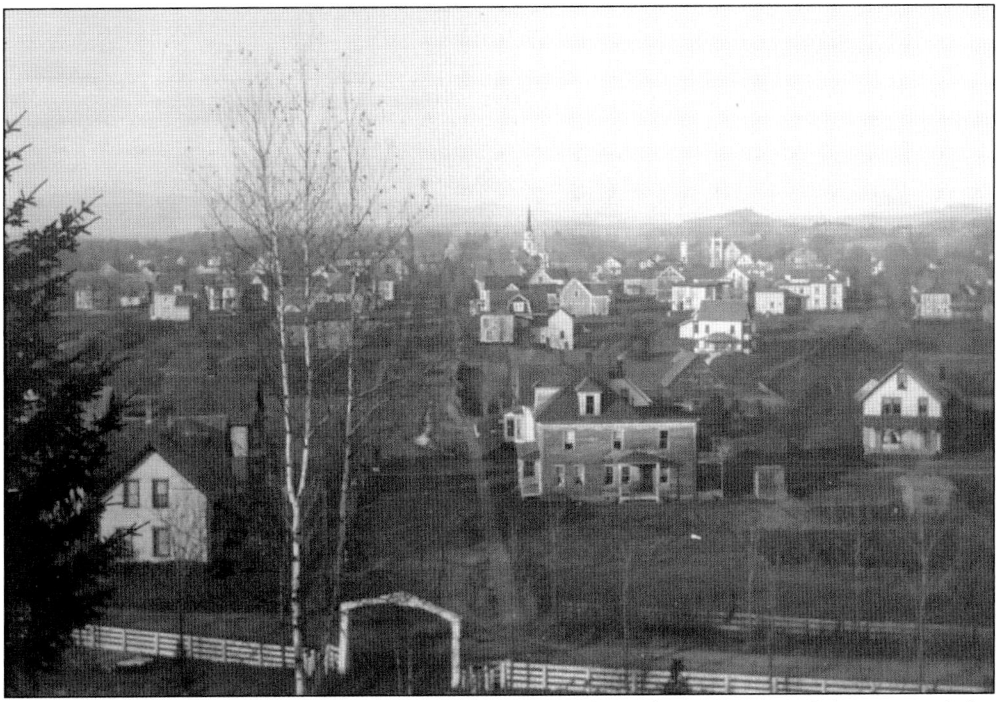

CONGRESS STREET, C. 1910. This view is looking northward on Congress Street toward the village. The Congress Street area remained fairly undeveloped for many years and was the site of the 1890 centennial celebration near Harrison Avenue. By 1910, a large number of homes had been built on Congress Street and other Morrisville side streets.

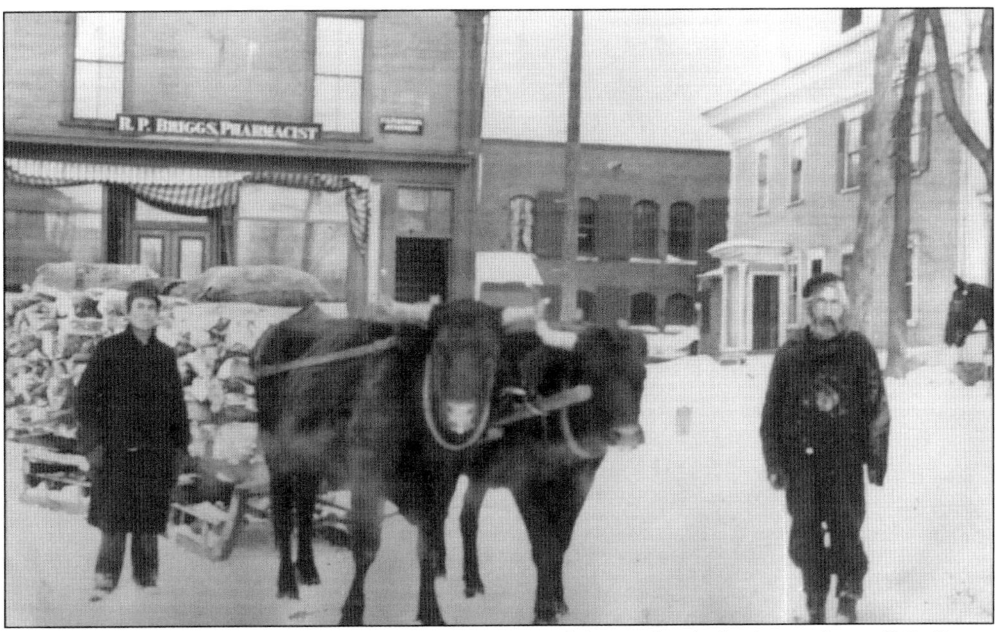

WOOD OPERATIONS, C. 1911. These men are about to deliver a load of pulpwood near R.P. Briggs Pharmacy during the winter of 1911. To the right is one-armed John McDermott. Wood delivery and operations were a good source of income in the late 19th and early 20th centuries.

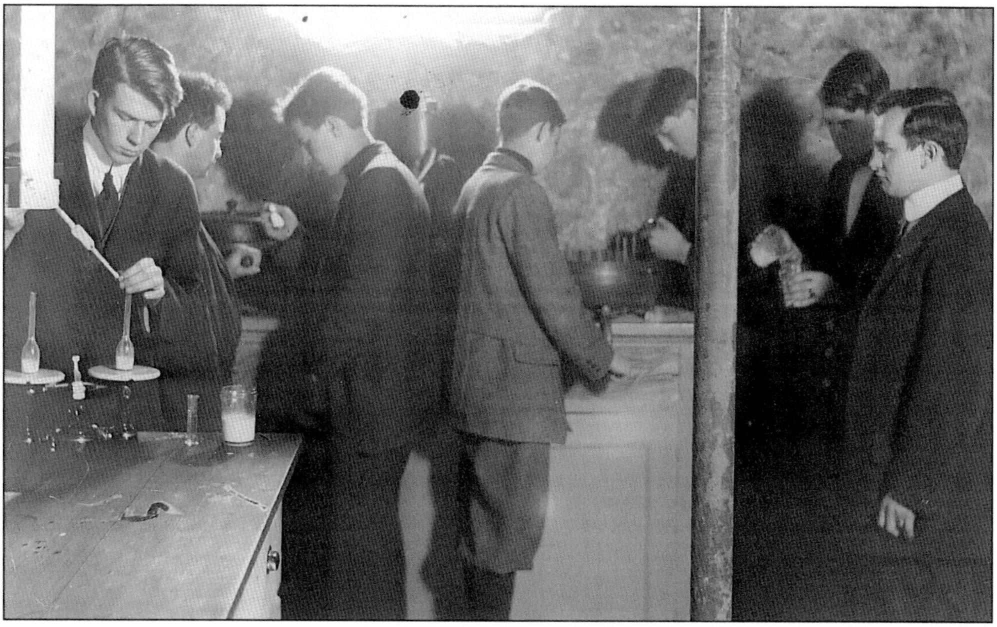

THE AGRICULTURE CLASS, 1913. Pictured here are members of Peoples Academy's agriculture class testing milk in 1913. This class was offered along with home economics and a teacher-training course in 1912 and 1913, as part of a curriculum expansion. Members of the agriculture class participated in a farm products and domestic arts contest on October 21, 1913.

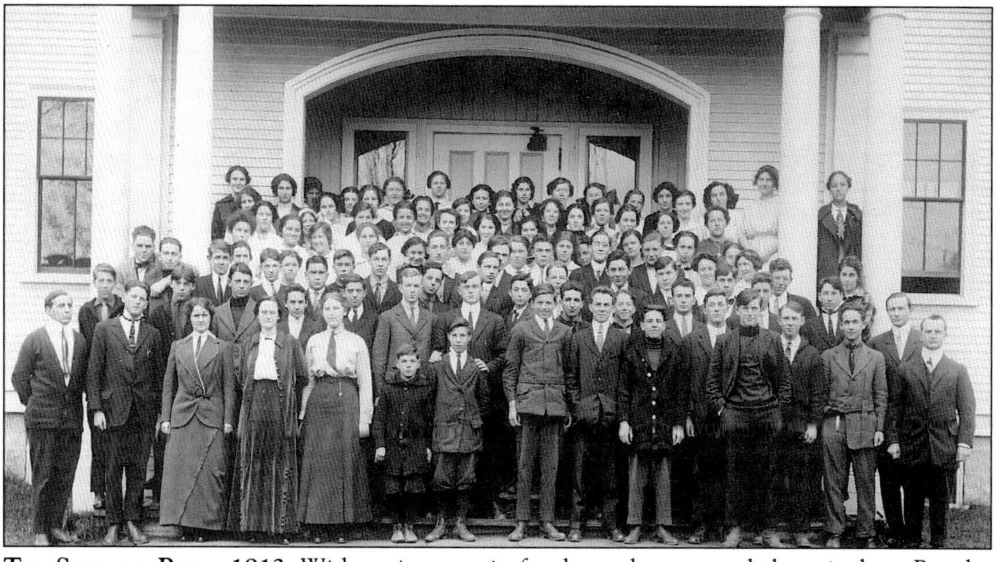

THE STUDENT BODY, 1913. With an increase in faculty and an expanded curriculum, Peoples Academy was better equipped to handle the steady growth in population that Morristown had undergone. Many rural Vermont towns were seeing a slight decrease in population; Morristown's, however, had increased from 1,897 in the 1870s to 2,652 in 1910.

THE SOLDIER'S MONUMENT, C.1911. The Civil War Memorial Monument was the brainchild of veteran Col. G.W. Doty. He made an appeal to the voters to construct some sort of monument to the soldiers who had fought in the Civil War. C.H.A. Stafford presented a resolution instructing the selectmen to give $1,500 toward the completion of a soldier's monument.

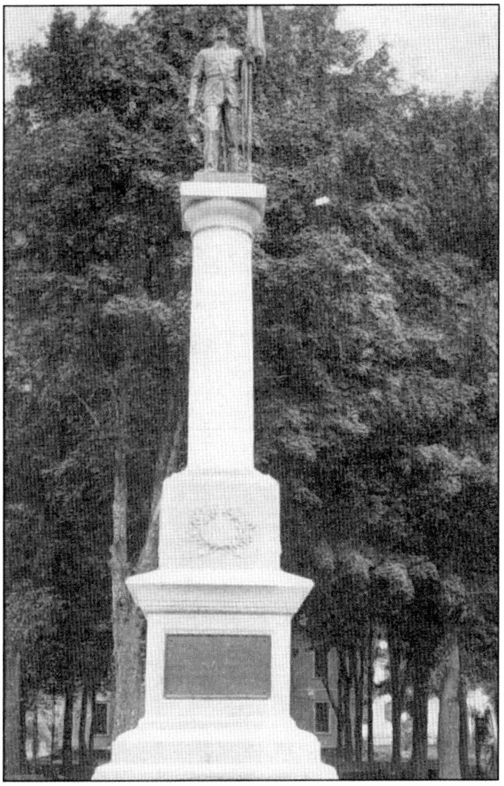

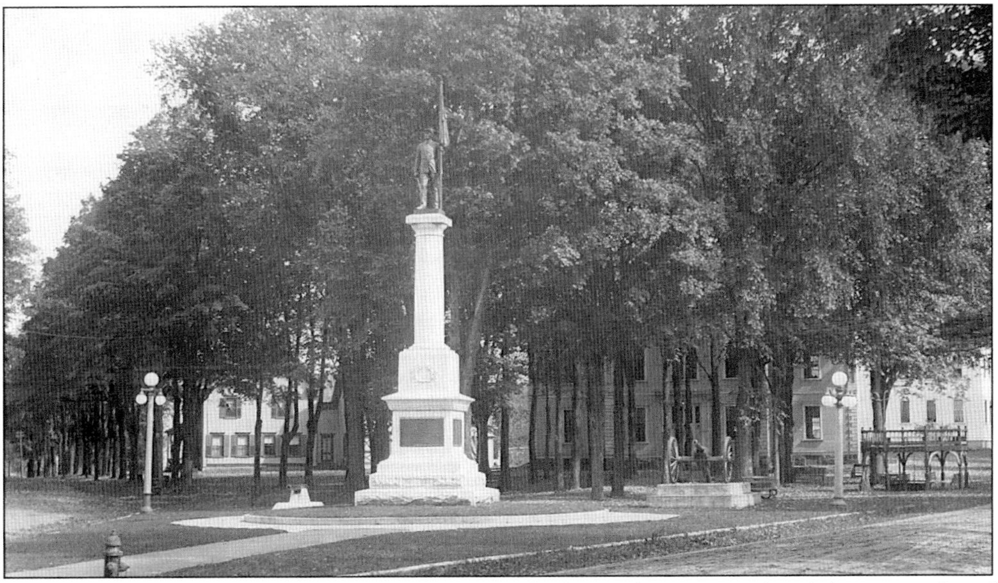

THE SOLDIER'S MONUMENT, C. 1911. C.H.A. Stafford's resolution passed and the remainder of the funds were raised by subscription. The 26-foot, six-inch monument was built with granite from Barre. It was topped with a 12-foot bronze soldier, and its sides contained the names of 172 Morristown volunteers and 85 members of the J.M. Warner Post No. 4 Grand Army of the Republic. A time capsule was inserted in the monument's foundation. The monument was dedicated on May 30, 1911.

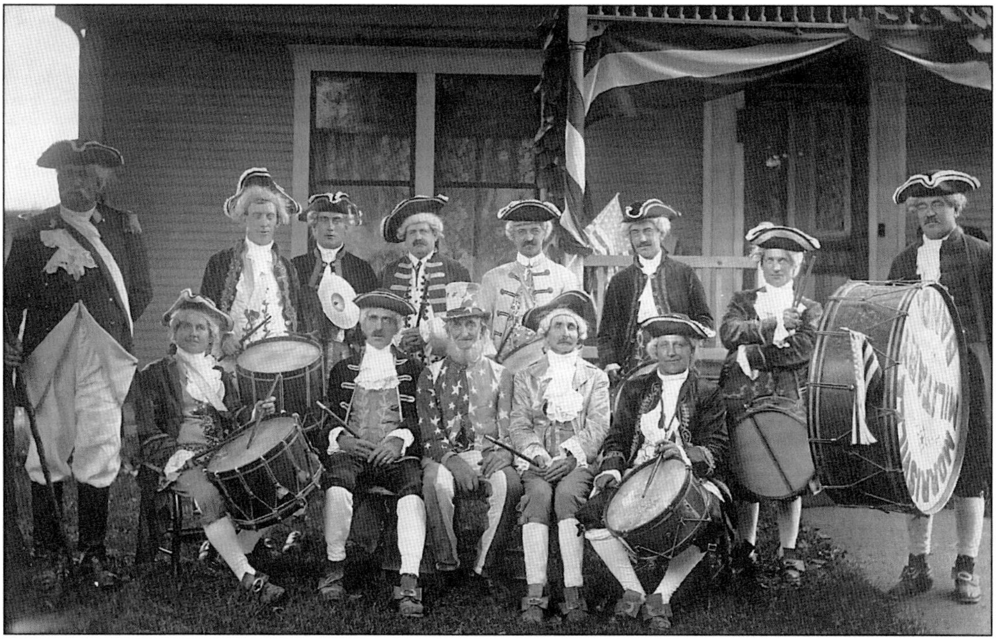

The North Hyde Park Drum Corps, 1912. This photograph of the North Hyde Park Drum Corps was taken on July 4, 1912. Members of the corps include five from the Morrisville Military Band, who joined the group after the Morrisville band disbanded following the loss of member Channing Greene and others. The North Hyde Park Drum Corps participated in Morrisville's Independence Day Parade on July 4, 1912.

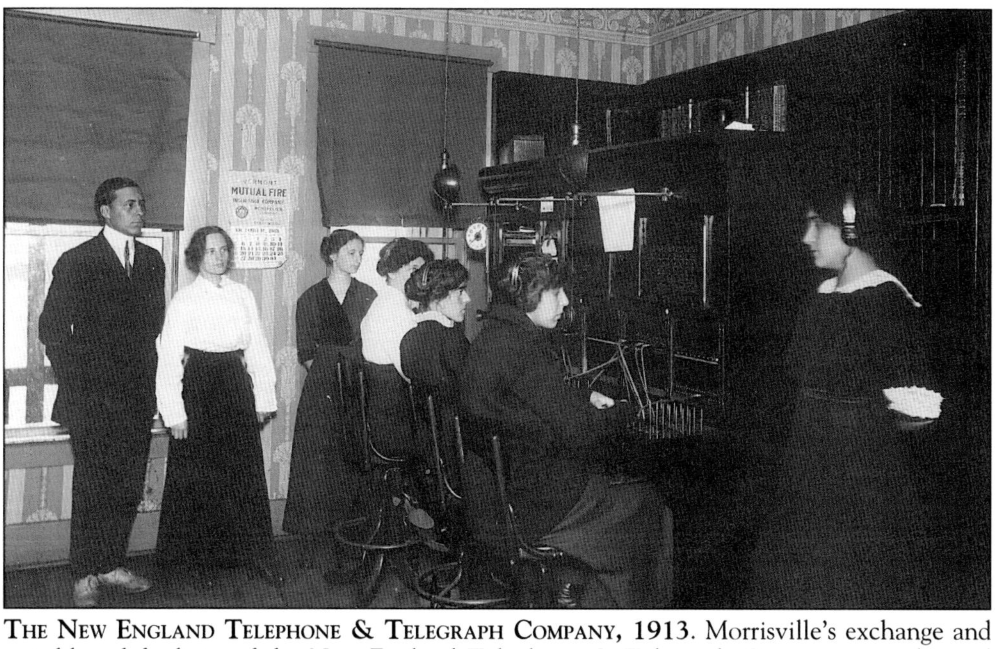

The New England Telephone & Telegraph Company, 1913. Morrisville's exchange and switchboard facilities of the New England Telephone & Telegraph Company were located on the second floor of the Centennial Block in 1913. Company personnel, from left to right, are William Meacham, Reba Delano, Bertha Durgin, Myrtle Durgin, Flora Tuliper, Hazel Sherman, and Juliaett Brooks.

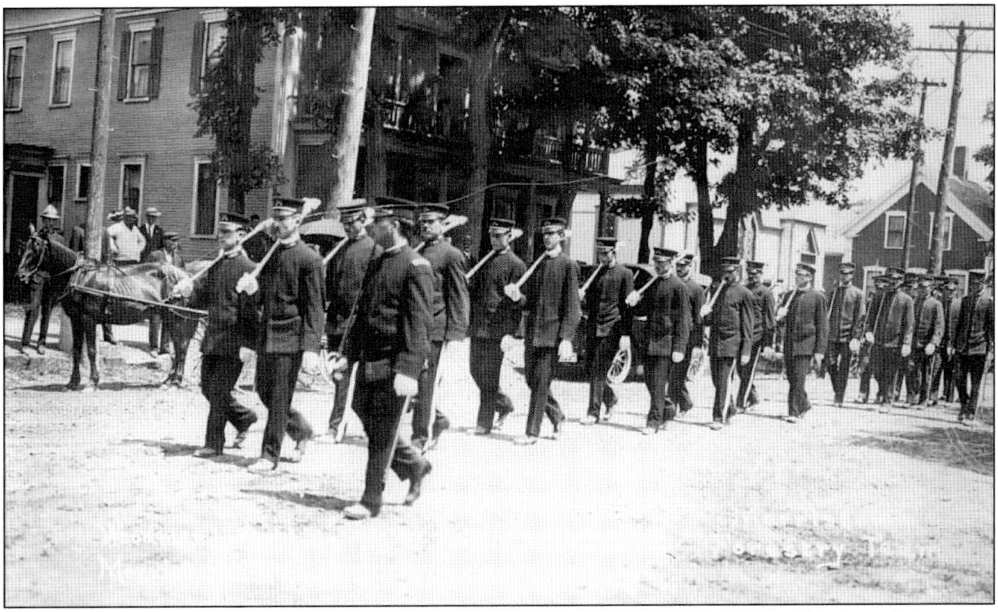

The Modern Woodsmen of America, 1911. In 1911, the Modern Woodsmen of America celebrated a Woodsmen Field Day with a parade through the streets of Morrisville. During 1912, in wintertime's negative temperatures, members of the Modern Woodsmen of America cut, split, and piled 40 cords of wood for a sick Howard McNall.

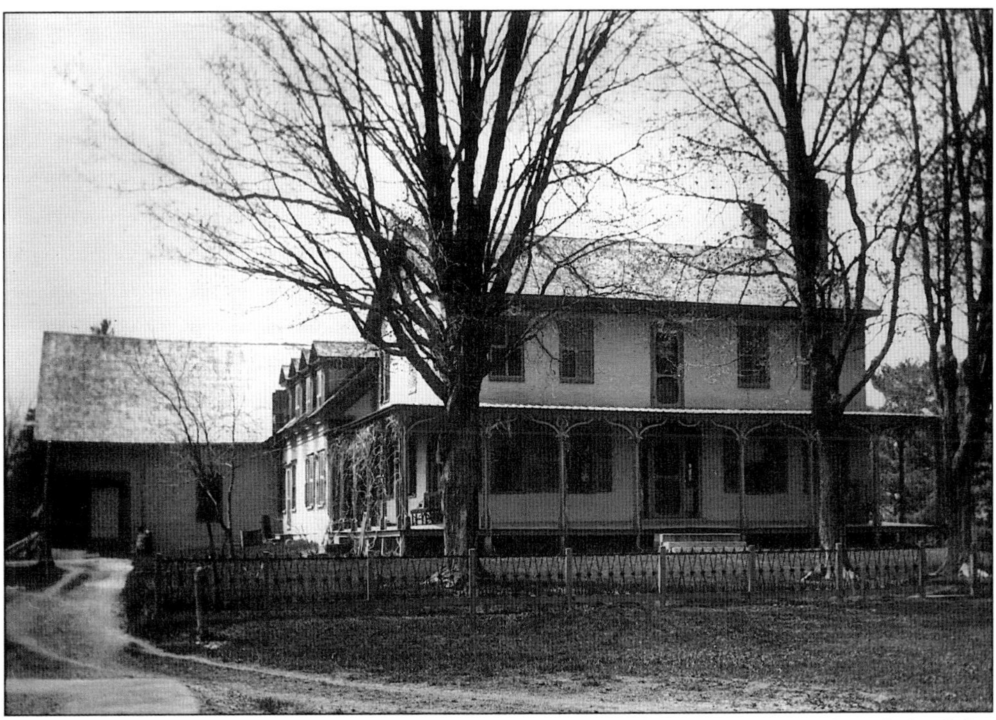

The Noyes House, c. 1910. In 1875, the Honorable Carlos S. Noyes purchased the John Safford House on Main Street. Noyes added the ell, carriage barn, and Victorian porch, and also renovated the house's interior.

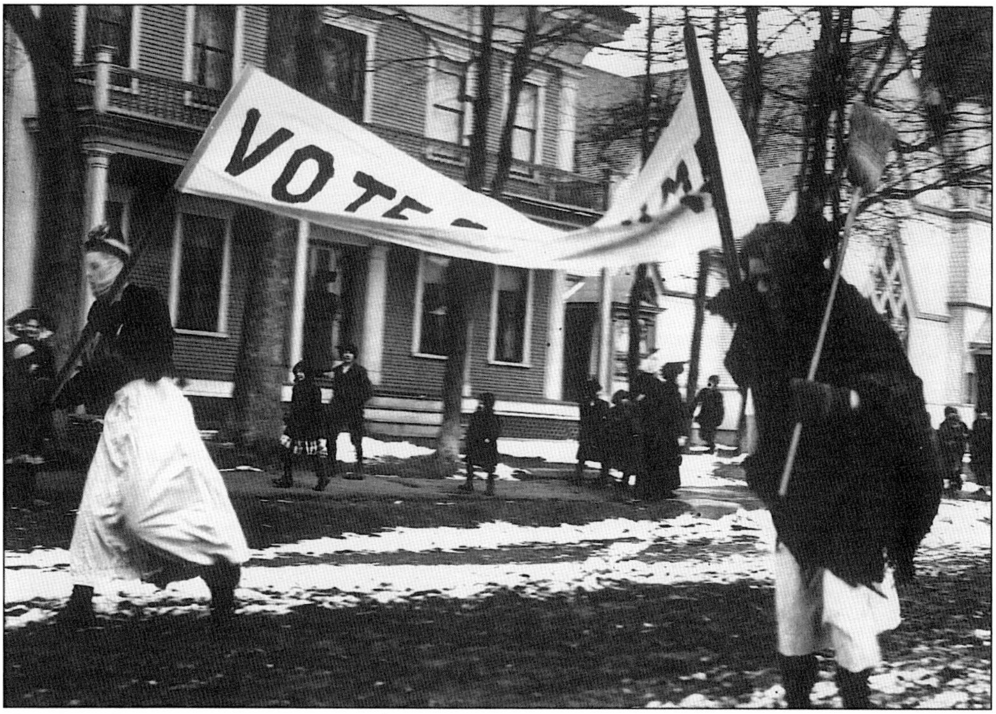

THE FUN PARADE, 1913. On March 28, 1913, Peoples Academy students marched through the streets of Morrisville in the Fun Parade. These marchers poked fun at the women's suffrage movement. The banner that they are carrying reads "Vote fer Wimen."

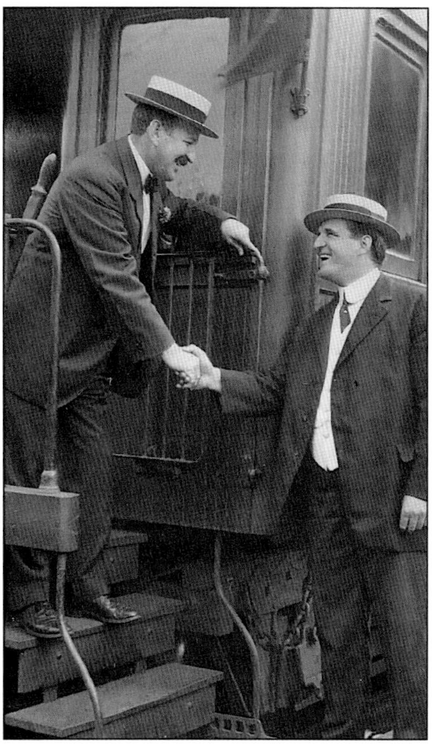

OUT WITH THE OLD, IN WITH THE NEW, c. 1911. This photograph depicts a send-off and a welcoming of Congregational ministers. Rev. Christopher C. St. Clare was pastor from 1903 to 1910. Next, the church welcomed Rev. Walter E. Baker, who served as pastor from 1911 to 1918. Here, Baker bids St. Clare farewell on the St. Johnsbury & Lake Champlain Railroad.

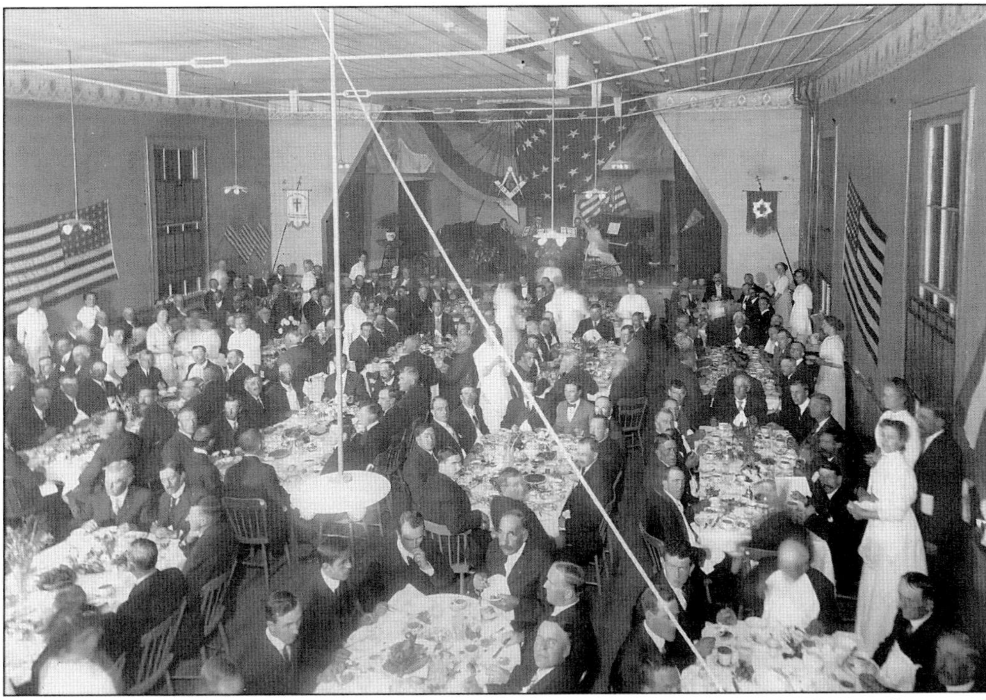

THE MOUNT VERNON LODGE ANNIVERSARY, 1913. This photograph shows the 100th anniversary banquet of the Mount Vernon Lodge No. 8, held on October 12, 1913. Included at the tables in the foreground are T.C. Cheney, Fred Mould, E.H. Olmstead, Capt. Frank Kenfield, and W. Irving LeBarm. The banquet was held at Morrisville Town Hall.

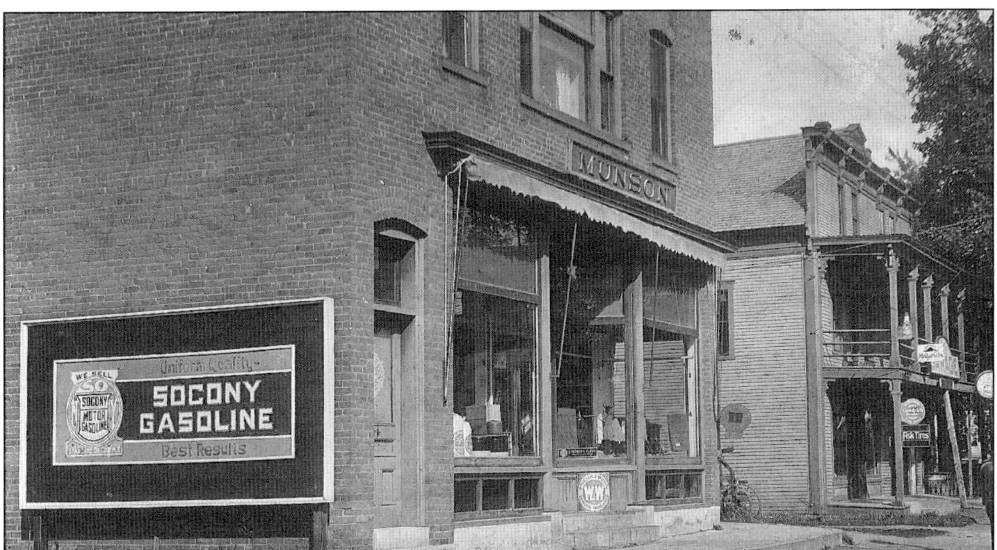

THE MUNSON STORE, C. 1914. Harlan P. Munson constructed this Main Street building in 1904. Munson died in 1914, and his son Levi Munson continued the business. To the right stands the former furniture and undertaking establishment of G.W. Doty.

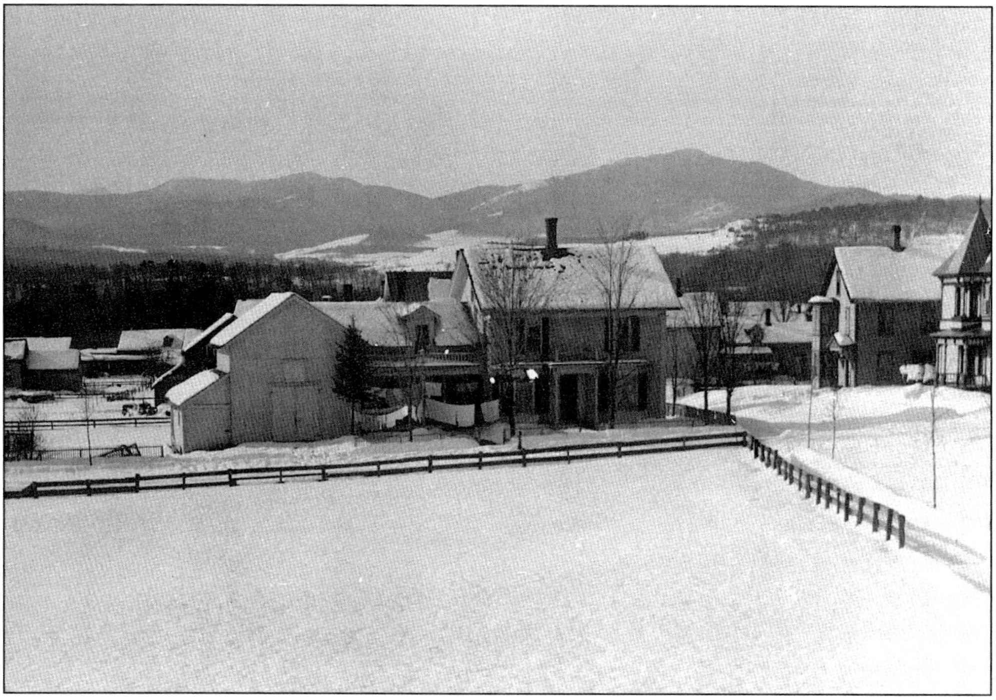

Congress and Union Streets, c. 1915. This photograph was taken from the Stafford House on Union Street, looking across Congress Street to Union Street, which runs along the right. The Bates house stands on the right, and the home of longtime Peoples Academy teacher Grace Tyndall is in the center.

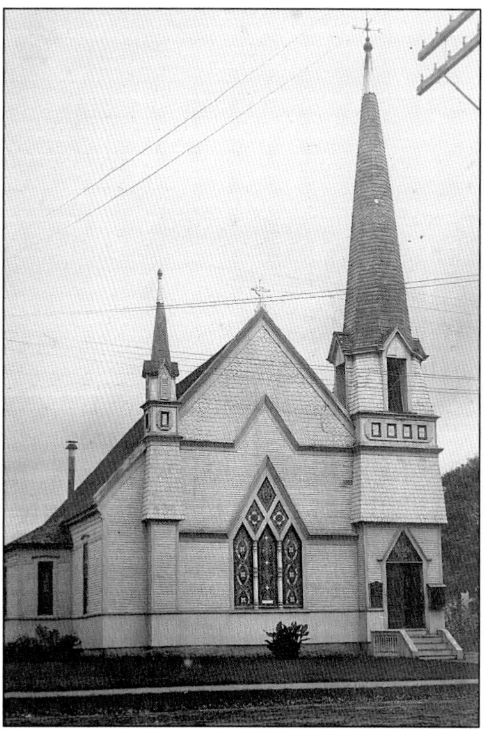

The Puffer Methodist Church, 1915. Named in honor of Rev. William R. Puffer, the Puffer Methodist Church was constructed in 1895 at a cost of $3,500. Early Methodists had shared the Union Church that was built in Morrisville in 1836. When the Universalists gained denomination, the Methodists built a church back at the town center in 1839. They came back to Morrisville in 1872 and occupied three other buildings before constructing this church. Puffer Methodist Church was enlarged under the direction of Rev. W.T. Best in 1912.

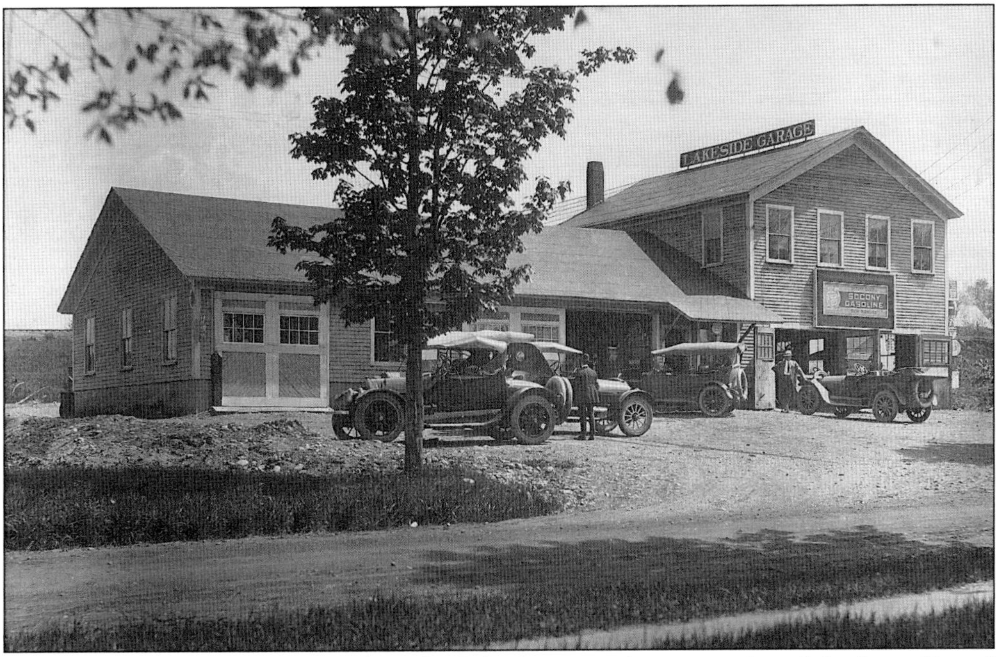

The Lake Side Garage, 1919. The Lake Side Garage took its name from Lake Lamoille and was founded in 1916 by James O. Reed and Fred C. Peck. Two years later Reed bought out Peck. The business serviced and repaired cars but did not sell them.

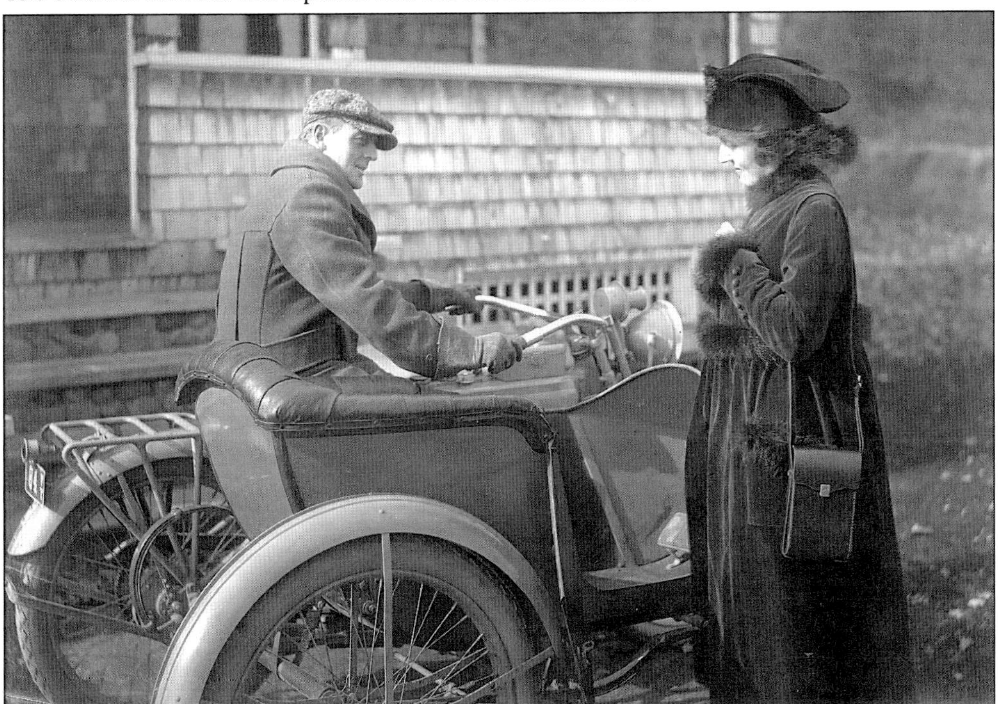

Frederick Child Jr. and Loeata Simpson, c. 1920. This photograph shows two local citizens, Frederick R. Child Jr. and Loeata Hill Simpson, with one of the only eight-horsepower Harley Davidsons in Morrisville. This cycle was registered to Leon E. Ward in 1917.

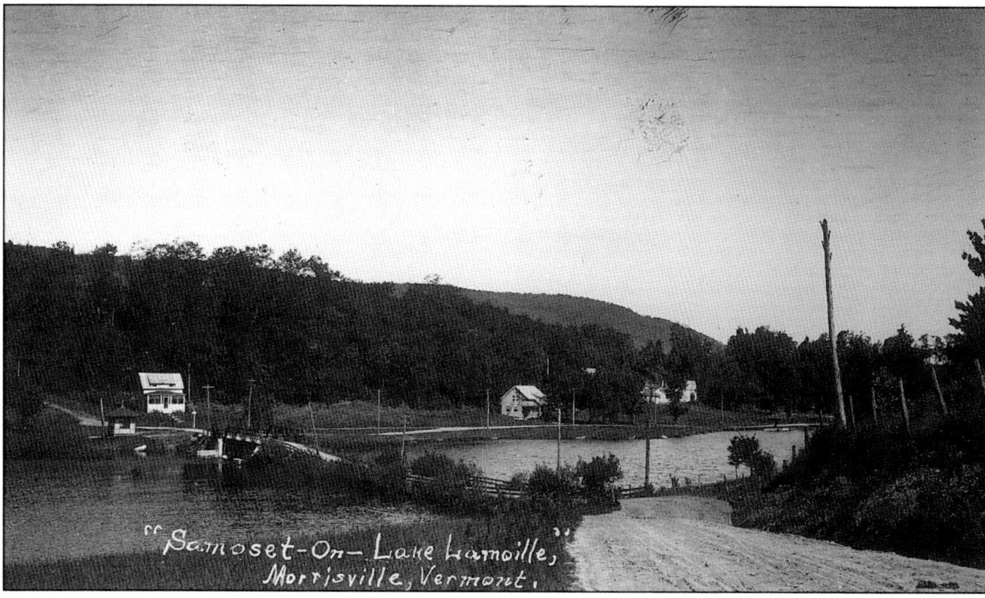

THE SAMOSET COLONY, ESTABLISHED 1908. Dr. William Taft Slayton had long envisioned a summer resort on Lake Lamoille. He established the Samoset Colony in 1908. Slayton began the project by improving the shores of Lake Lamoille. He then built a central dining hall, a clubhouse, and 20 cottages.

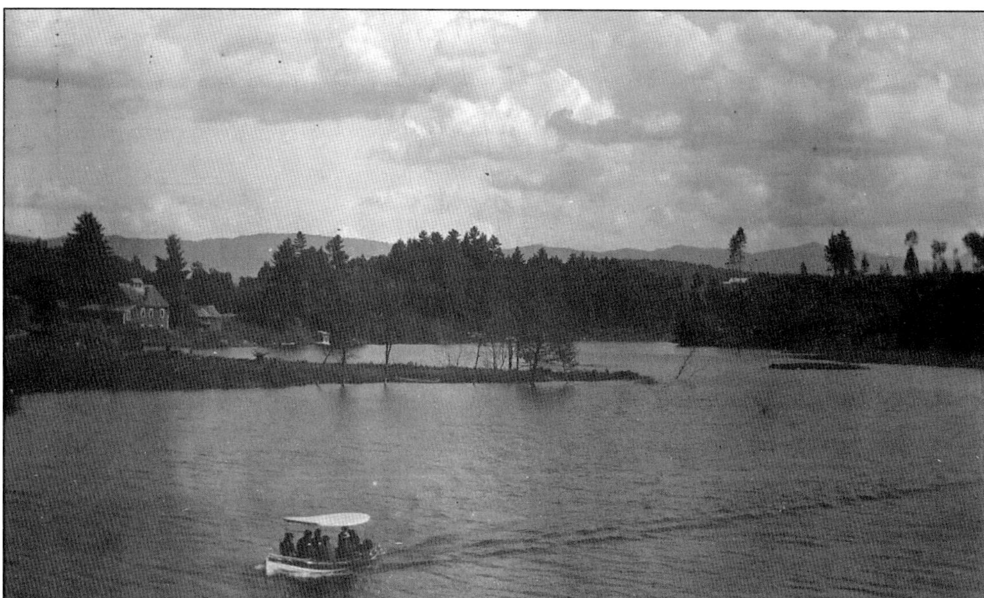

"DREAMWORLD" ON LAKE LAMOILLE. Dr. William T. Slayton called his Samoset resort "Dreamworld." It attracted many summer residents to the heart of Lamoille County for relaxation, fishing, and swimming.

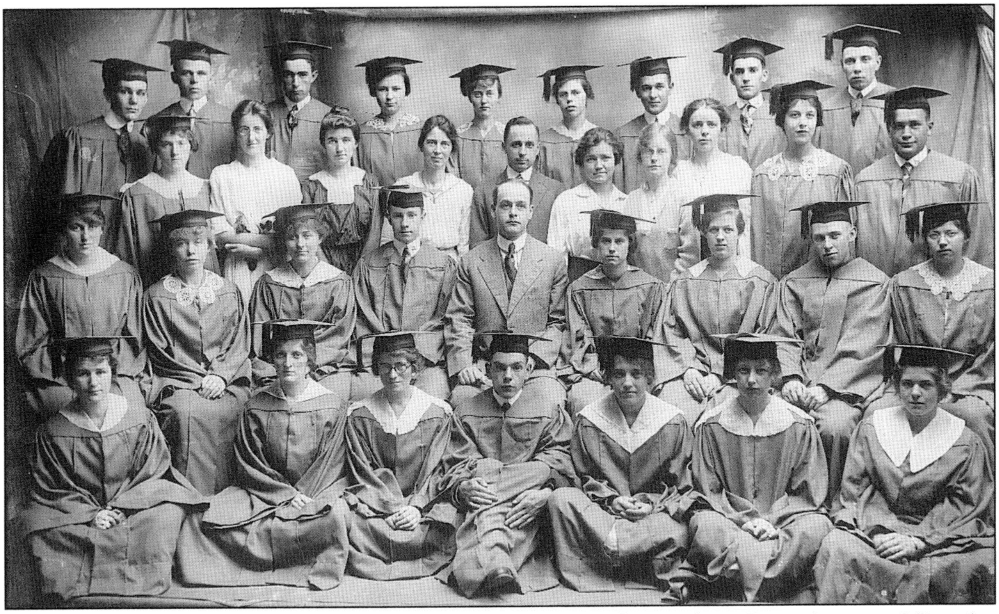

The Graduating Class of 1917. This photograph shows the 27 graduates of Peoples Academy's Class of 1917. Also pictured are seven teachers and Principal J. Thatcher Sears, who filled the vacancy after the resignation of Principal Rollo G. Reynolds. These students most surely benefited from the new library that had opened in 1913 on Main Street near Academy Park.

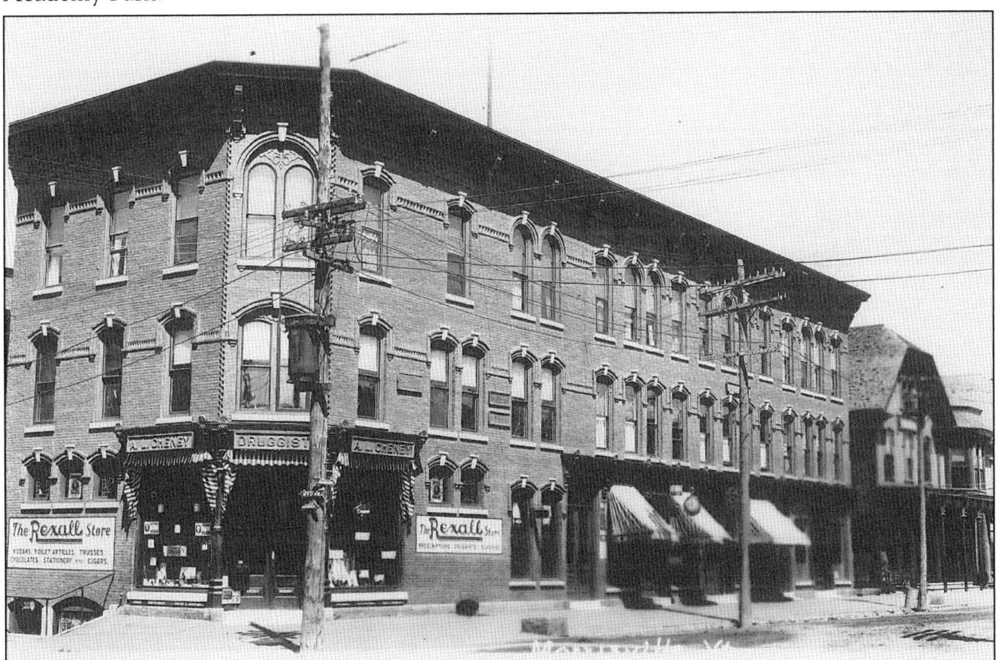

A.L. Cheney, Druggist, c. 1920. A.L Cheney had established his drugstore in the Centennial Block shortly after its completion in 1891. Over the years his product line steadily increased and he became affiliated with the Rexall Company. Seen here is the Centennial Block, with signs advertising the Rexall Store, owned by Cheney.

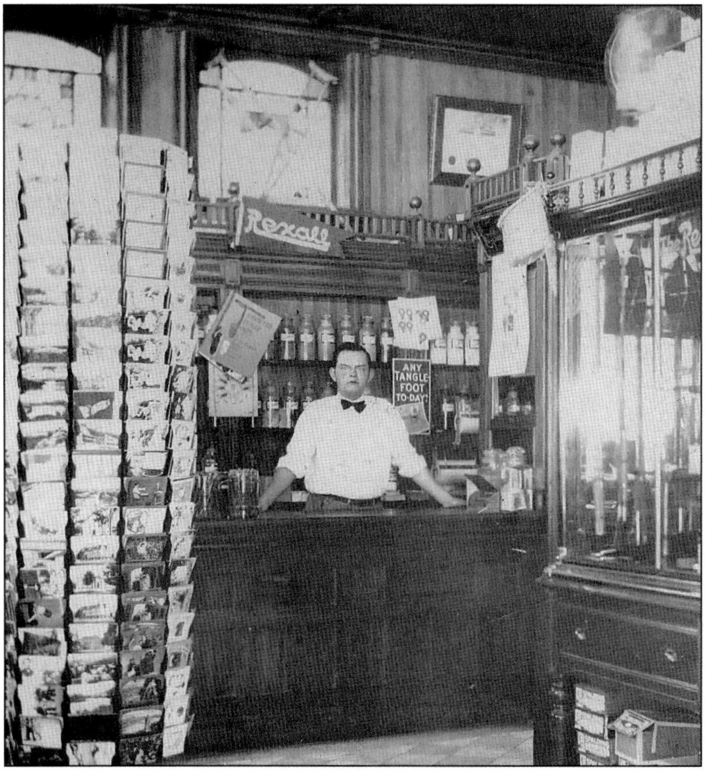

A.L. Cheney, Druggist, c. 1920. A.L. Cheney's store advertised prescriptions, Kodaks, toilet articles, trusses, chocolates, stationery, and cigars. In 1921, it was sold to Elwyn J. Wheeler, who installed a classic soda fountain. Seen here is the interior of Cheney's store sometime prior to 1921.

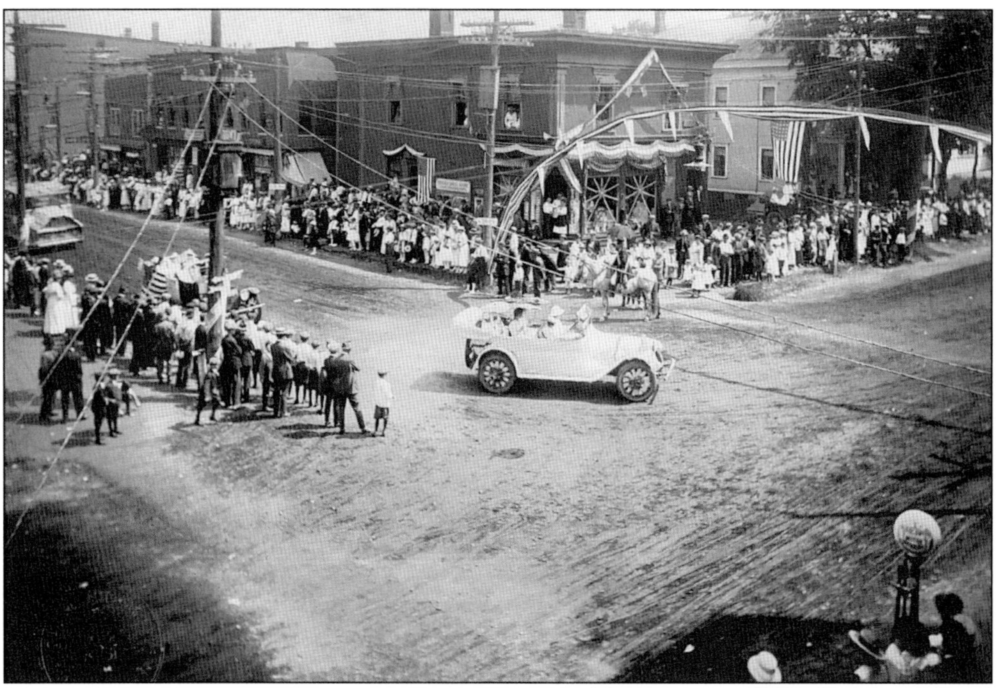

The Independence Day Parade, c. 1920. Taken from the Randall Hotel and looking at the corner of Main and Portland Streets, this photograph shows the Independence Day Parade of 1920 or 1921. Briggs drugstore can be seen in the Fleetwood Building at the corner.

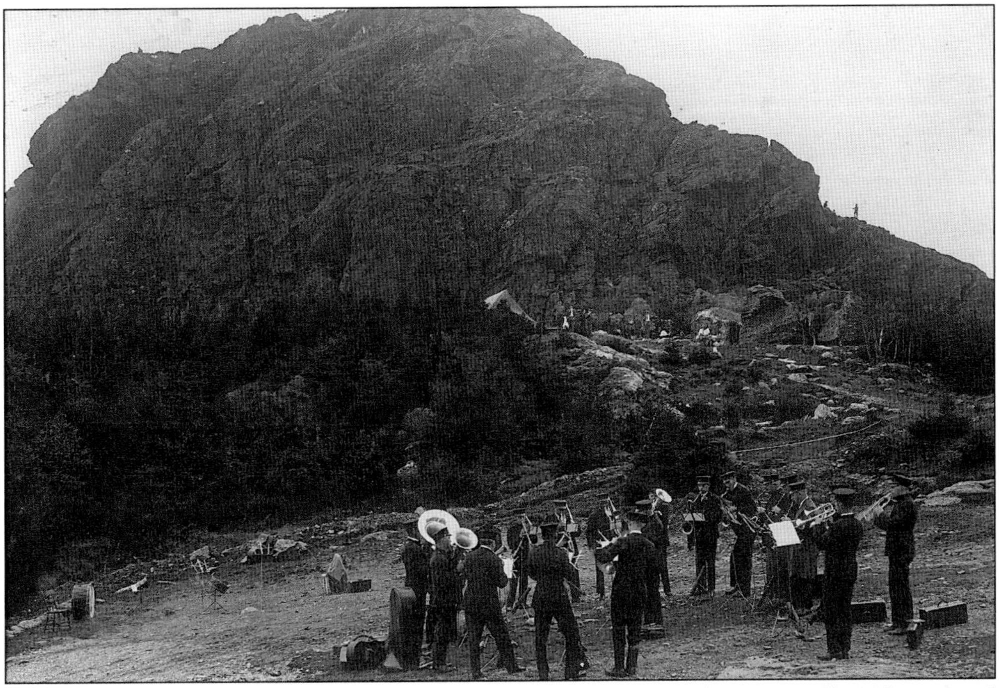

The Morrisville Military Band, 1922. On Labor Day of 1922, the Morrisville Military band played atop Mount Mansfield to commemorate the completion of a new road to the summit ridge. This photograph was taken from the porch of the Summit House Hotel.

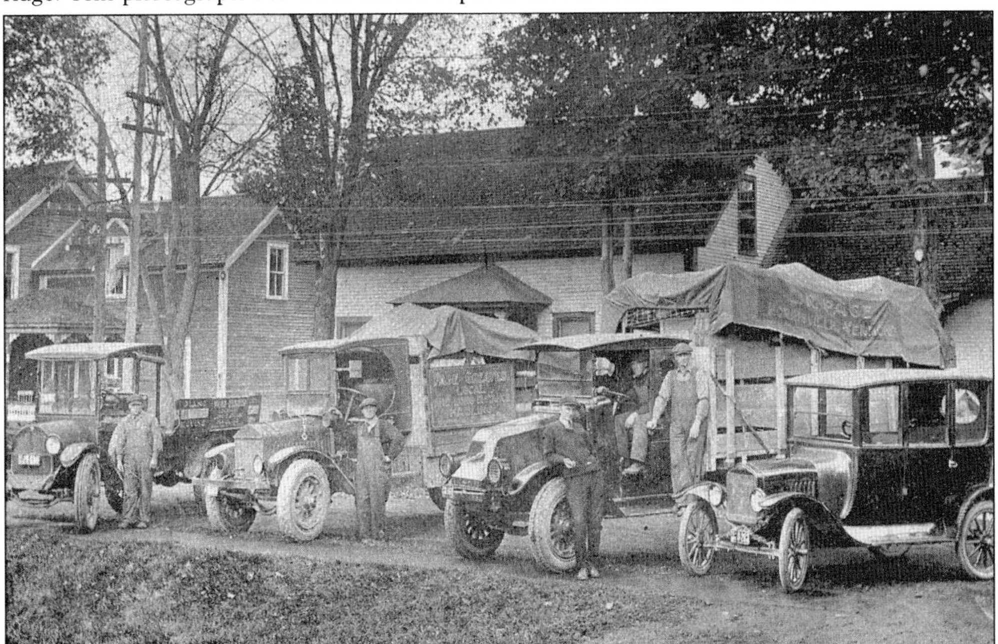

Page's Trucking, 1921. This Maple Street trucking business was owned by L.R. Page. Page's Trucking offered local and long-distance hauling. The service may have been used by Clifton Greaves (left), who operated a commercial dairy. With Greaves are Paul Carrell (center) and Lynn R. Page (right).

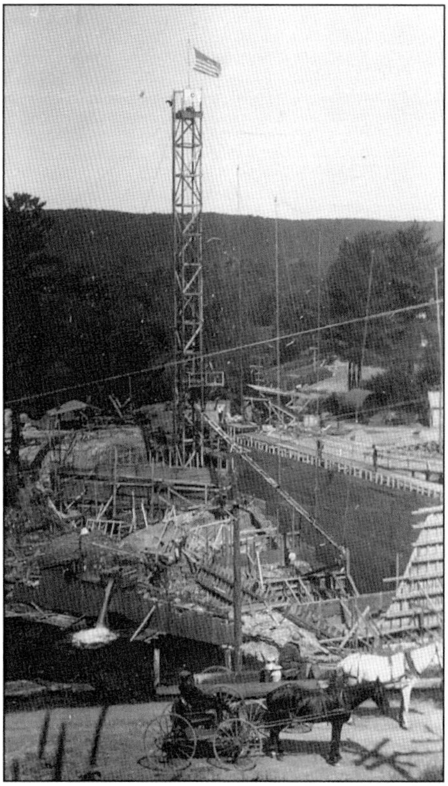

The Morrisville Water & Light Department, 1924. The Morrisville Water & Light Department constructed this dam in 1924. The dam was built to form the Morrisville Falls, which was to accompany a power-generating plant built near the site. The large tower was used to anchor various support cables while loads of concrete were moved and positioned as needed.

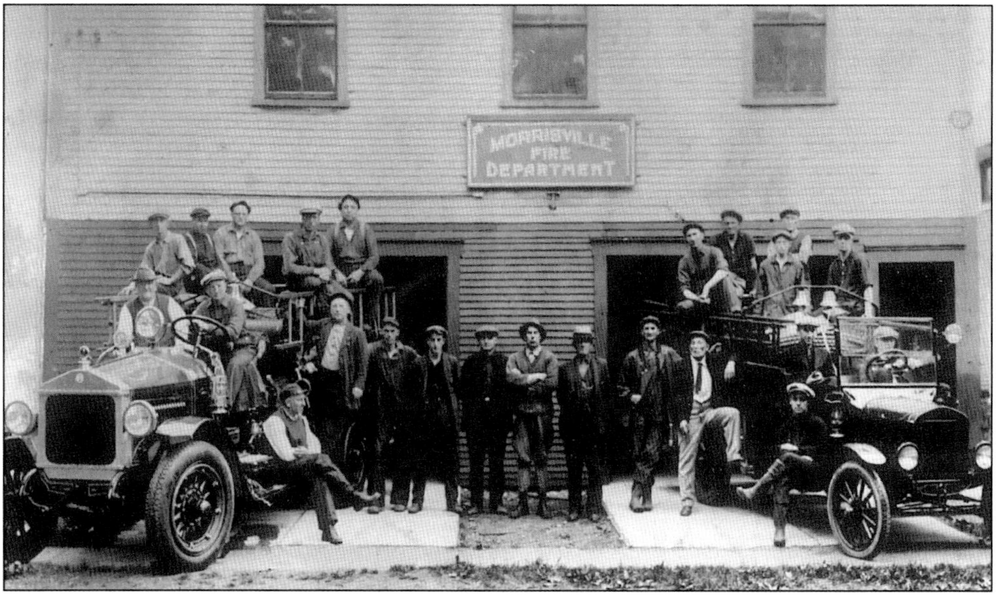

The Morrisville Fire Department, 1924. Members of the Morrisville Fire Department pose in front of the Union Street station in 1924. The two trucks were the first motorized trucks owned by the department: a 1924 Maxim and a 1923 Ford "mongrel" truck.

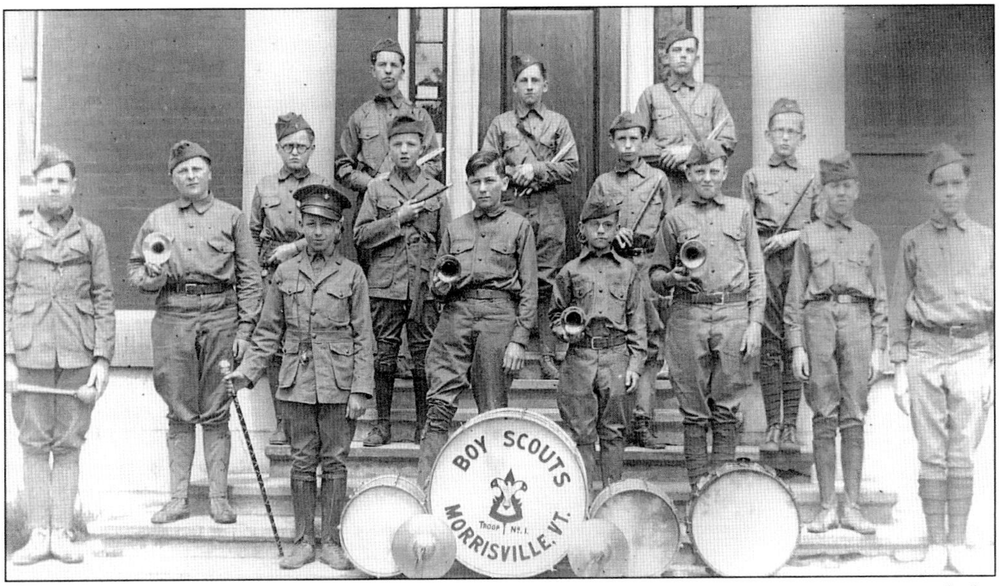

The Morrisville Boy Scouts, 1926. Members of Morrisville's Boy Scout Troop No. 1 include, from left to right, the following: (front row) S. Isham, ? Goodwin, W. Leba, unidentified, R. Davis, and Rice ?; (middle row) L. Parks, Ransom McNally, C. Stafford, D. Davis, W. Forocham, and M. Thomas. In 1917, the Boy Scouts were instrumental in the distribution of food rations and conservation cards throughout the town.

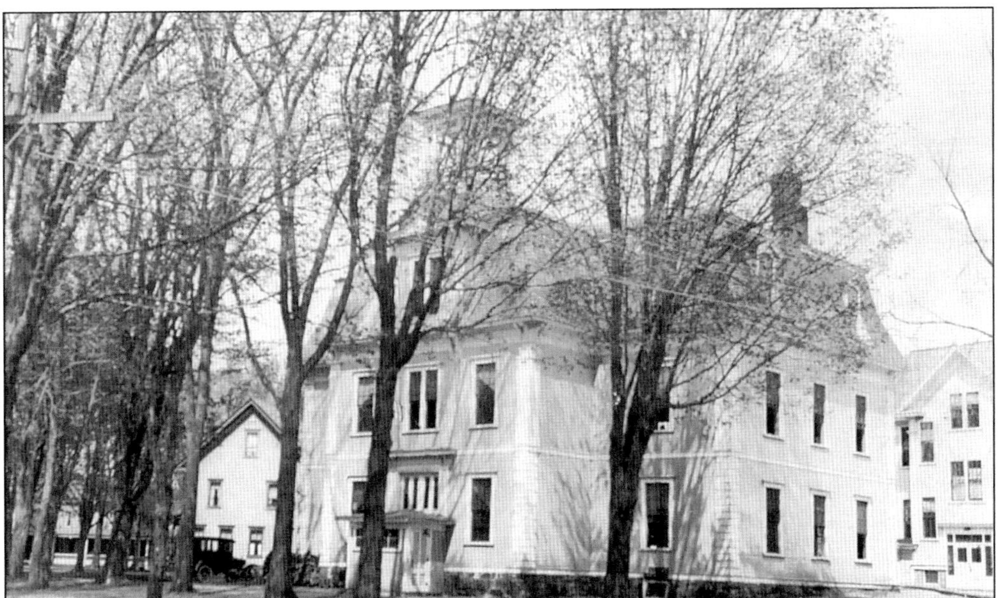

Peoples Academy and Morrisville Graded Building, c. 1920. For years, Peoples Academy was the head of the school system of District No. 1. In 1892, the districts were abolished and the tuition paid by students who were not from the district ended. Then, children from the entire town could take advantage of the superb schooling, since everyone was required to pay a school tax.

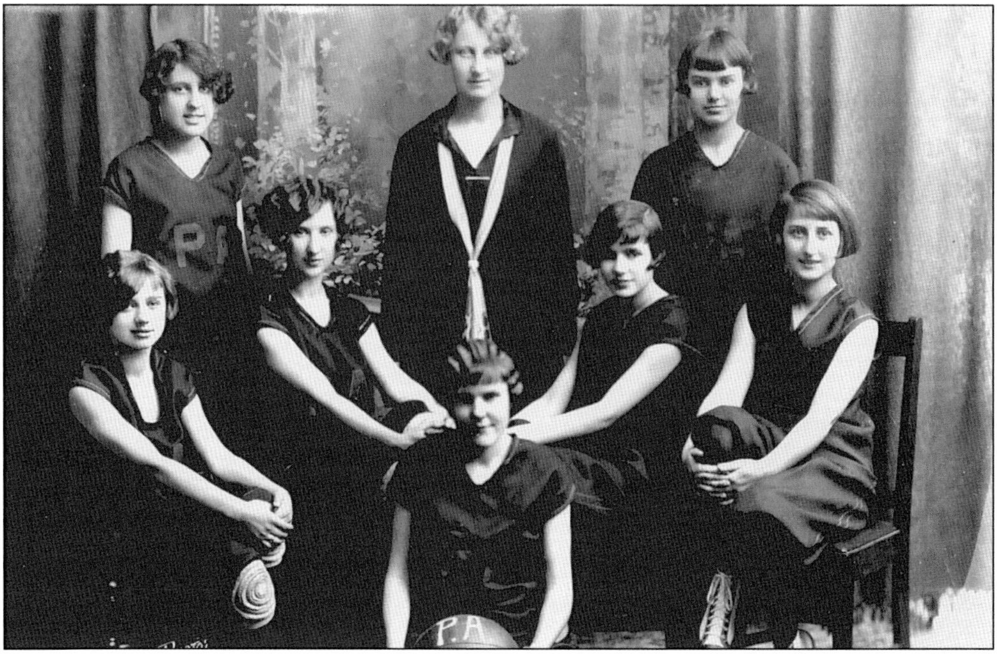

THE GIRLS' BASKETBALL TEAM, 1925. At Peoples Academy the girls' basketball team of 1925 was made up of, from left to right, the following: (front row) May Clark; (middle row) Mildred Fortier, Harriet Johnstone, Marion Goodrich, and Rena Reed; (back row) Katherine Valleau, Katherine Aldrich, and Reba Kinsley.

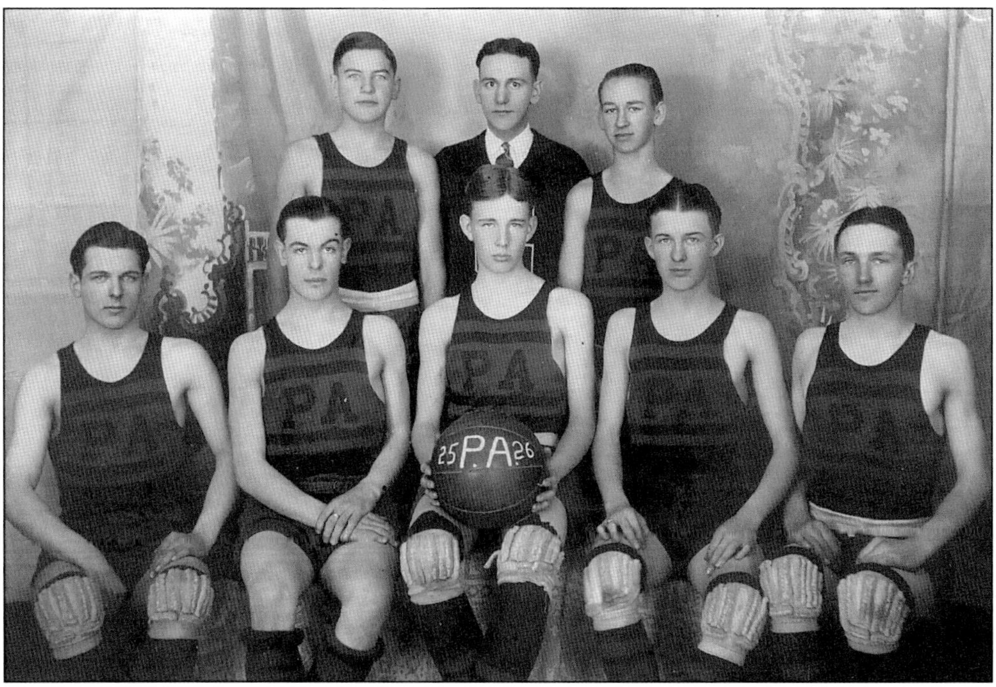

THE BOYS' BASKETBALL TEAM, 1925. The boys' basketball team of 1925 at Peoples Academy consisted of, from left to right, the following: (front row) Jay Foss, George Foss, Walter Sargent, Phil Smith, and Ed Welch; (back row) George Drowne, the coach, and Phil King.

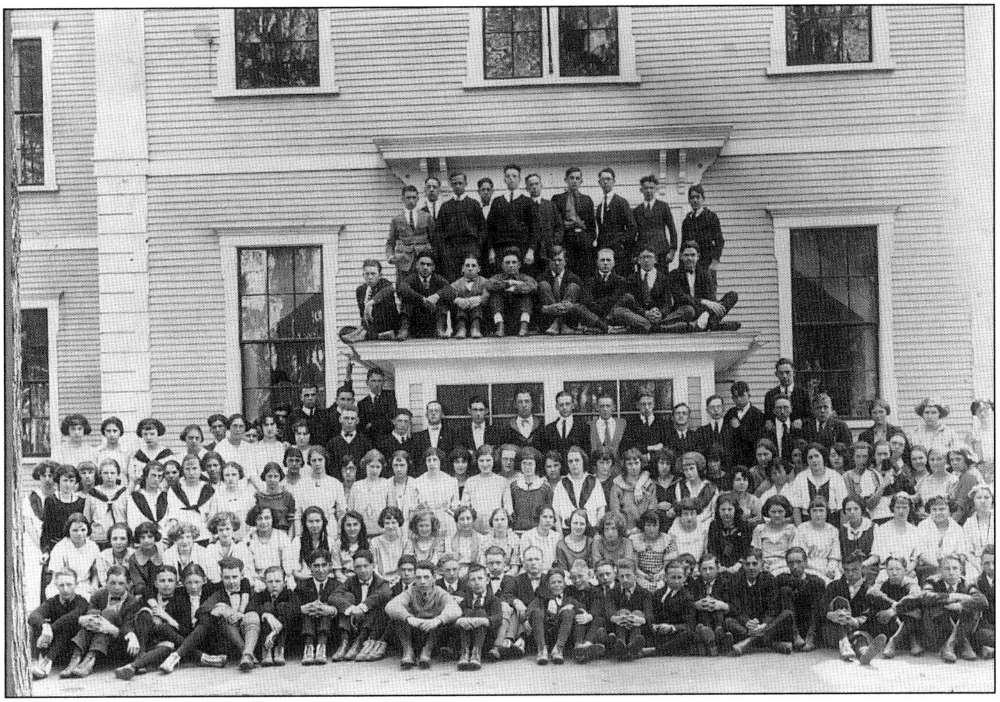

The Student Body, 1923. Shown is the student body of Peoples Academy for the 1923–1924 academic year.

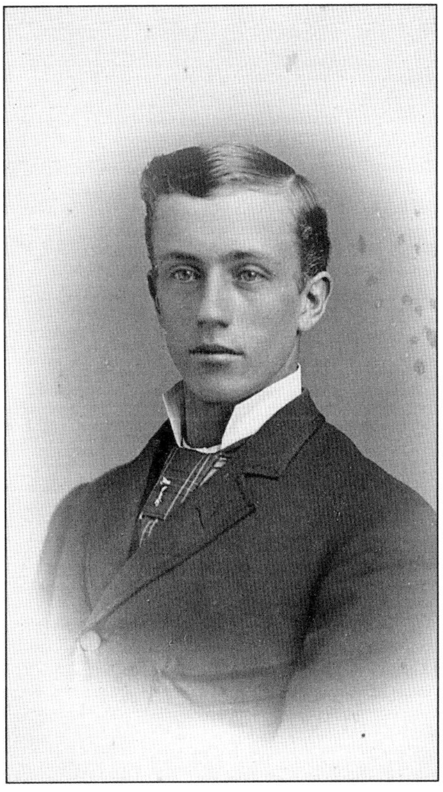

Alexander Hamilton Copley, 1856–1948. Alexander Hamilton Copley was born in the Morrisville House in 1856 to the widow of F.L. Matthews. An orphan during his childhood, the boy was shipped between relatives, some being in Elmore, at the age of 10. After learning the pharmaceutical trade by working in the pharmacy of A.O. Gates, Copley traveled to Boston, Massachusetts.

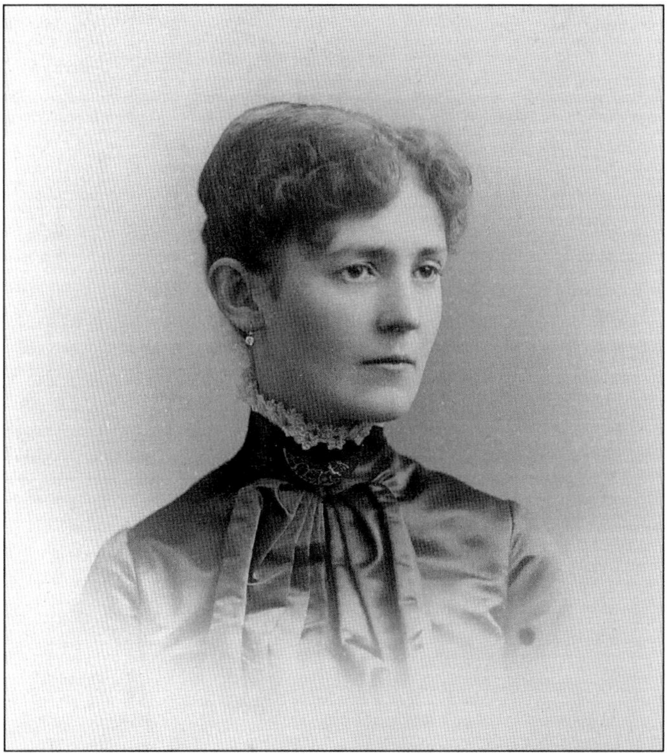

LUCY PAGE, C. 1900. Alexander Copley returned to Vermont to marry Lucy Page of Hyde Park on February 18, 1886. In 1901, Copley purchased a lot of land, which was known as Thomas Hill. His plans to build a summer home atop the hill were changed when his wife died suddenly in 1906. For some time afterward, Copley considered making a large gift to the town of his birth.

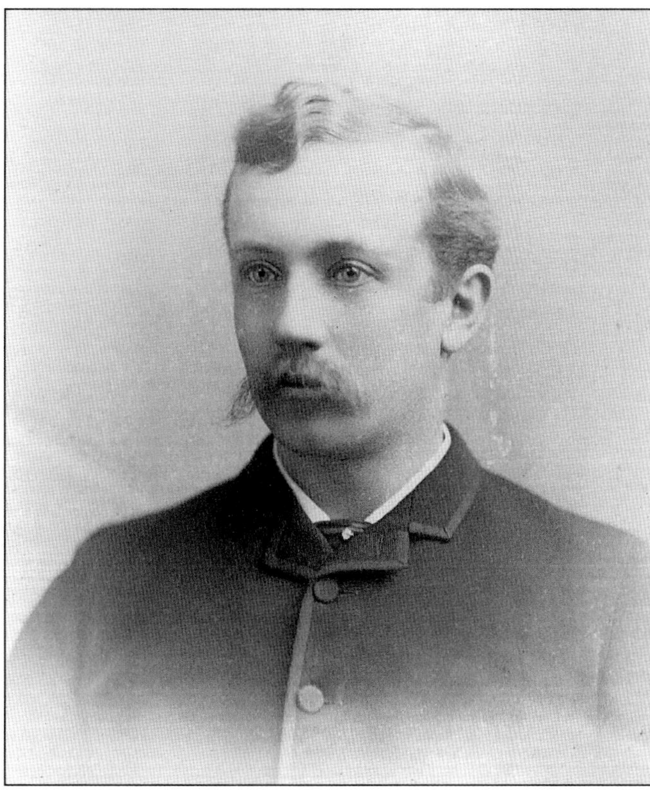

ALEXANDER HAMILTON COPLEY, C. 1900. Finally, Alexander Copley decided that the facilities at Peoples Academy had to be improved. He offered to construct a large, modern building on Thomas Hill and present it to the town with the condition that the old building be removed from Academy Park. Morristown accepted his offer with open arms and, in 1928, construction was under way on the structure, rumored to cost $250,000.

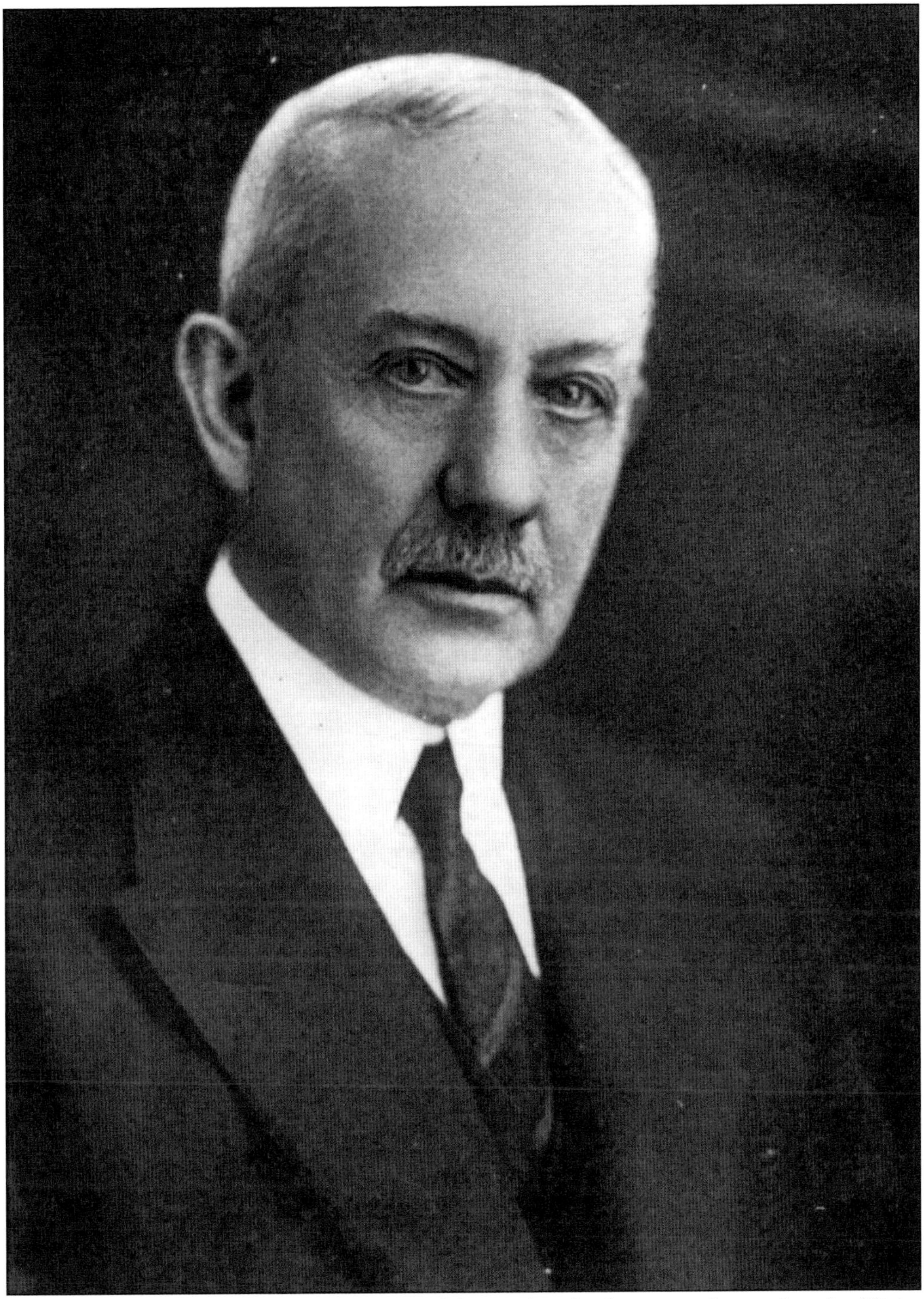

Alexander Hamilton Copley, 1927. "He didn't wish to be famous or desire a lot of publicity because of his gifts. I think he was truly and sincerely desirous of just being generous to his old hometown," lawyer Clifton G. Parker said of Alexander Copley. Copley's generosity did not end with Peoples Academy. Copley blessed Morristown many times with large donations, several trust funds, and the Copley Fund before his death on May 22, 1948.

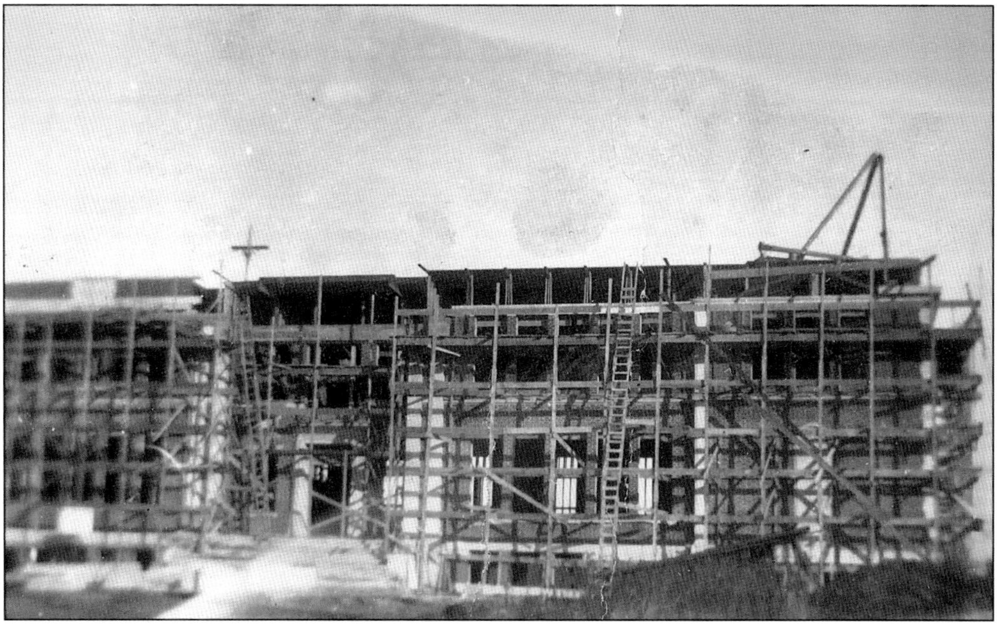

PEOPLES ACADEMY CONSTRUCTION, 1928. The 60- by 145-foot building atop Thomas Hill was constructed of tapestry brick and granite trimmings. Indiana limestone was used to create the large front pillars.

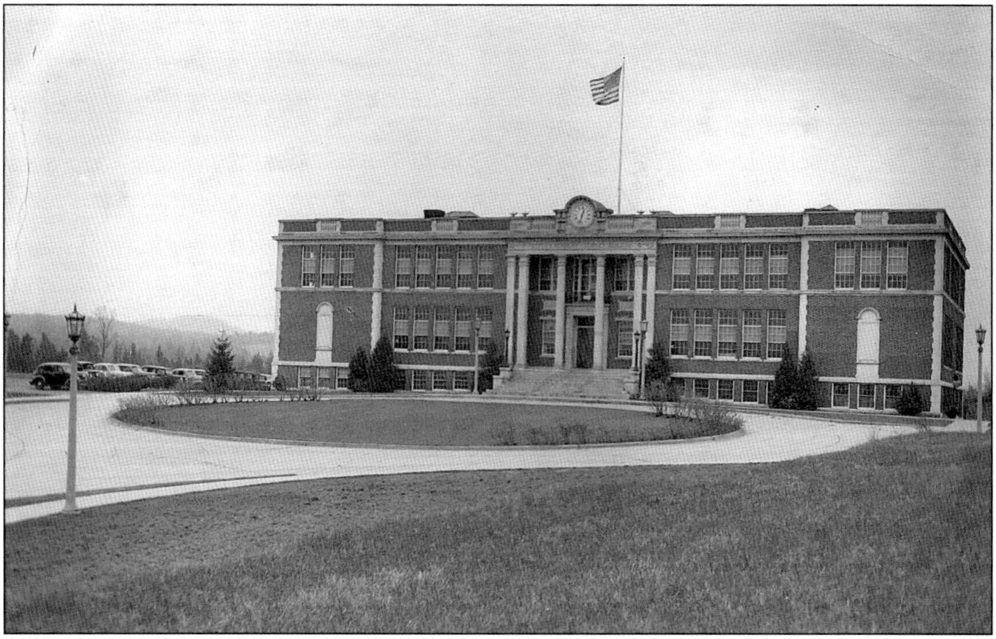

PEOPLES ACADEMY III, 1929. Construction of Copley's Peoples Academy was completed in 1929. The modern building featured study rooms, modern labs, a drafting room, commercial rooms, sewing rooms, a large basement lunchroom, locker rooms, a gymnasium, and an auditorium capable of seating 450. The third Peoples Academy opened for use on September 11, 1929 and was dedicated during the June 16, 1930 commencement.

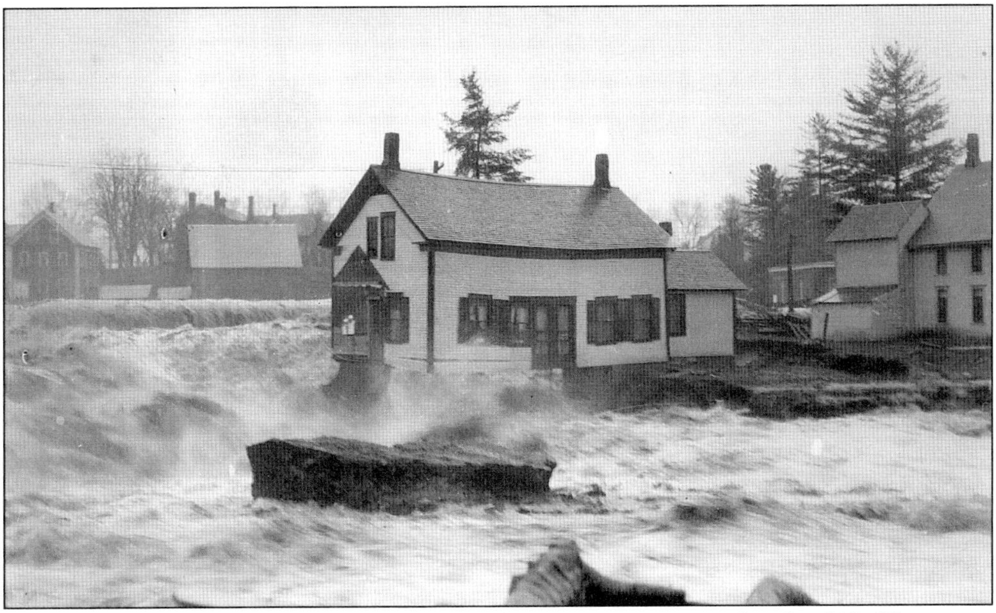

The Flood of 1927. Disastrous flooding struck Vermont on November 3, 1927. The waters of the Lamoille River began their destruction after 40 hours of steady rain. Four feet of water flowing over the new dam caused it to eventually give way. Another dam measured a flow rate of 36,600 cubic feet of water per second. There were no Morristown fatalities; however, the destruction caused by the flooding was unimaginable.

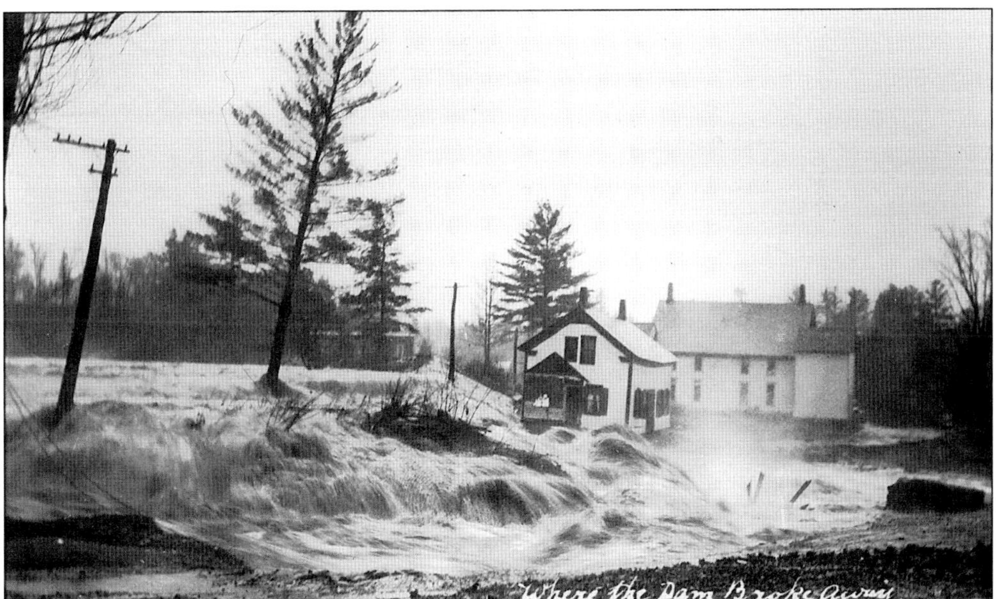

The Flood, 1927. The savage river cut a chasm 40 to 60 feet deep and 16 feet wide south of Bridge Street. Initially, six homes were lost; two more were demolished later because of major damage. River Street was completely washed away and was never rebuilt.

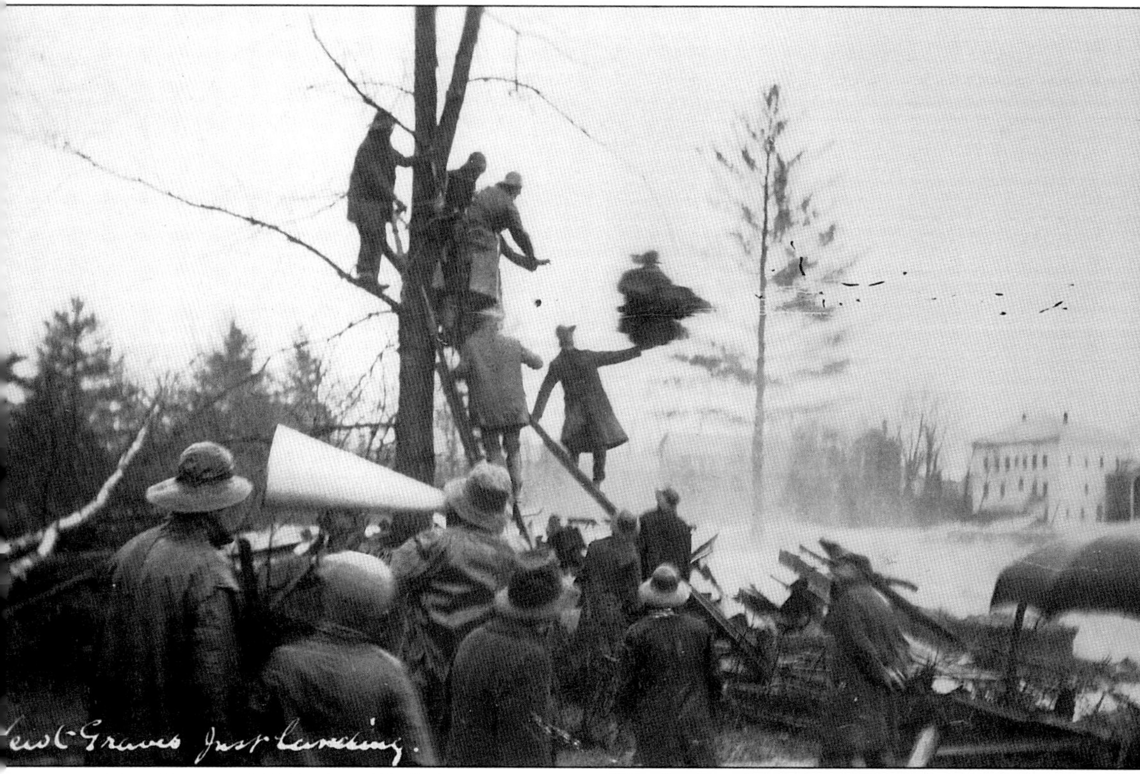

The Flood, 1927. The Clark Park property off Bridge Street was lost and abandoned. This photograph shows Newton Graves coming across a cable. On an island created by the flowing river, 27 people were stuck. All were rescued when a rope was stretched across the chasm and tied to a tree on each side.

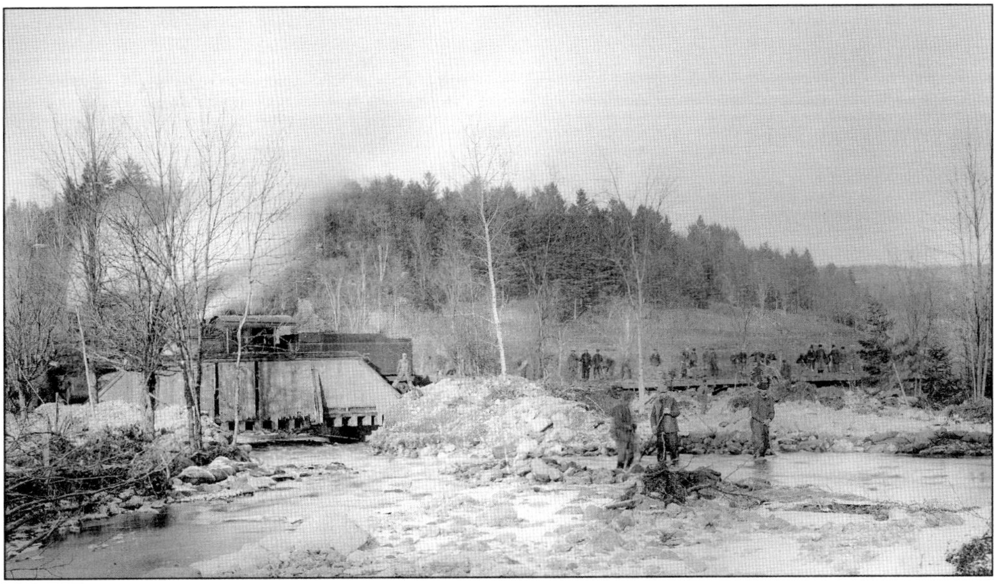

The St. Johnsbury & Lake Champlain Railroad, 1927. In 1925, a group of men acquired the line and put much thought and work into it so that it could continue to run. Morristown and its neighbors realized the seriousness of the situation, and there was a great spirit of cooperation among towns through which the line ran. Thanks to good management, the railroad survived and soon business increased. For the first time in years, the railroad paid its operating expenses. However, the floor of 1927 wrought havoc on the railroad.

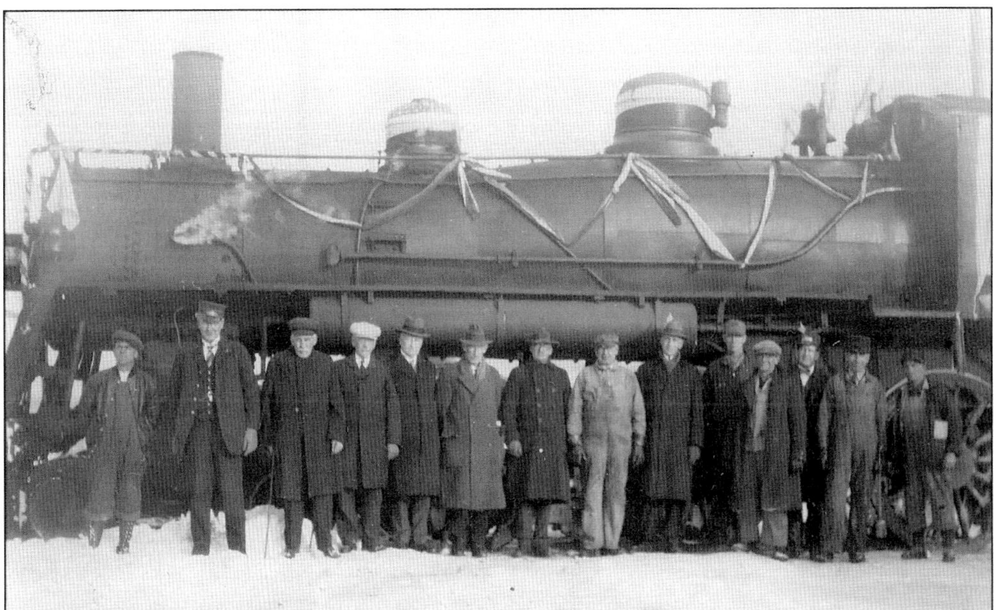

The Return of the Rail, 1927. No trains ran from the time of the November 1927 flood until December 26, 1927, when this photograph was taken. The cost to restore the rail system, which had suffered 160 washouts, lost 6 culverts and 12 bridges, and had endured 24 landslides, was $500,000. A loan of $300,000 was obtained to help with repairs, thanks to Morrisville residents T.C. Cheney and Justice G.M. Powers.

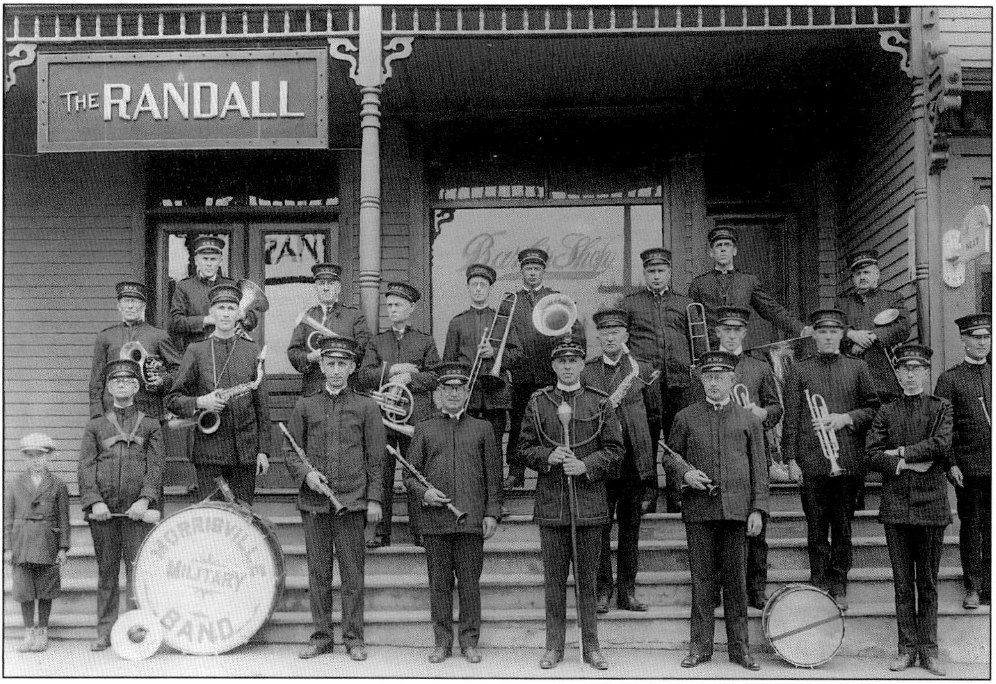

The Morrisville Military Band, 1925. After a number of rocky years, the Morrisville Military Band underwent reorganization and its membership began to increase. In 1926, the band received a $500 town appropriation. The band began to operate on a commercial basis, and its members received 50¢ per rehearsal and $1 per concert. The band is pictured here in front of the Randall Hotel.

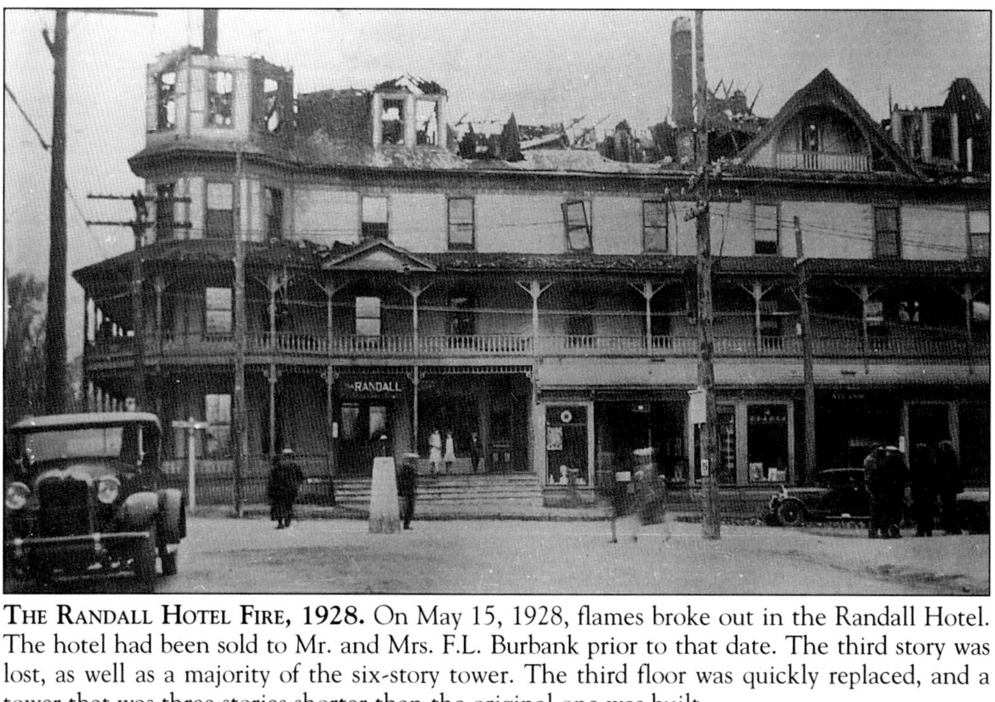

The Randall Hotel Fire, 1928. On May 15, 1928, flames broke out in the Randall Hotel. The hotel had been sold to Mr. and Mrs. F.L. Burbank prior to that date. The third story was lost, as well as a majority of the six-story tower. The third floor was quickly replaced, and a tower that was three stories shorter than the original one was built.

The Universalist Church, 1928. The Universalist church was built on the same lot that was home to the shared Methodist and Universalist Union Church. The Union Church burned in 1852. This photograph shows steeple of the Universalist church undergoing major repairs in 1928.

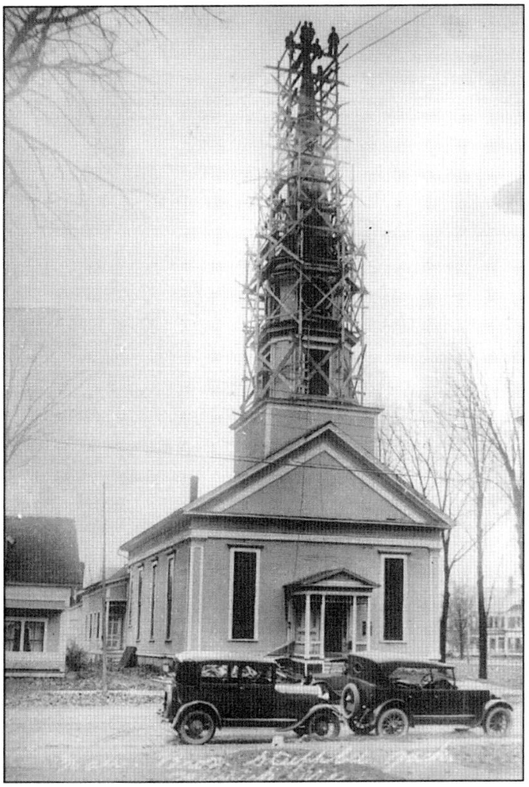

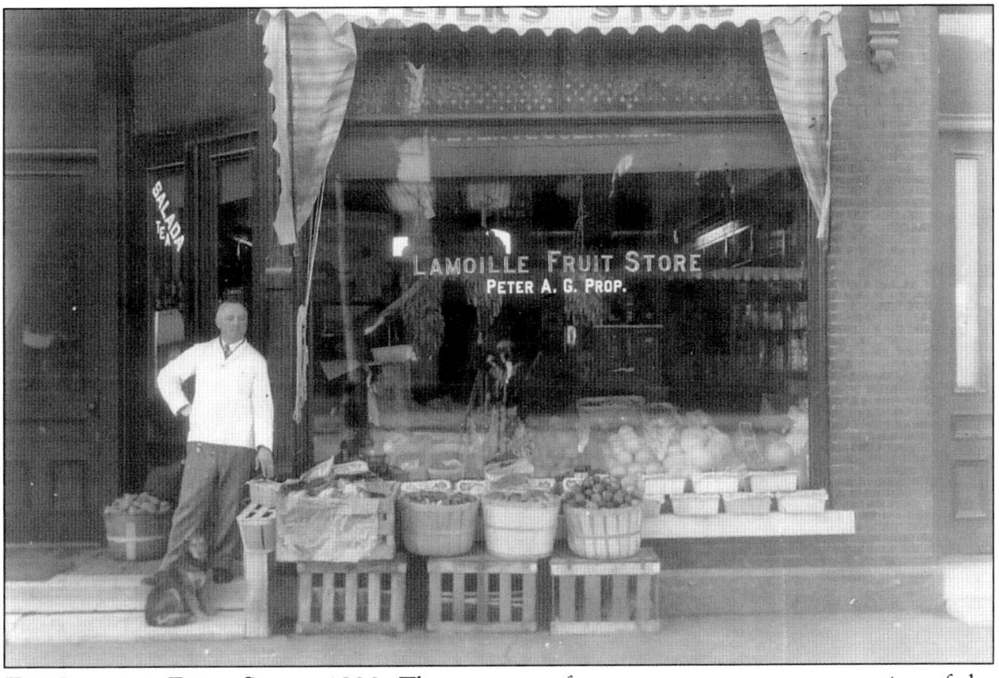

The Lamoille Fruit Store, 1929. This was one of many stores to occupy a section of the Centennial Block's first floor. The Lamoille Fruit Store was owned and operated by Peter A. Guirnieri, standing on the left.

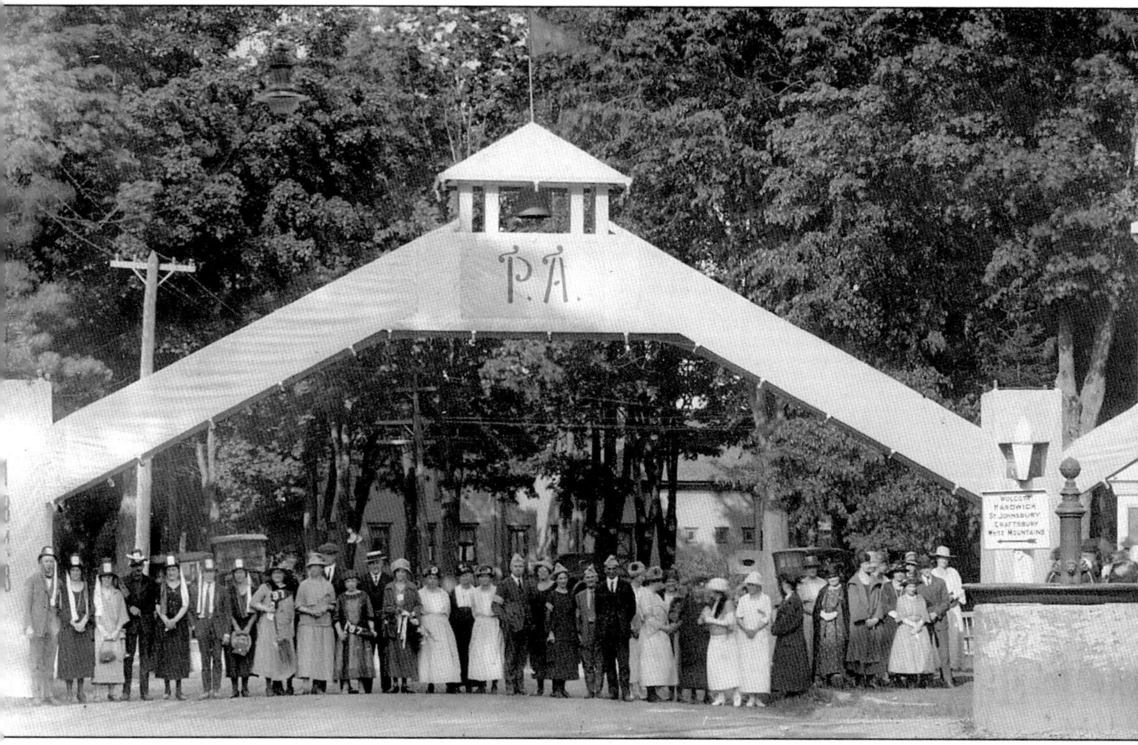

The 75th Anniversary of Peoples Academy, 1923. On June 12, 1923, efforts of the Peoples Academy Alumni Association paid off. A giant arch, spanning Park Street and Main Street, was built at the foot of Academy Park, and businesses throughout Morrisville decorated their

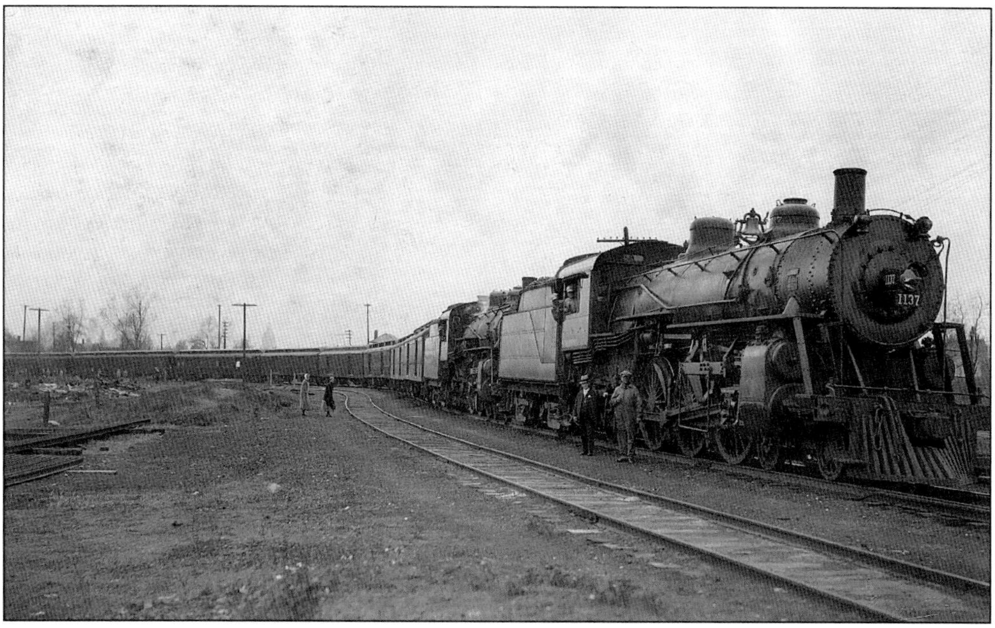

The Railroad, c. 1930. Despite the popularity of the railroad, the advent of automobiles put stress on the passenger rail business. After the Flood of 1927, the railroad continued operating at an annual deficit, which became a serious problem, and the line was almost abandoned.

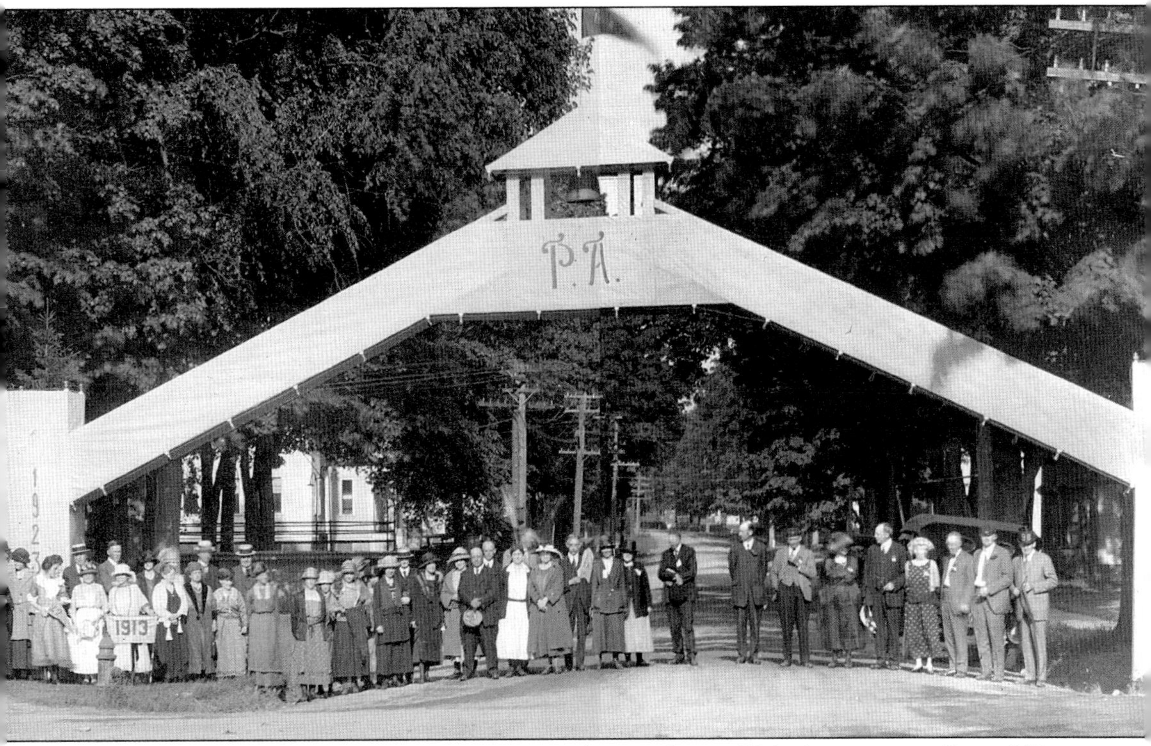

storefronts with green and gold in honor of Peoples Academy's 75th Anniversary. Some 350 Peoples Academy alumni and friends attended the anniversary events, which included a large banquet and ball.

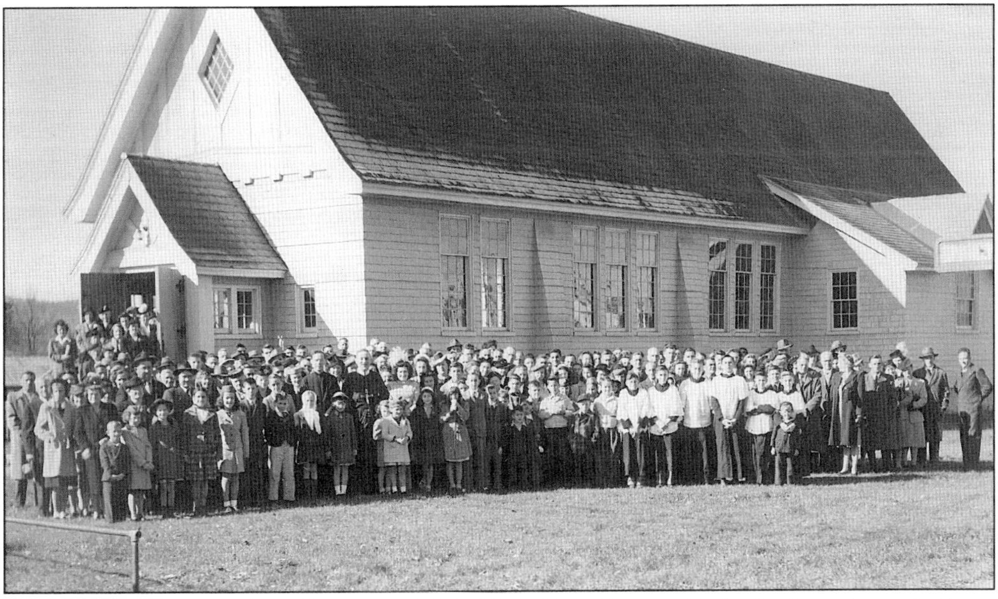

THE CHURCH OF THE HOLY CROSS, C. 1931. Holy Cross Roman Catholic Church was built on Brooklyn Street in 1913. There were no records of any Roman Catholics among Morristown's early settlers. Seen here are the church's parishioners gathered during a weeklong mission at the church held in October 1931.

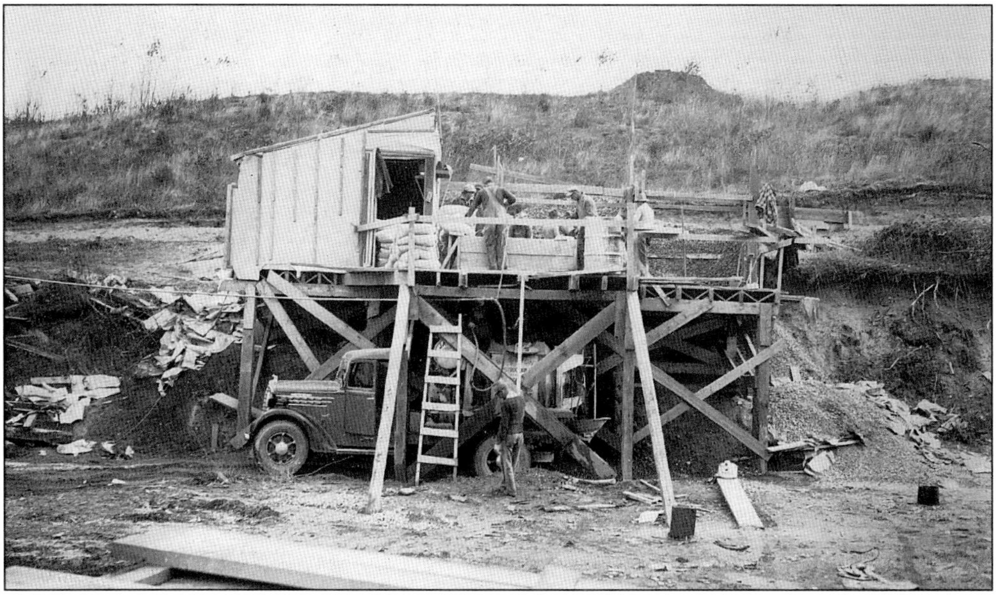

Morrisville Street Paving, c. 1929. Morrisville residents voted in favor of a major street-paving program in 1929. The project to pave with concrete Bridge, Main, Congress, and Park Streets, as well as Copley Avenue, got under way shortly. Curbing and sidewalks were also included in the project. Forty feet of Lehigh cement was laid between the curbs.

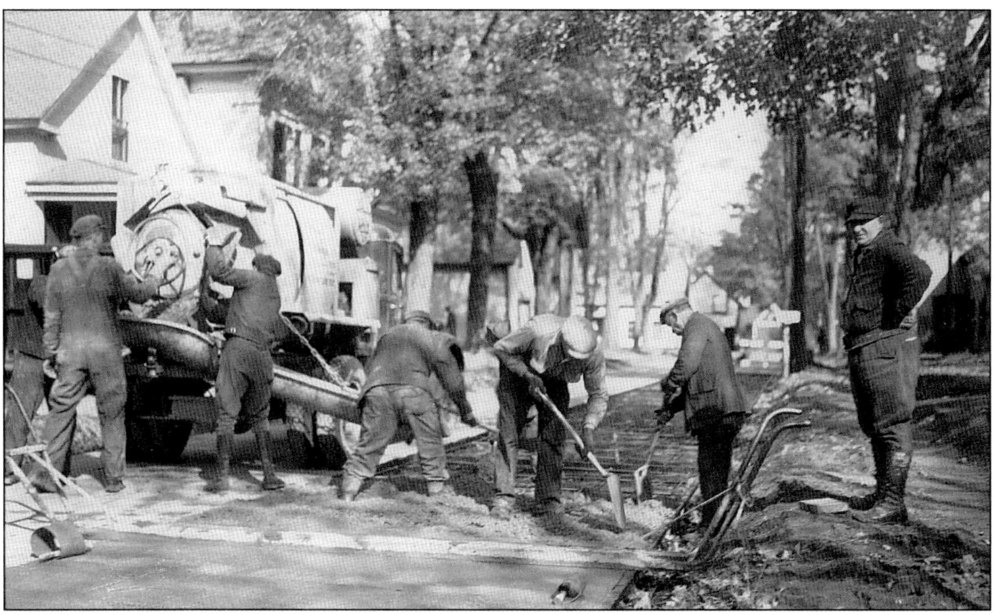

Morrisville Street Paving, c. 1929. Fred W. Densmore of Claremont, New Hampshire, was in charge of the project. Morrisville paid $2.57 per square yard. That price included the excavating. The Lehigh cement was laid seven inches thick and met all state of Vermont specifications. Morrisville advertised its cement streets proudly, as paved streets were seen as truly a sign of progress.

Two

THE MID-20TH CENTURY, 1930–1960

According to Esther Swift, Morristown is the only town in Lamoille County to have gained in total population by each census since it was created, with the exception of a minor decrease in 1850. By 1930, Morristown's population had grown to 2,939. However, times were not easy for Morristown residents; the Great Depression forced many Morristown employers to layoff employees. Money was tight everywhere. Morristown voted to purchase a Randolph Road farm and made arrangements to build cottages on it to accommodate families with children during the difficult years. Morristown survived and continued to grow. By 1940, its population had reached 3,130.

Soon to follow was World War II, in which 16 Morristown men gave their lives. On the home front, Morristown residents took turns atop Peoples Academy on airplane-spotting duty. "We were afraid of being bombed," said Marguerite Woods. "They had a night watch at Peoples Academy. My husband would do his stint every week and watch for airplanes during the night . . . the war . . . was an awful, awful thing." Others said that if Morrisville were ever bombed, the war would certainly be lost. Morrisville also conducted a very successful scrap metal drive and rationed gasoline and food to help the war effort.

"This past . . . school year has been a memorable one. Peoples Academy has gone to war. Many have left—never to return. They make us realize the part we must play in the ensuing months. The last words of the Declaration of Independence read: 'And for the support of this declaration . . . we mutually pledge to each other our lives, our fortunes, and our sacred honor.' In the spirit of . . . our forefathers we dedicate ourselves to that pledge which has made America truly the land of the free."—Principal Ralph A. Eaton, 1943.

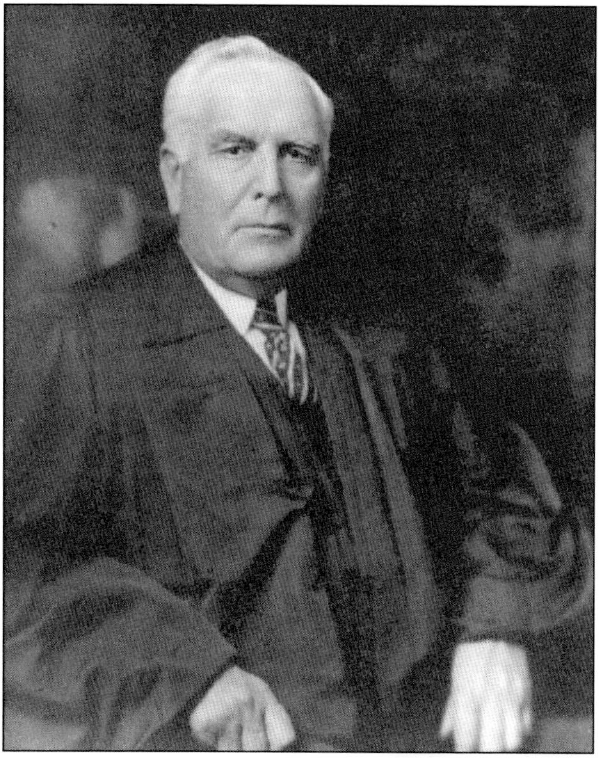

Chief Justice George M. Powers, 1930. Born in 1861, George M. Powers was educated at Peoples Academy and graduated from the University of Vermont in 1883. At the age of 43, he began his judicial career and, in 1906, he was elected judge of the superior court. He served as chief justice of the Vermont Supreme Court for several years. This photograph was taken in 1930.

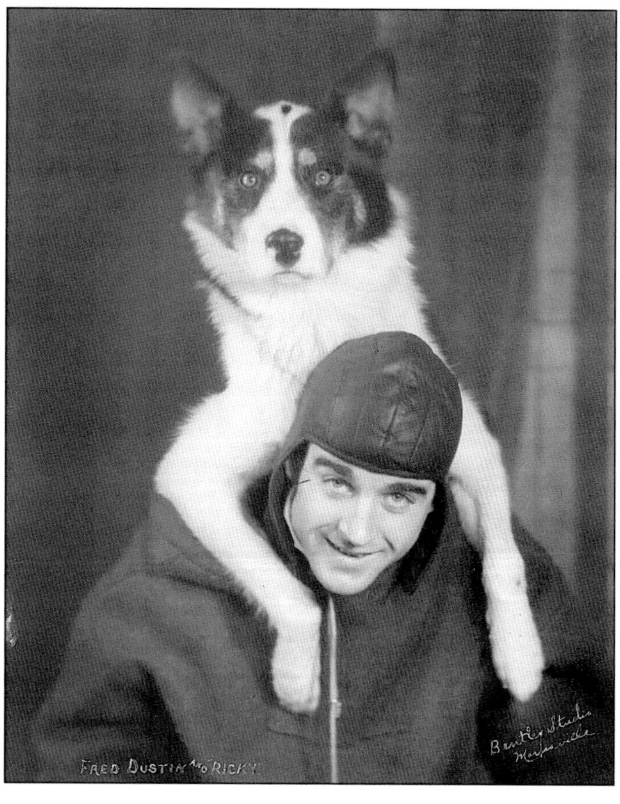

Fred G. Dustin and Ricky, c. 1936. Although Fred Dustin was from Massachusetts, he had friends in Morrisville and knew the town well. He gained recognition serving aboard the *Jacob Rupert* on Rear Adm. Richard Byrd's second expedition to Antarctica, in 1935. Dustin agreed to fly a Peoples Academy banner over the South Pole and returned a local hero. He is seen here with his dog Ricky.

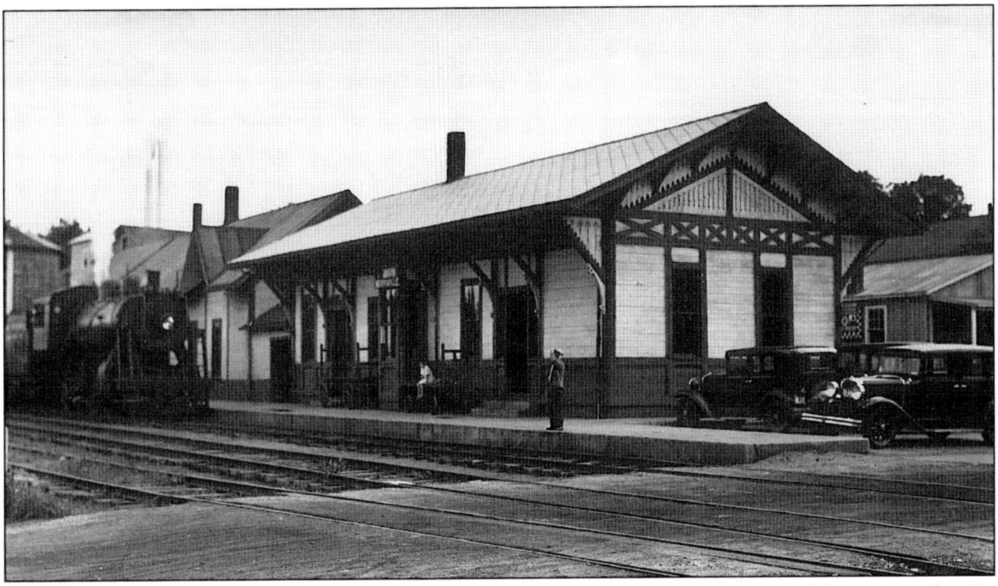

The Morrisville Railroad Depot, 1935. The Flood of 1927 had been unable to stop the St. Johnsbury & Lake Champlain because of the railroad's good management and strong willpower. However, times continued to be tough for the railroad, and it became more and more evident that bankruptcy might have to be declared.

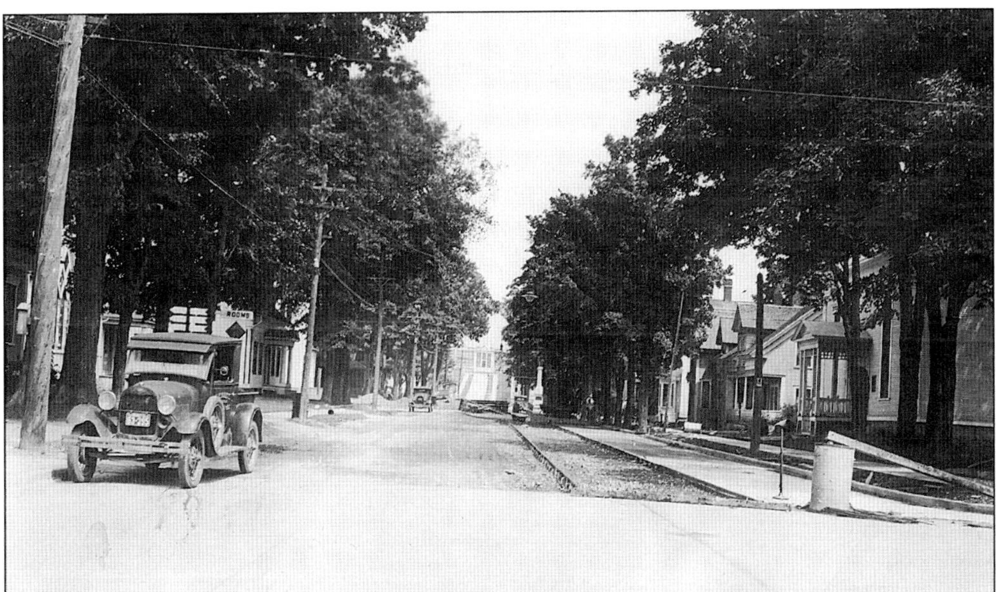

Main Street, 1931. This photograph shows evidence of Morrisville's major street-paving project, which was completed in 1931. Copley Avenue and Peoples Academy can be seen atop the former Thomas Hill.

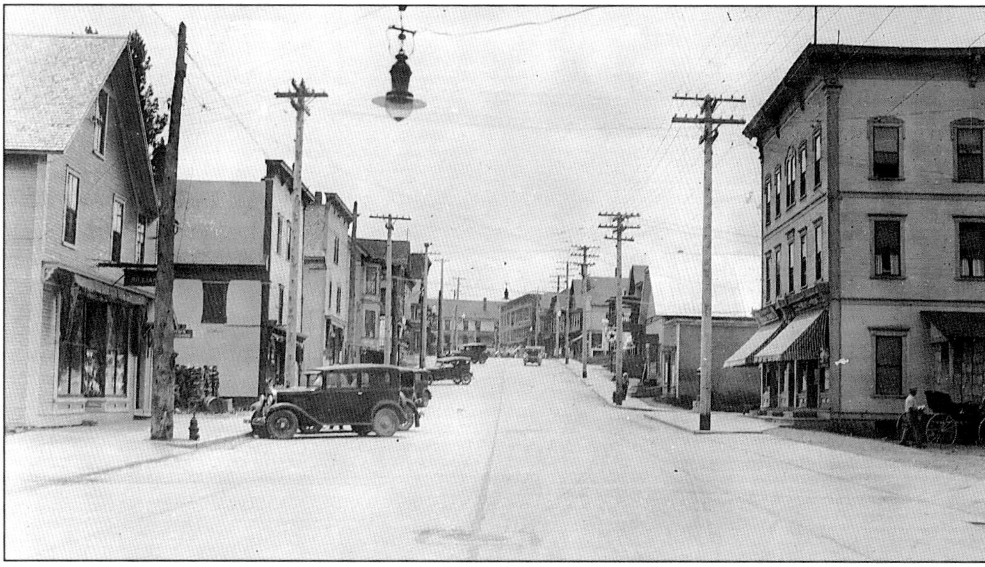

PORTLAND STREET, 1931. Fred Densmore of New Hampshire had done a wonderful job excavating and paving the streets of Morrisville. This photograph shows the finished product on Portland Street.

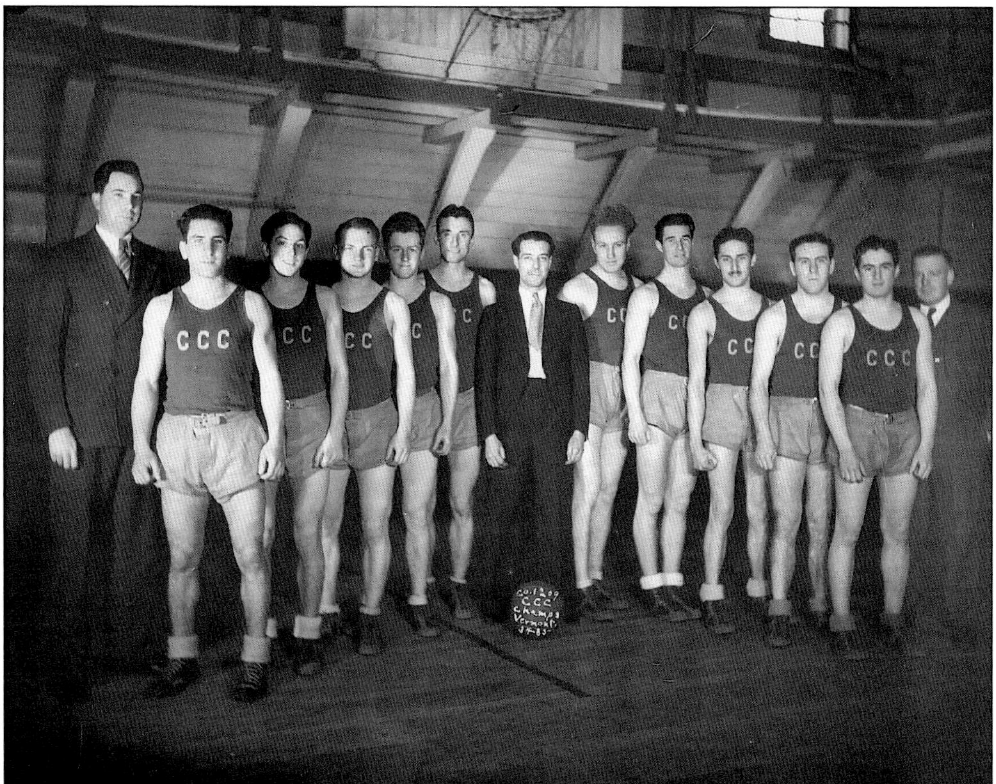

THE CIVILIAN CONSERVATION CORPS, 1935. The Civilian Conservation Corps was a federal program established during the Great Depression. This unit was based in Elmore and often played basketball at the Morrisville Gymnasium, off Main Street, as in this 1935 team photo.

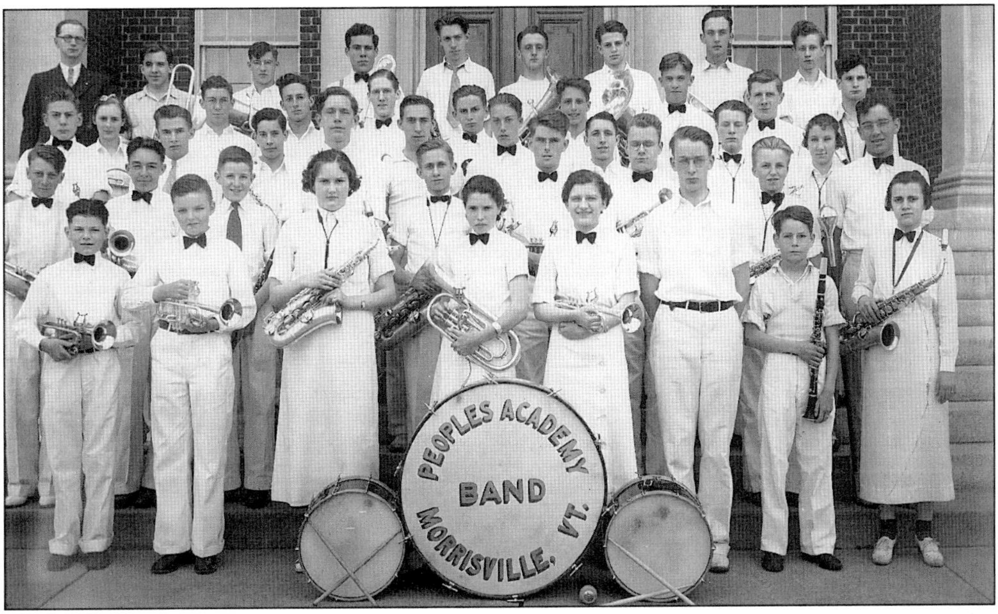

THE PEOPLES ACADEMY BAND, 1935. Under the direction of Willard K. Sanders, the Peoples Academy Band was established in 1930. This photograph was taken prior to a concert on May 29, 1935, most likely to celebrate Memorial Day.

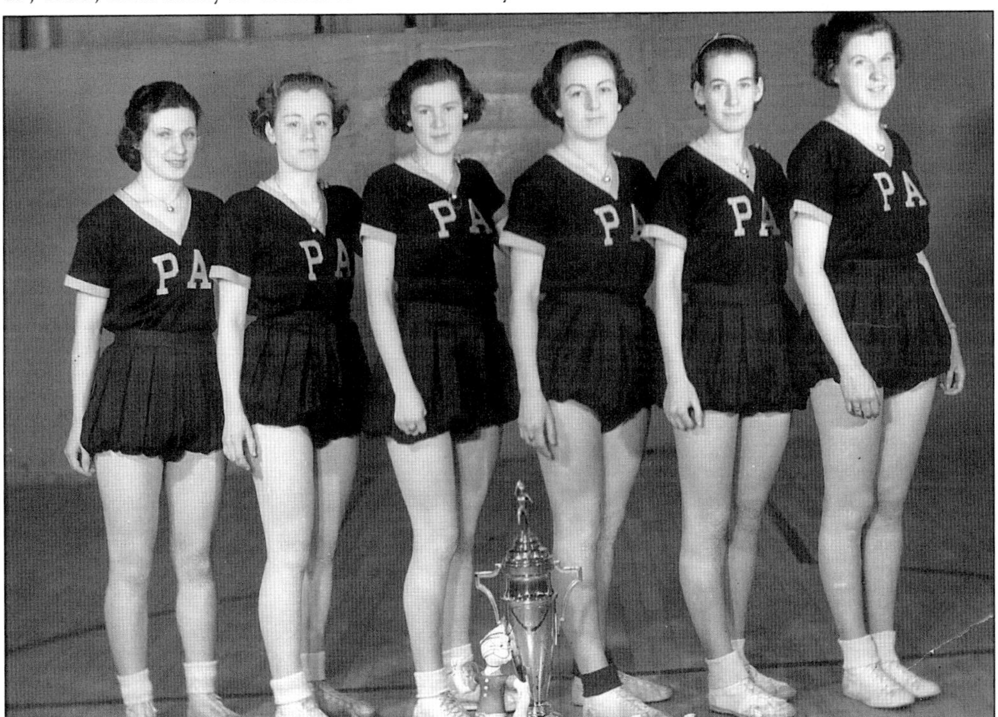

THE GIRLS' BASKETBALL TEAM, 1936. This 1936 team brought the state championship to Peoples Academy. The players, from left to right, are Frances Raymond, Alice Hagar, Mora Stetson, Edna Dewey, Eleanor Eaton, and Shirley Waite. The Popeye doll in the foreground was the team's mascot.

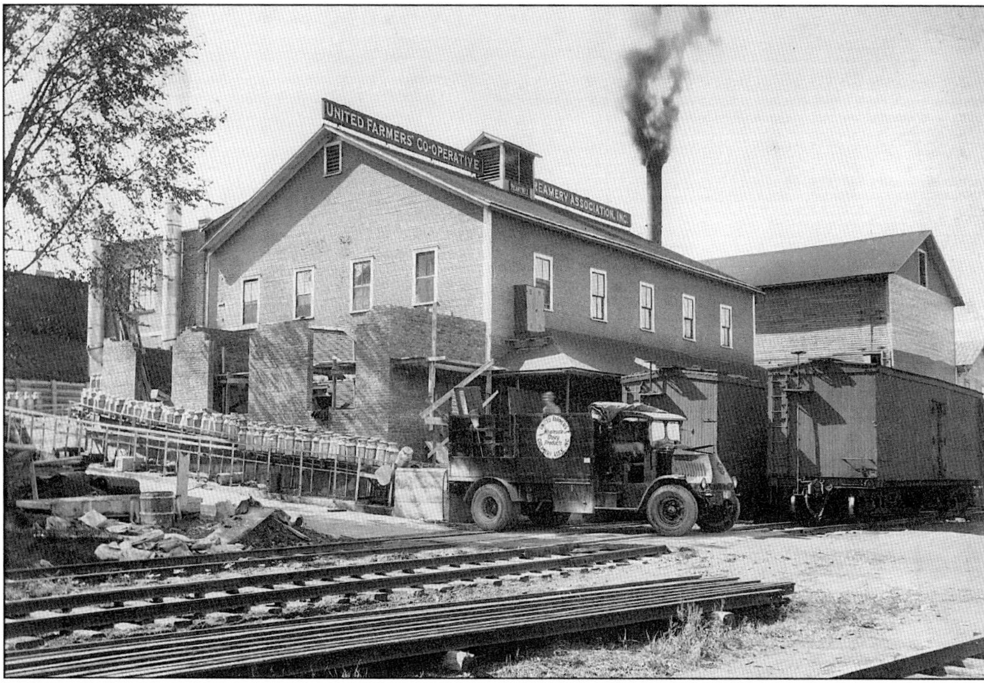

The United Farmers Cooperative Creamery, c. 1933. The United Farmers Cooperative Creamery Association was established in 1919 and had grown to an enormous size, thanks to a major plant built on Railroad Street in 1925. It was said to be the most up-to-date creamery in Vermont, if not in all of New England. The creamery offered a diverse array of products, including condensed milk, cottage cheese, buttermilk, powdered skim milk, and ice cream.

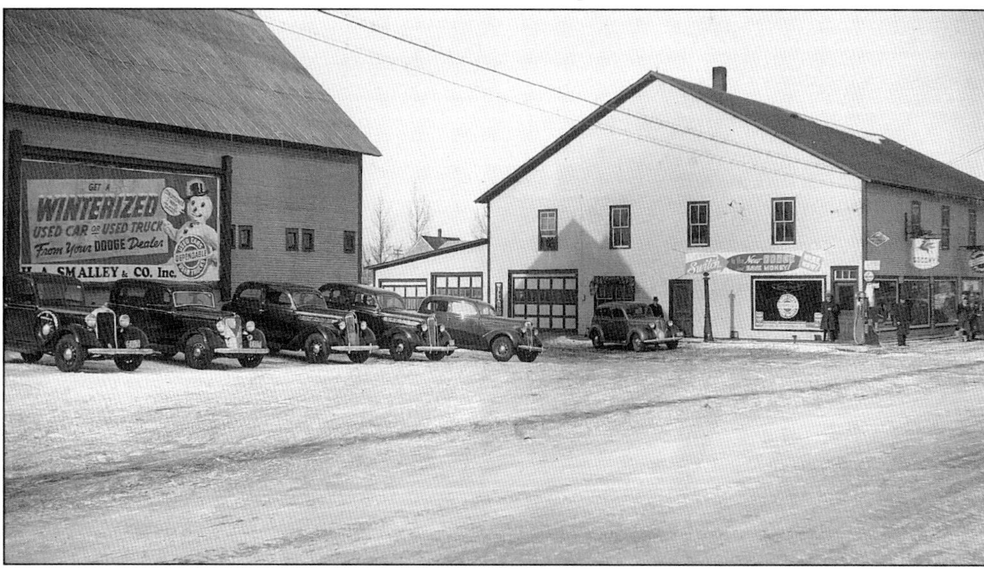

H.A. Smalley & Company, 1936. A company that once took aim at automobiles soon was dealing in them. In 1907, H.A. Smalley & Company was selling horses and buggies from a Bridge Street stable. In 1928, Herbert Smalley established a corporation and stopped dealing in horses altogether in 1932. His garage offered sales and service. He dealt mainly in Dodge automobiles.

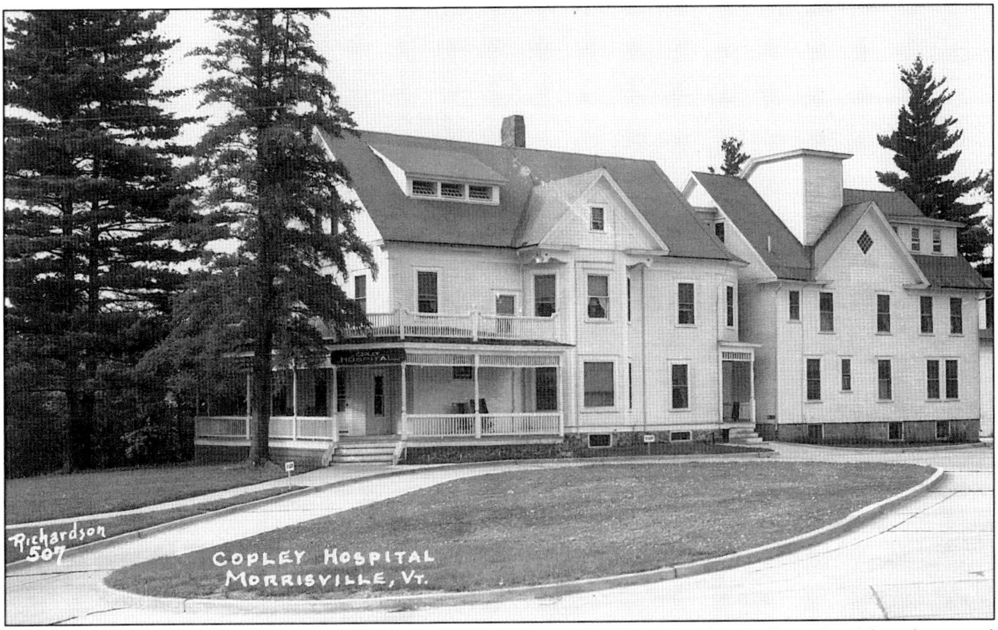

COPLEY HOSPITAL, C. 1932. Alexander Copley had initially planned to build a hospital east of the village until he chose to build instead the third Peoples Academy. He remained interested in the project and acquired the summerhouse that was built by Addison P. Wheelock of Connecticut in 1896. Copley equipped and renovated the building, and it was ready for inspection as Copley Hospital on September 26 and 27, 1932.

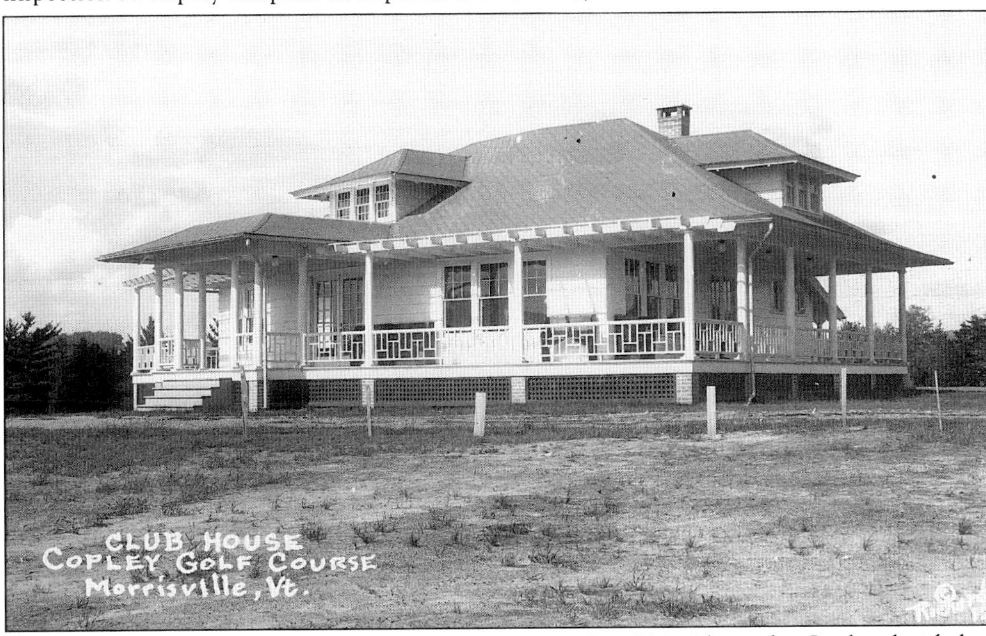

THE COPLEY COUNTRY CLUB AND AIRFIELD, C. 1937. In 1934, Alexander Copley decided to deed to the town 38 acres slightly east of Maple Street. His intent was an airfield, and a golf course was soon added to the project. Two runways were built, both 1,800 feet long, as well as a clubhouse for the nine-hole golf course, which opened in May 1936 with a par of 34. The airfield opened for use on June 6, 1936.

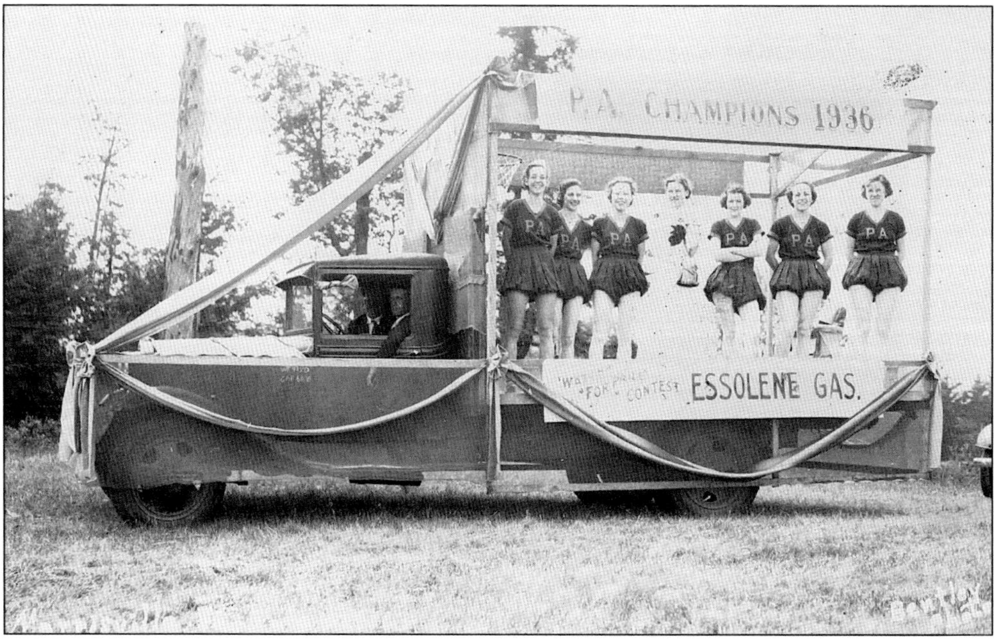

The Independence Day Parade, 1936. Peoples Academy's state champion girls' basketball team of 1936 rode through the streets of Morrisville during the Fourth of July parade that year.

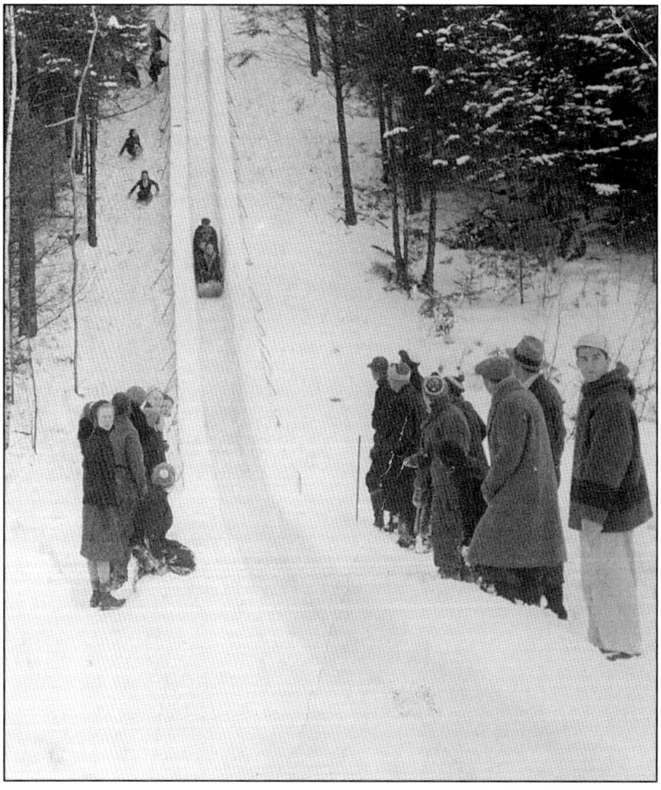

The Toboggan Chute, c. 1936. This exciting toboggan run was built by the Lamoille Valley Winter Sports Club on Kelley Point in the mid-1930s.

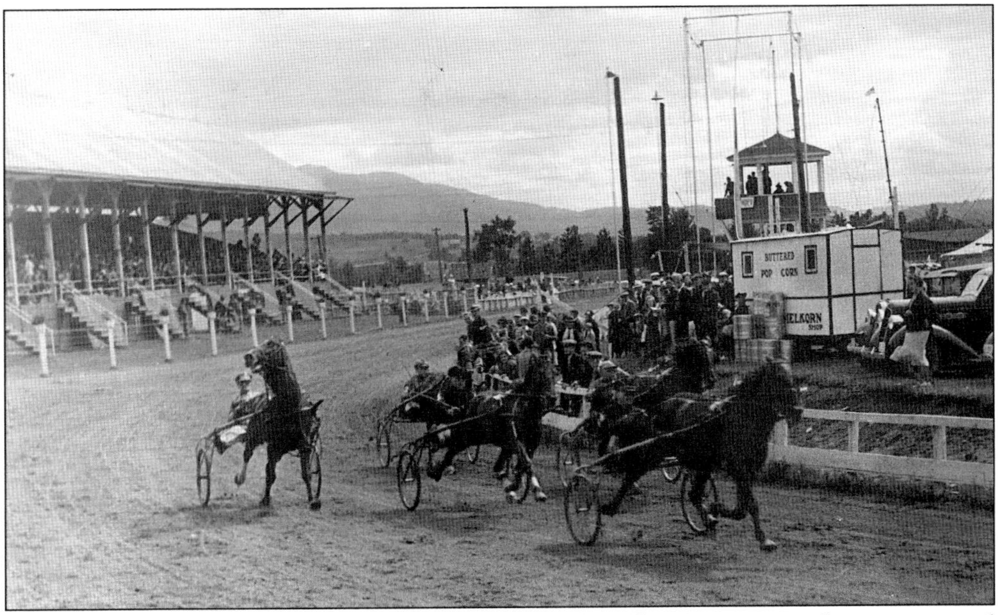

THE LAMOILLE VALLEY FAIR, LATE 1930S. The Lamoille Valley Fair continued every year until World War II, with a few exceptions. This photograph, taken by Leon M. White, shows the trotters coming around a bend during a harness race on the fairground's racetrack. It was World War II that brought an end to the fair. The plan was to resume the fair after the war was over, but that plan never materialized.

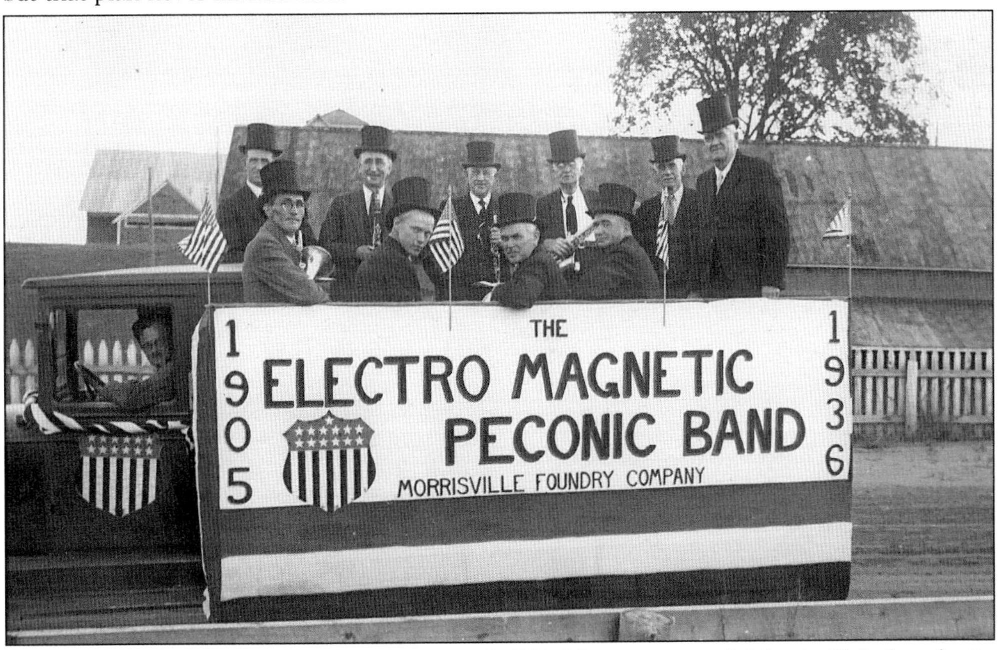

THE MORRISVILLE FOUNDRY COMPANY, 1936. E.B. Merriam started Morrisville's foundry in 1872 after the arrival of the railroad was an assured fact. It was one of Morrisville's longest established, continuously operating manufacturing businesses. In 1930, the foundry brilliantly manufactured the dome for the observatory at Peoples Academy. Shown is the Electro Magnetic Peconic Band, a Morrisville Foundry production.

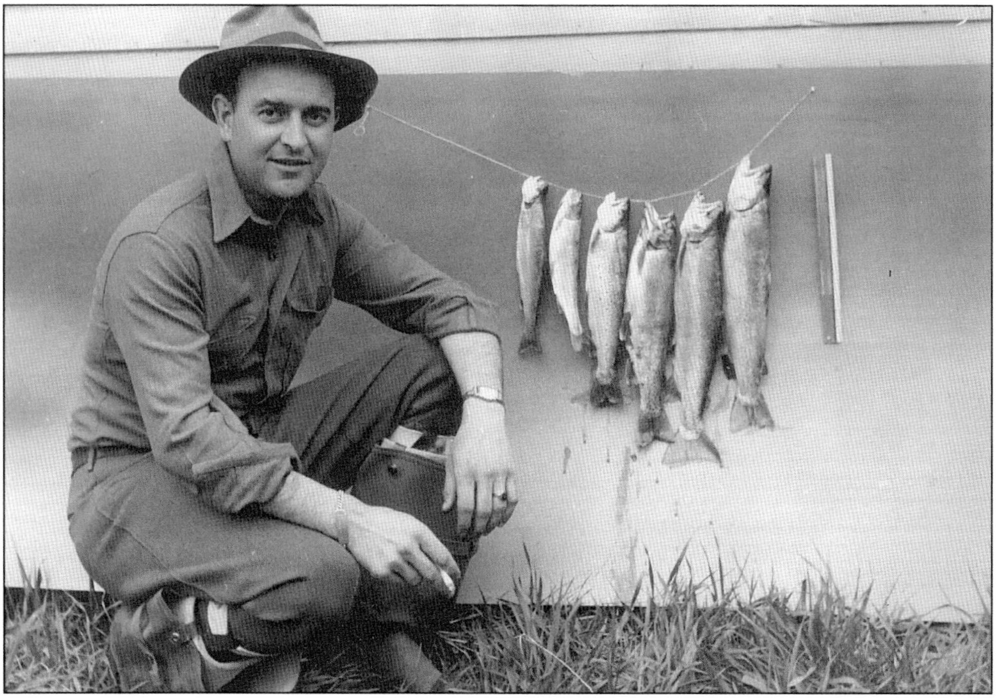

CLYDE A. LIMOGE, C. 1946. The Vermont Fish & Game Department called the Lamoille River Basin one of the best watersheds in Vermont for trout in the early 1940s. The river began to be used more for recreation than for water-powered industries in the 1930s. By 1935, most of those industries had closed. Clyde Limoge, seen here with a large trout, was the son of Arthur Limoge, who acquired the *News & Citizen* in 1942.

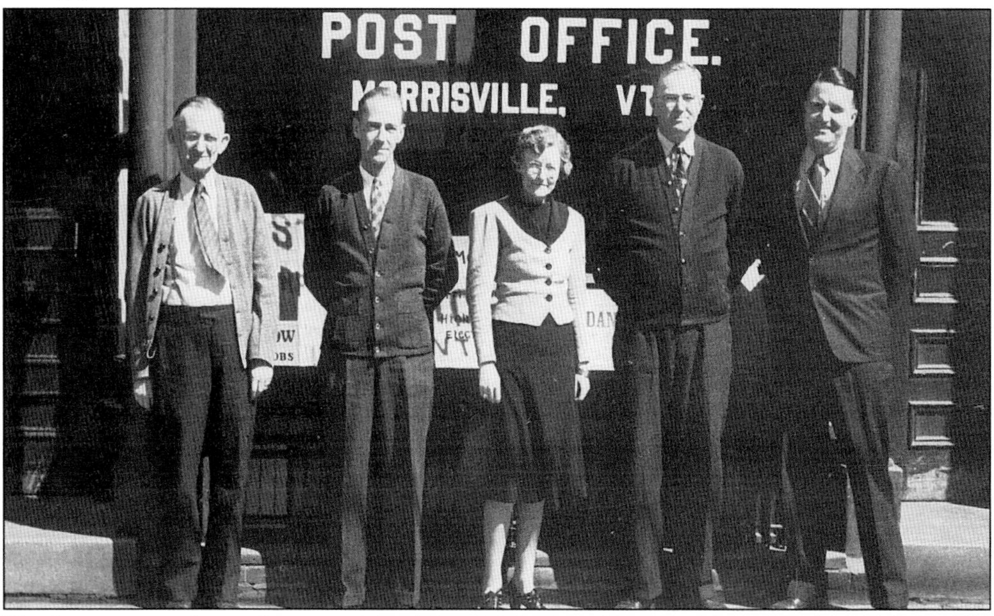

THE MORRISVILLE POST OFFICE, 1941. After the Drowne Block was completed, the Morrisville Post Office moved there. Pictured is the post office's 1941 staff, from left to right, Claude Fisher, Henry Smilie, Mary Gates, Ballou Towne, and John Stewart, postmaster.

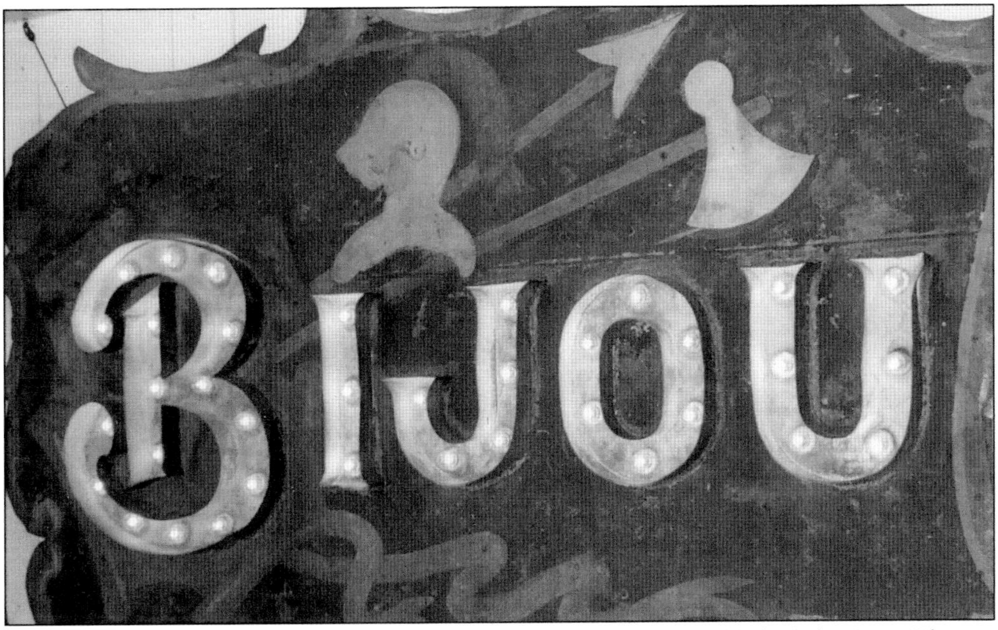

THE BIJOU THEATRE, 1937. Leon C. Emmons and W.C. Laird established the Bijou Theatre in a space at the Randall Hotel in 1902. The Bijou moved down Portland Street in 1909 to the corner of Portland and Brigham Streets. Just one year later, Emmons moved the Bijou to a wood-frame building where Portland and Bridge Streets intersect. By the 1930s, silent movies were out and talkies were in. Emmons was among the first in Vermont to install sound equipment in 1930.

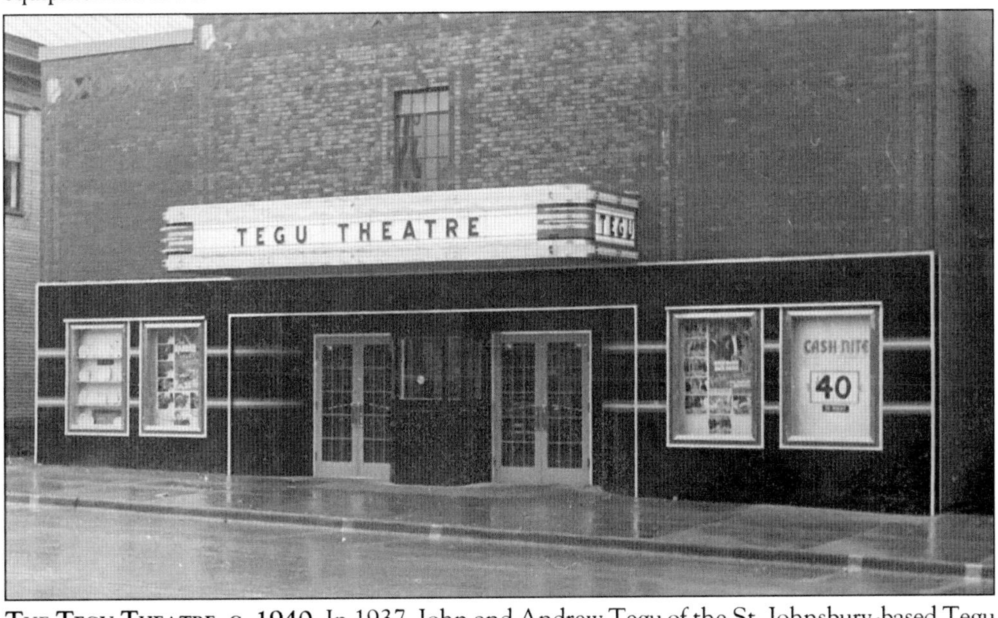

THE TEGU THEATRE, C. 1940. In 1937, John and Andrew Tegu of the St. Johnsbury-based Tegu Theatre Circuit, bought the Portland Street Burke Block. They demolished the old building and constructed a 650-seat, modern movie theatre, which was called "VT's Little Radio City." The Tegu provided much competition for the Bijou Theatre. It offered Saturday matinees that, according to Ethelda Graves, were "a favorite of Morrisville youngsters."

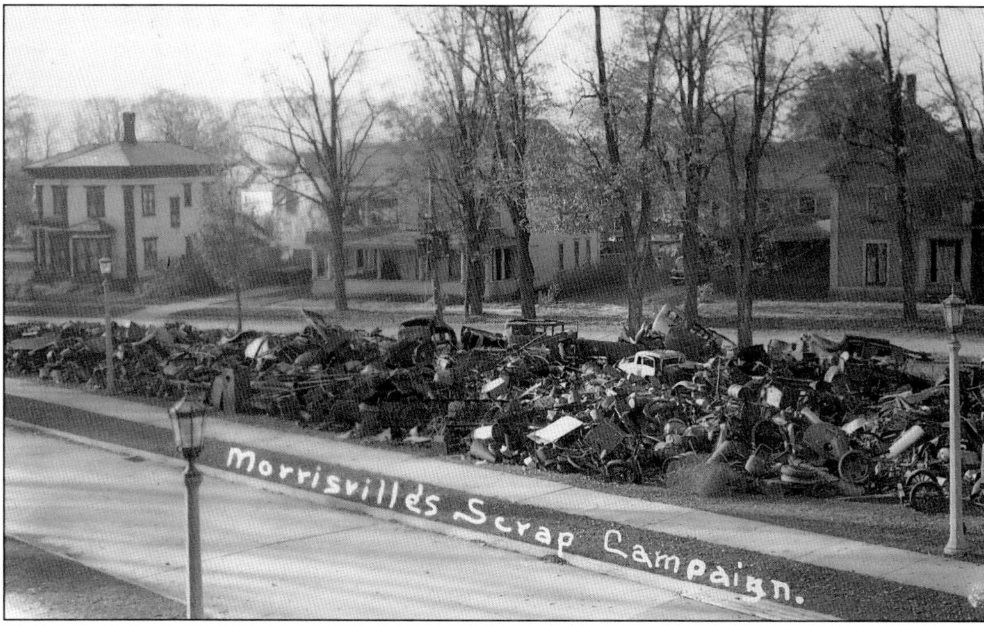

MORRISVILLE'S SCRAP CAMPAIGN, 1942. Morrisville residents collected scrap metal on an open area between the intersection of Park Street and Copley Avenue in 1942. The scrap metal campaign was part of a national home front effort during World War II. The street lamps that can be seen along Copley Avenue in this photograph were gifts of Alexander Copley.

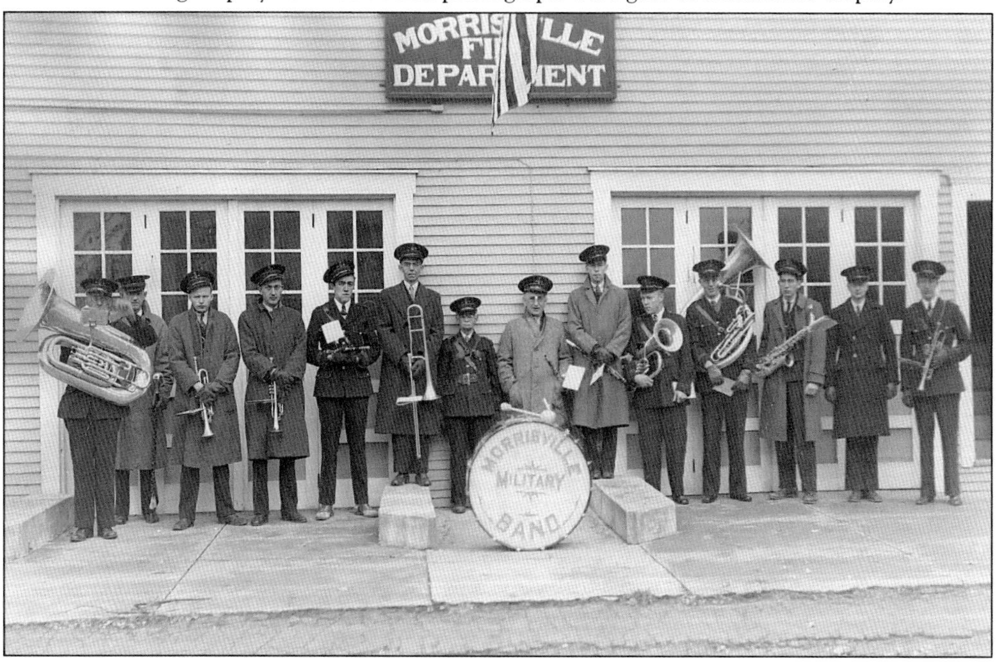

THE MORRISVILLE MILITARY BAND, 1942. The Morrisville Military Band's membership dropped radically from 1942 to 1946; however, after the conclusion of World War II, the band flourished. The band gained its first female member in 1946, when Mary Sanders Mitchell decided to begin playing. Although some members were opposed to the idea, the fact that her father, Don A. Sanders, and brother Willard K. Sanders were in the band helped get her in.

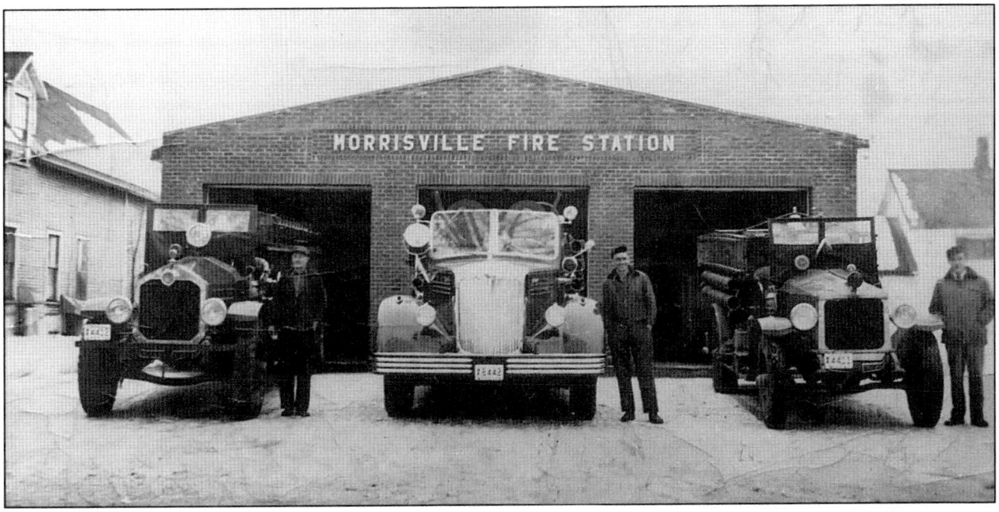

The Morrisville Fire Department, c. 1949. A new fire station was built on the former site of the Charles R. Page house, on Upper Main Street, in 1949. These two photographs show the station shortly after completion; the lower one was taken during the dedication ceremony.

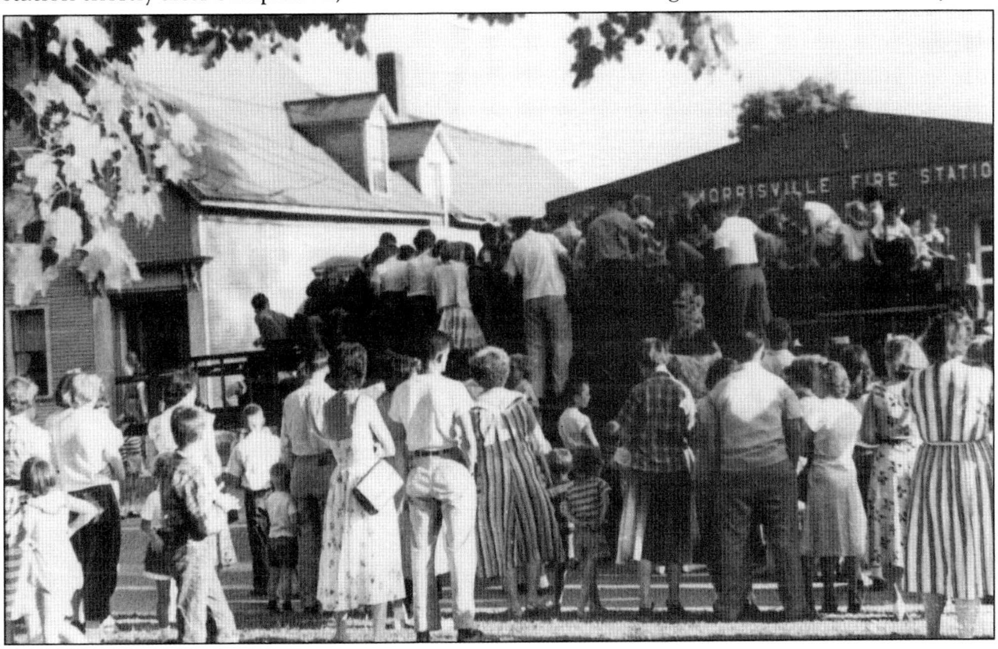

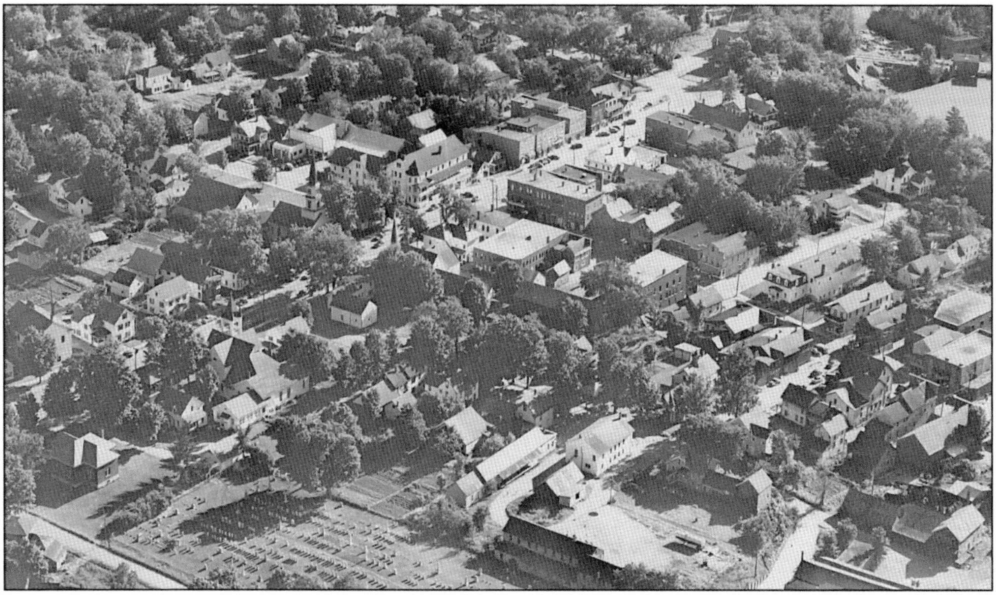

MORRISVILLE FROM THE AIR, EARLY 1950S. Much had changed in Morrisville by the early 1950s, when this aerial photograph was taken. Morristown was still undergoing much growth that had sparked development in the north end of town. However, Morrisville still remained the economic, commercial, and social center of Morristown. Unbeknownst to Morristown residents, much more was soon to change.

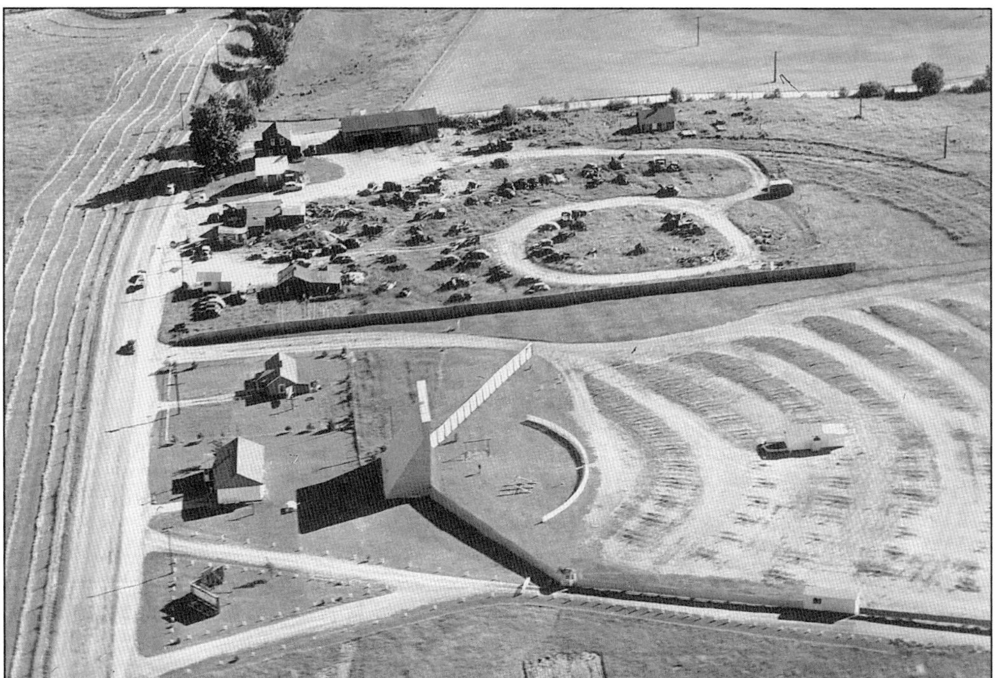

THE MORRISVILLE DRIVE-IN, C. 1950. Morrisville's third movie theatre came in the form of a drive-in when Green Mountain Drive-In Theatres purchased a large lot off Brooklyn Street on the former fairgrounds. Morrisville's Drive-in Theatre opened to the public on August 5, 1949.

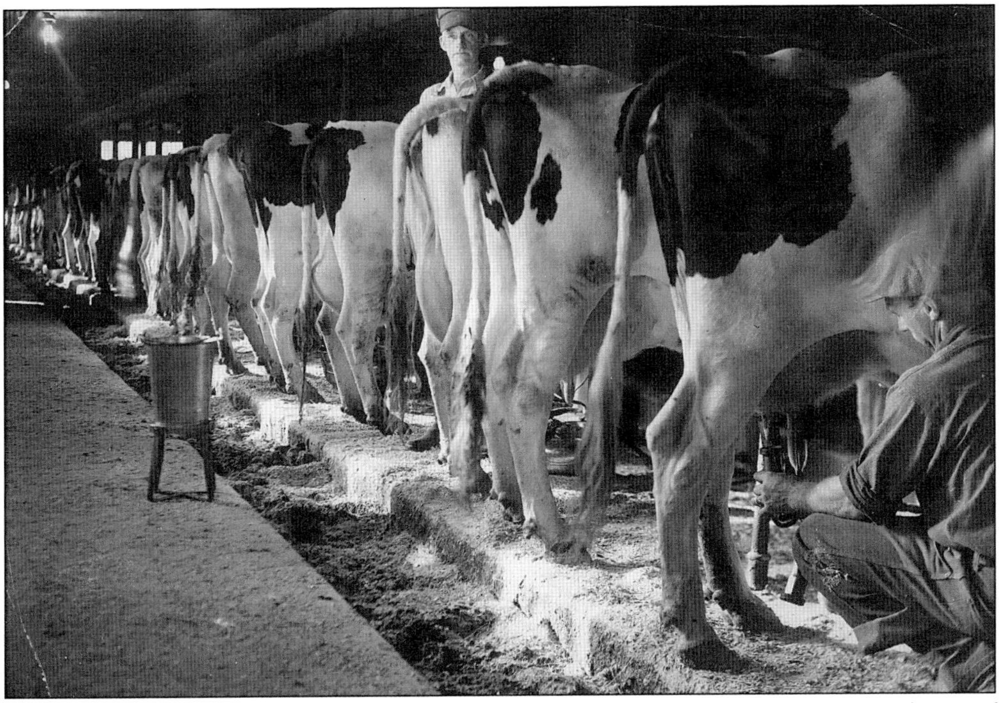

THE FARMING COMMUNITY, c. 1950. Farming and agriculture had long been a vital part of Morristown's economy; however, with the arrival of the railroad, manufacturing came to the region in full swing. Beginning in 1929, Morristown saw a decline in the number of farms. Through the decades, family-owned farms began to shut down across the county.

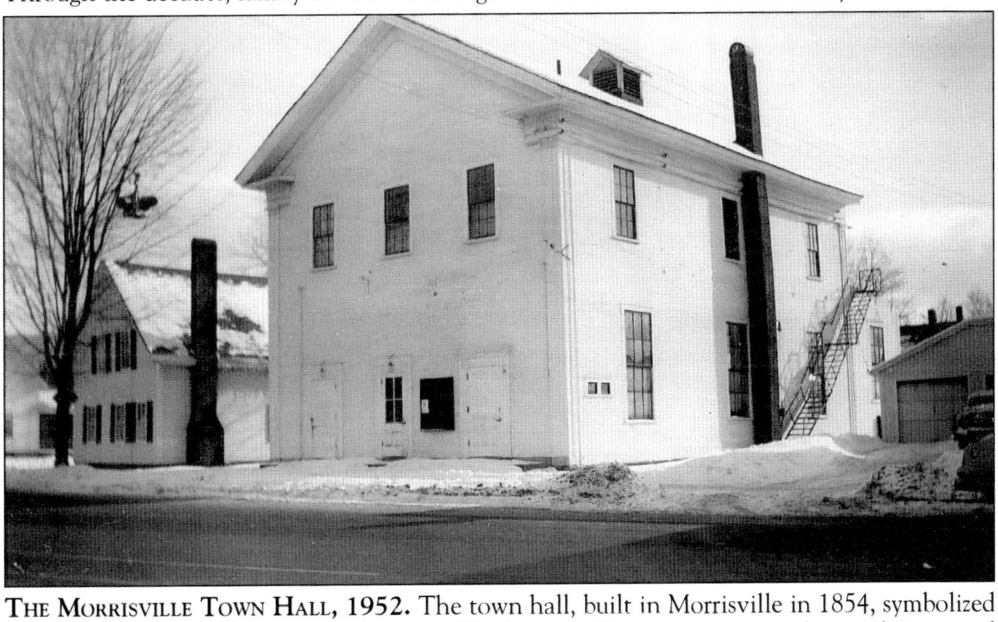

THE MORRISVILLE TOWN HALL, 1952. The town hall, built in Morrisville in 1854, symbolized the shift of Morristown's center of gravity. The large building was renovated several times and finally saw its end in 1968. The year 1951 marked the beginning of the end for the old hall when, due to increased space at Peoples Academy, recreational activities and town meeting were moved there.

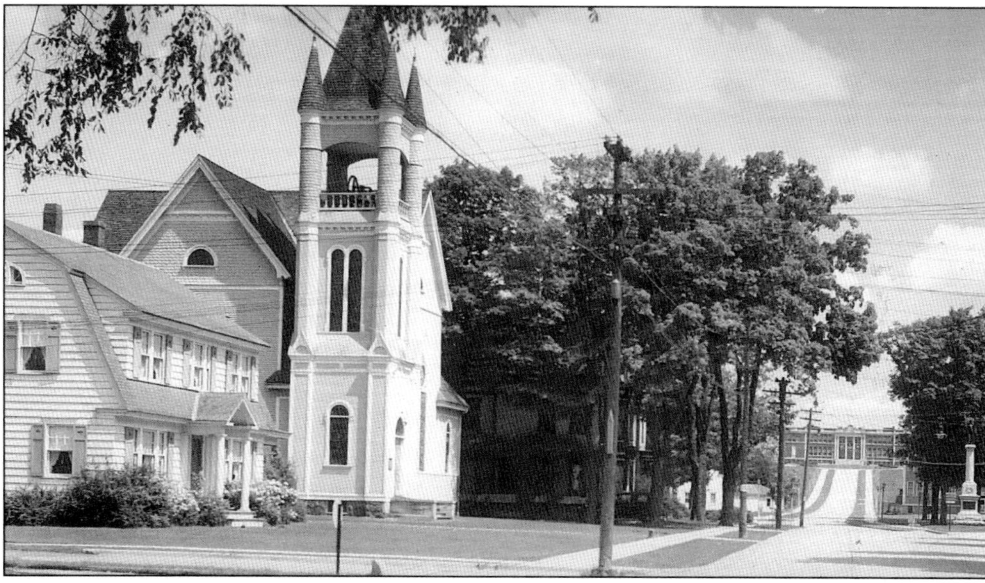

The First Congregational Church, United Church of Christ, c. 1950. In 1875, the First Congregational Church was moved back and was turned at a right angle. It became the vestry of the new church pictured here. In 1949, Sunday school rooms were constructed and, in 1957, there was another major renovation project. The 1950s marked the end of Rev. George E. Goodliffe's 33 years of service as pastor, the longest in the church's history.

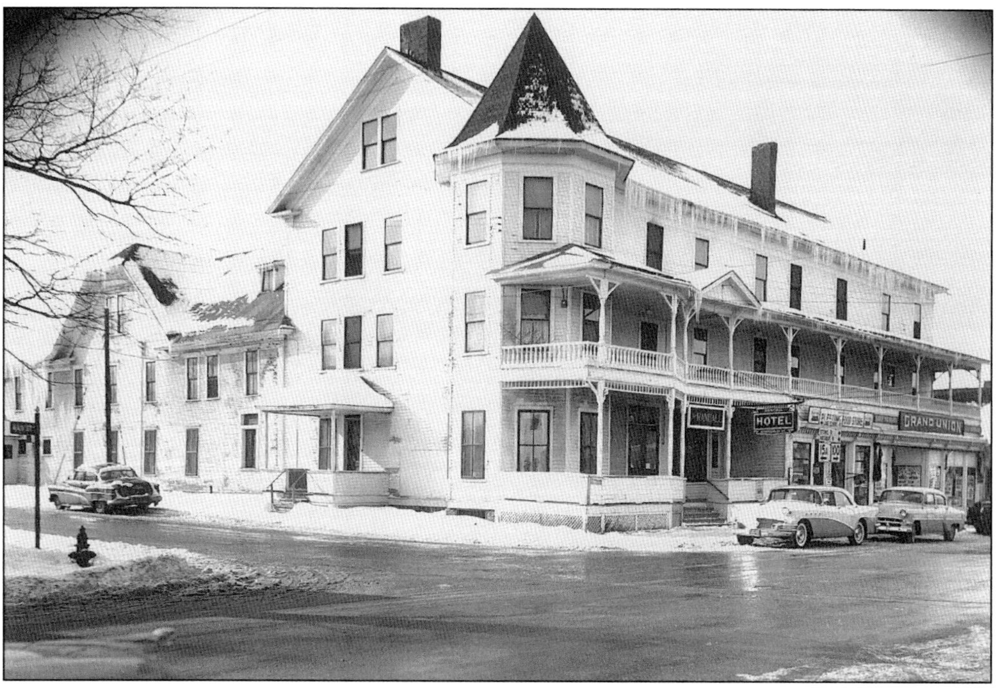

The Randall's Final Days, 1956. Prior to the 1950s, the Randall continued to be a popular Morrisville hotel. It went through several owners, all of whom made modifications. The final owner, Erwin D. Miller, sold the property to Edward R. McMahon of Stowe. McMahon planned to use the lot as a car dealership.

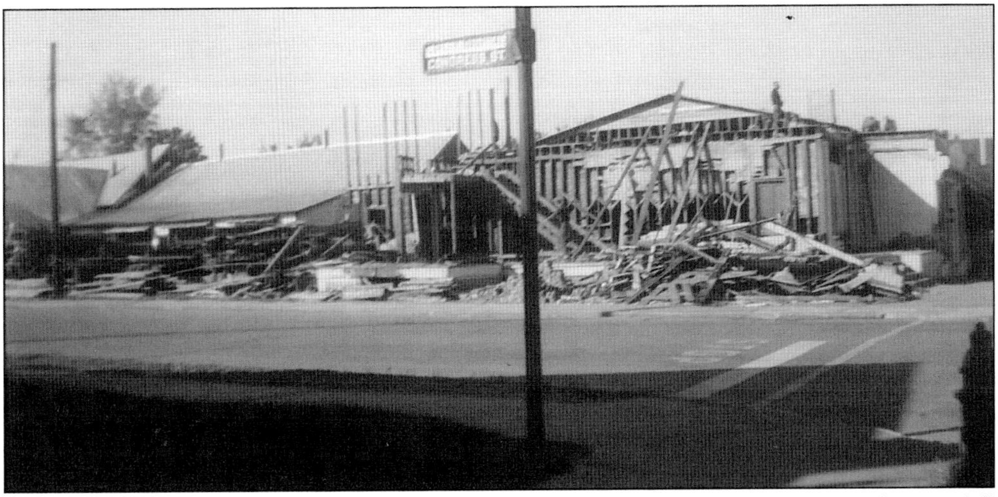

The Randall No More, 1956. In July 1956, the walls came tumbling down. The Randall Hotel, which for so long had stood at the corner of Main and Congress Streets, is shown during its demolition. Edward McMahon changed his mind about the car dealership and built on Brooklyn Street instead. The Randall lot soon became a service station.

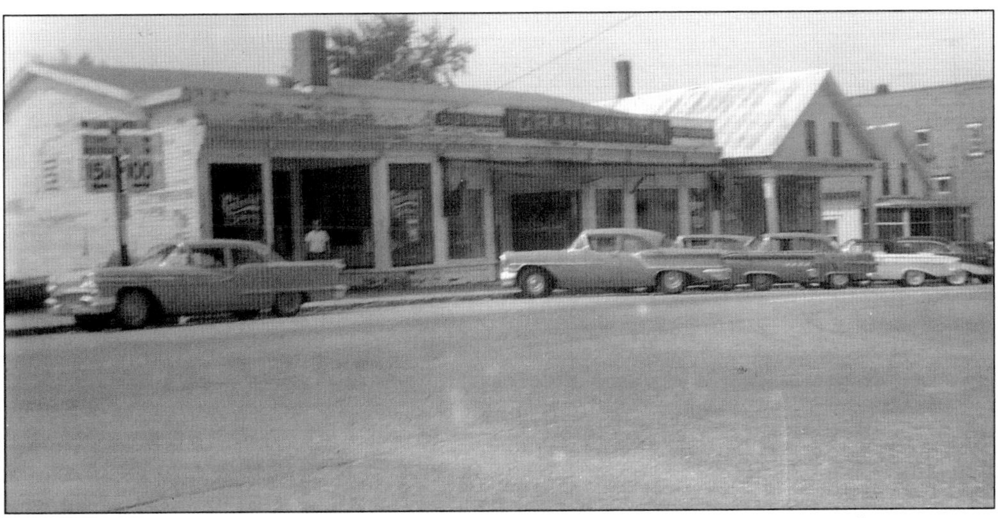

The Last Trace, 1961. Although the actual hotel was gone, the bottom floor was not demolished. In this photograph the remaining section can be seen as the home of a Grand Union Company store. The *News & Citizen* building can be seen on the right.

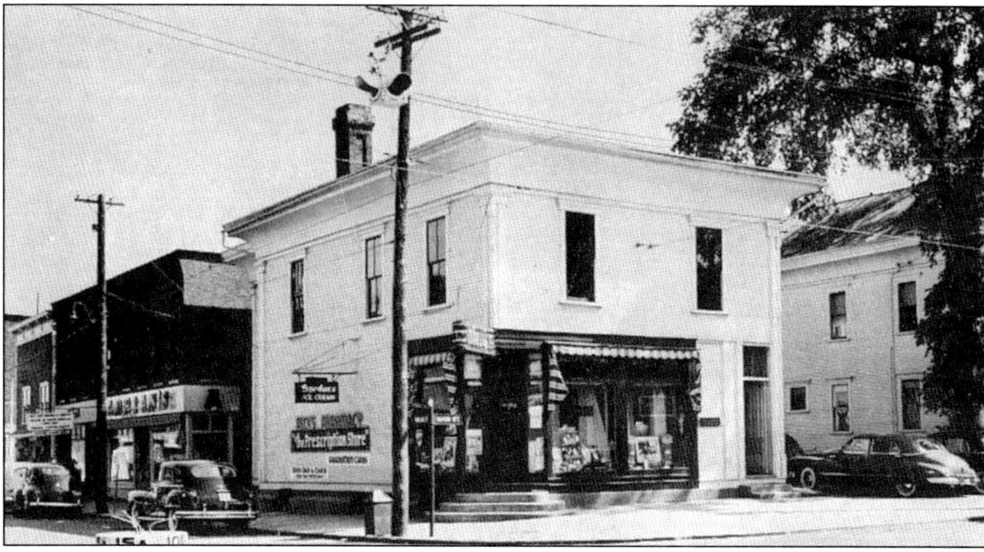

THE FLEETWOOD AND DROWNE BUILDINGS, C. 1959. In 1930, Fred and Jean Peck took over an existing pharmacy in the Fleetwood Building and opened Peck's Pharmacy. W. Wallace Peck took over the business in 1939, when his father died. To the left is Adrian's Store, run by Rethel C. West. In 1959, West's son, Adrian West, joined in the management. A Ben Franklin Store, in the Kelley Block, was also owned by the Wests.

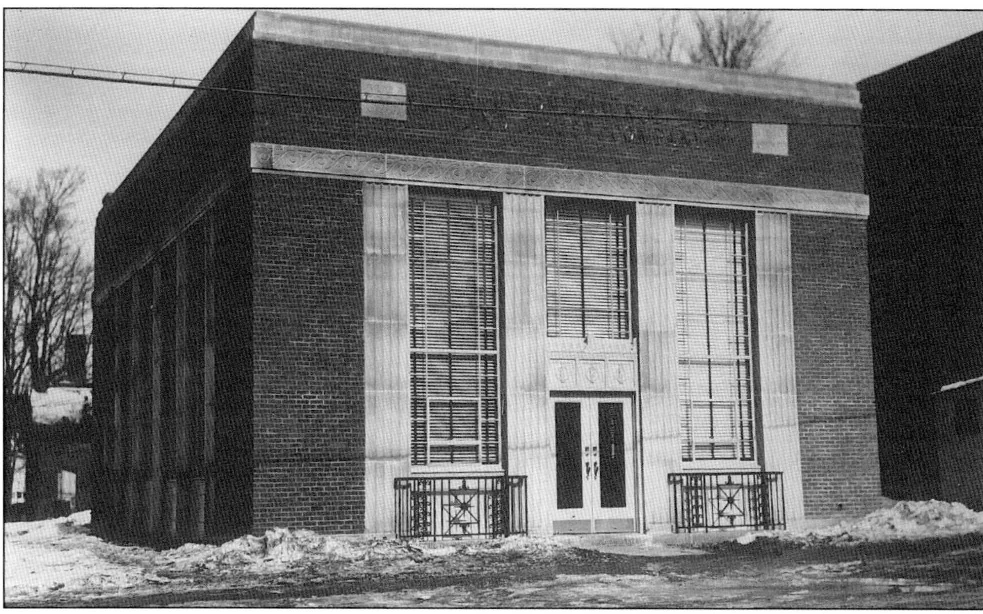

THE UNION SAVINGS BANK & TRUST COMPANY, THE 1950S. In 1940, the Union Savings Bank & Trust moved from its Main Street building, which had opened in 1892, to a new building next door. The former John Miles House, which had already been moved twice to make way for new buildings, was moved a third time to Union Street. By the 1950s, the Union Savings Bank had opened branches in Jeffersonville and Stowe.

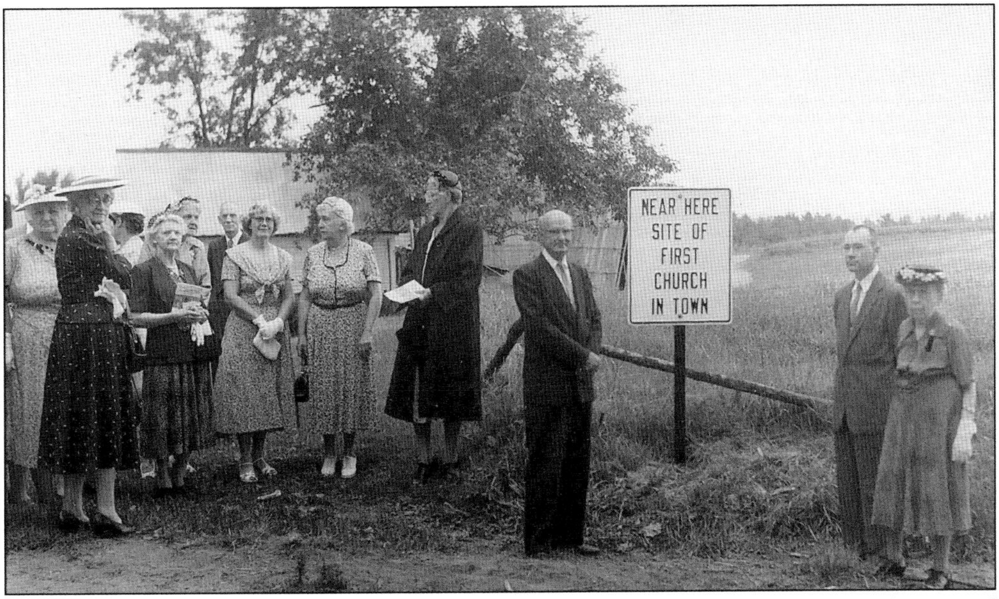

THE SESQUICENTENNIAL CELEBRATION, 1957. This photograph shows a members and principal figures of the First Congregational Church gathered for the July 14, 1957 dedication of a sign marking the site of the first church building in Morristown as part of the church's sesquicentennial celebration. On the right, from left to right, are Rev. Frank Stockwell, Rev. Walter Cooley, and Anna L. Mower.

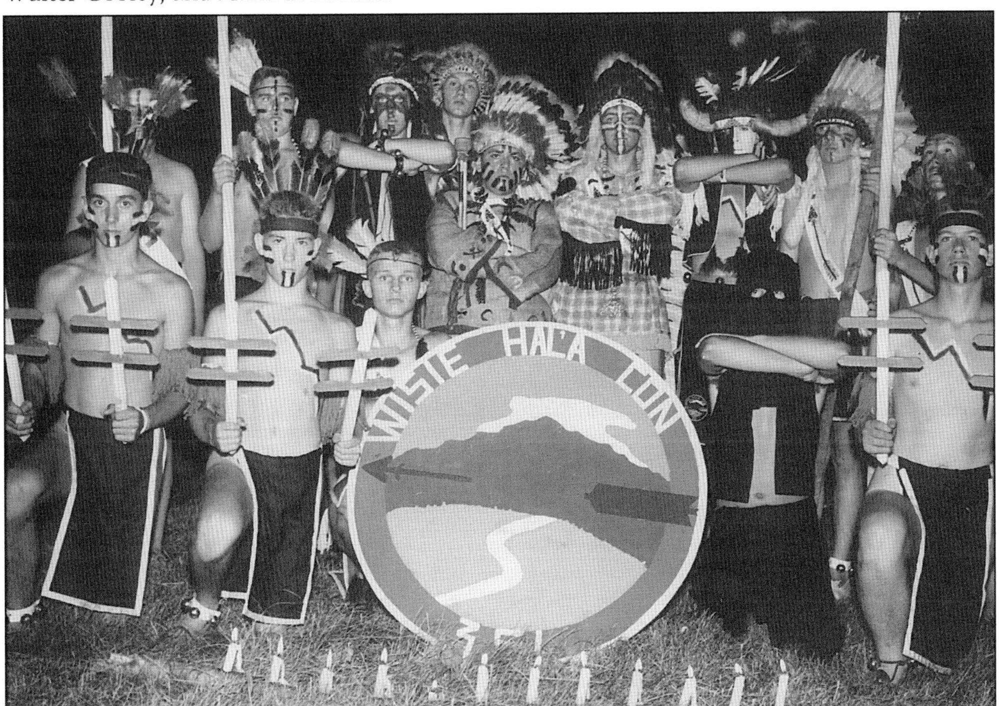

ARROW SCOUTS, 1959. Arrow Scouts of the Long Trail Council took part in an Indian pageant for the Morristown Historical Society's celebration of the Champlain Festival. The Scouts staged a devil dance on the shores of Lake Lamoille.

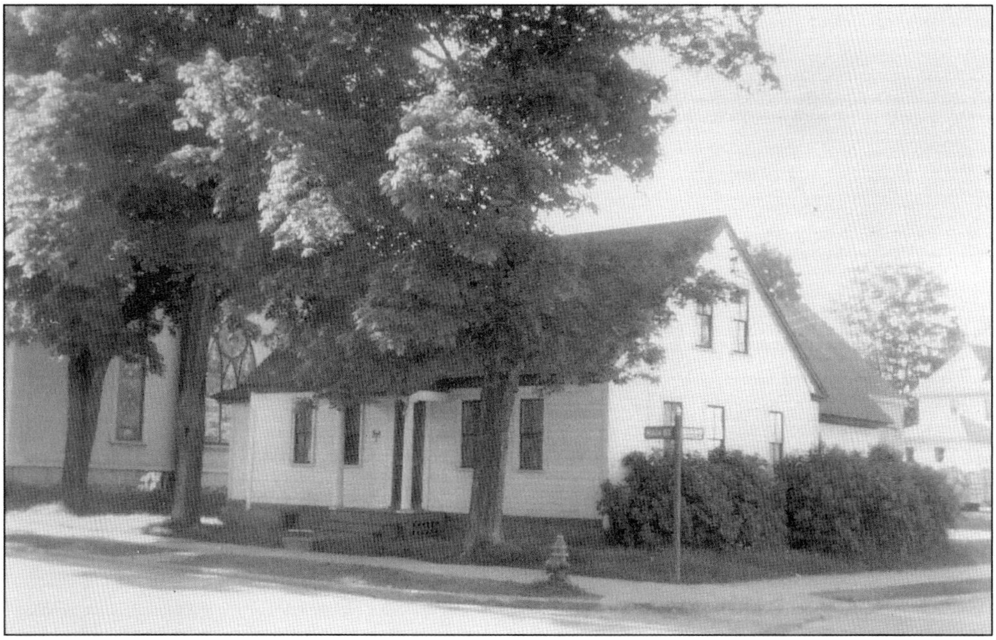

The Tinker-Powers House, 1959. Dr. Almerin Tinker constructed his Main Street home in 1839. The house was owned by Gertrude Powers in 1959. She sold the house to Fred A. Ribolini of Montpelier, who then moved the house a short distance down Congress Street and sold the lot to other parties. The corner lot was soon converted to an automobile service station.

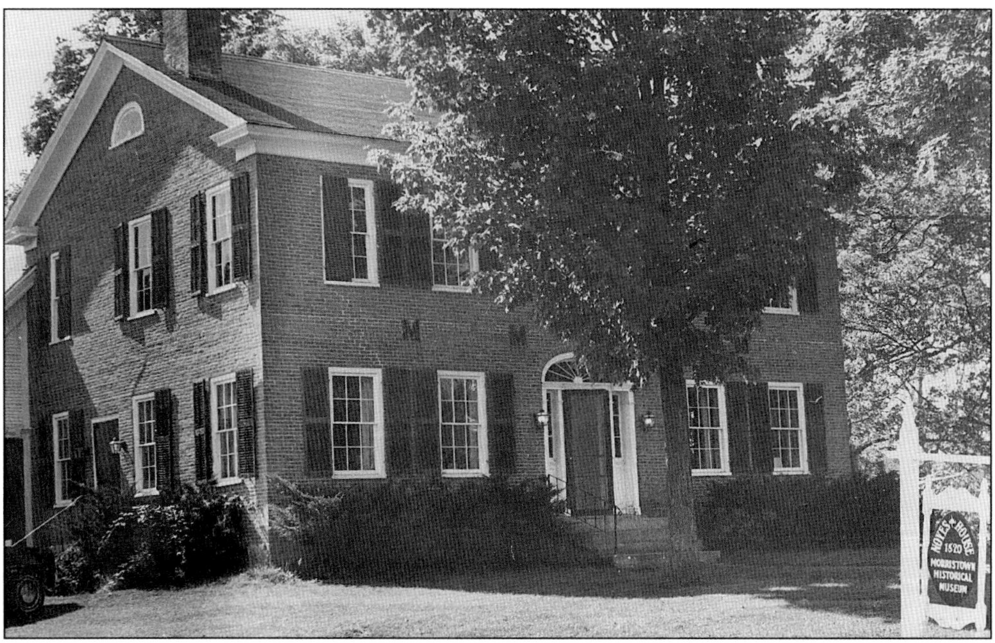

The 1820 Noyes House, 1950s. Originally built by John Safford in 1820, this Main Street building was renovated by Carlos Noyes, the father of Lamoille County banking. The house stayed in the Noyes family until 1948. After serving as apartments for several years, the house was leased by the town to the Morristown Historical Society for operation as a museum.

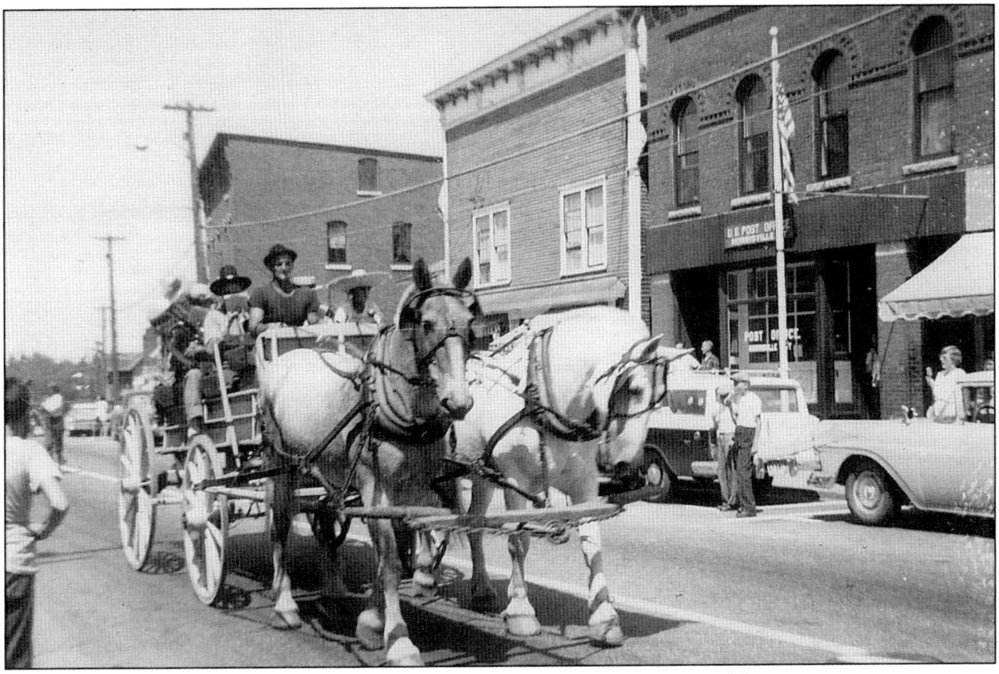

Morristown on Wheels, 1959. Mount Mansfield Company's old-time mountain wagon is drawn by Edgar Emery's team of grays. This wagon is shown appearing in the Morristown Historical Society's Morristown On Wheels Parade on July 29, 1959. The wagon contains members of the Morrisville Military Band.

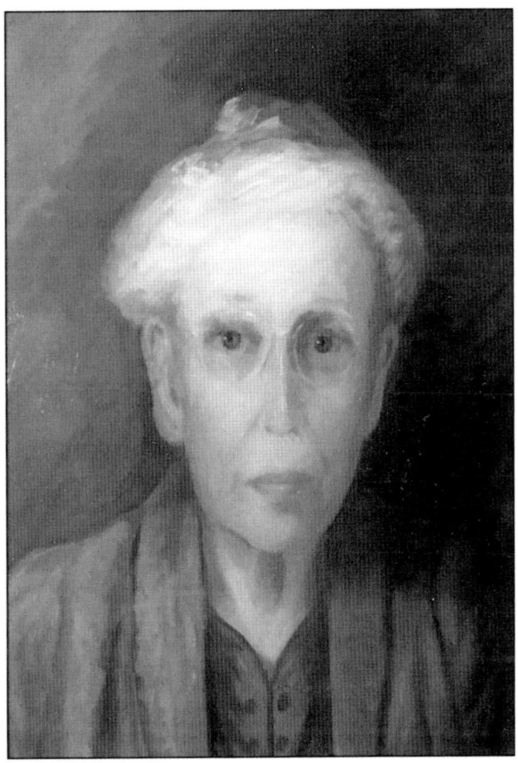

Anna L. Mower, 1876–1966. Anna Louise Mower lived in Morristown her entire life. A Peoples Academy graduate, she later taught at Peoples Academy before becoming a librarian at the Morristown Centennial Library, a job that she dearly loved and kept for 42 years. She organized and led the Morristown Historical Society and authored the *History of Morristown, Vermont*, which was published in 1935.

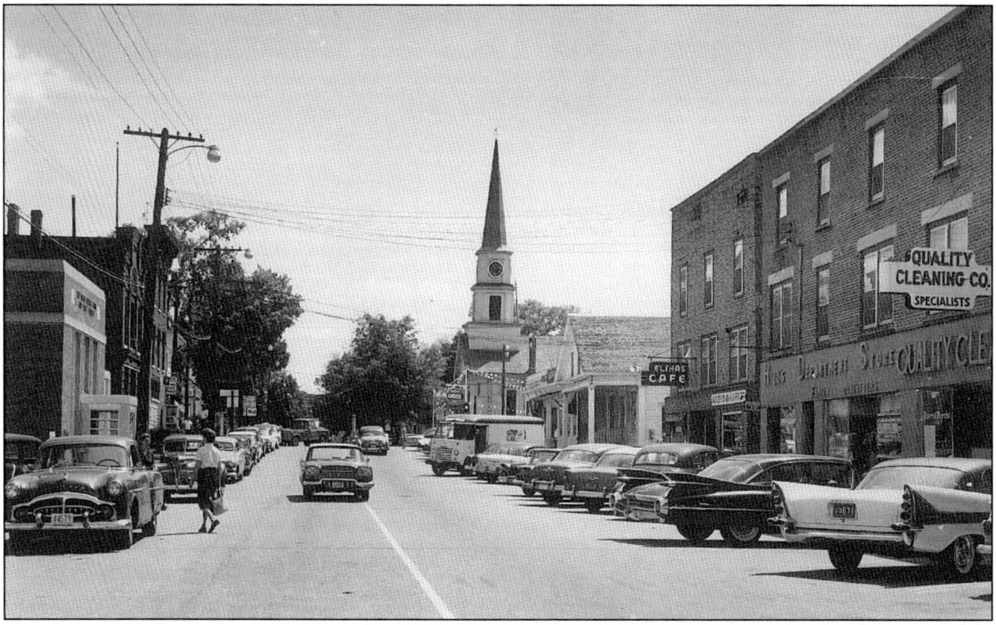

MAIN STREET, LATE 1950S. This photograph shows the Main Street Ferris Block, the home of Hill's Department Store and Quality Cleaning Specialists.

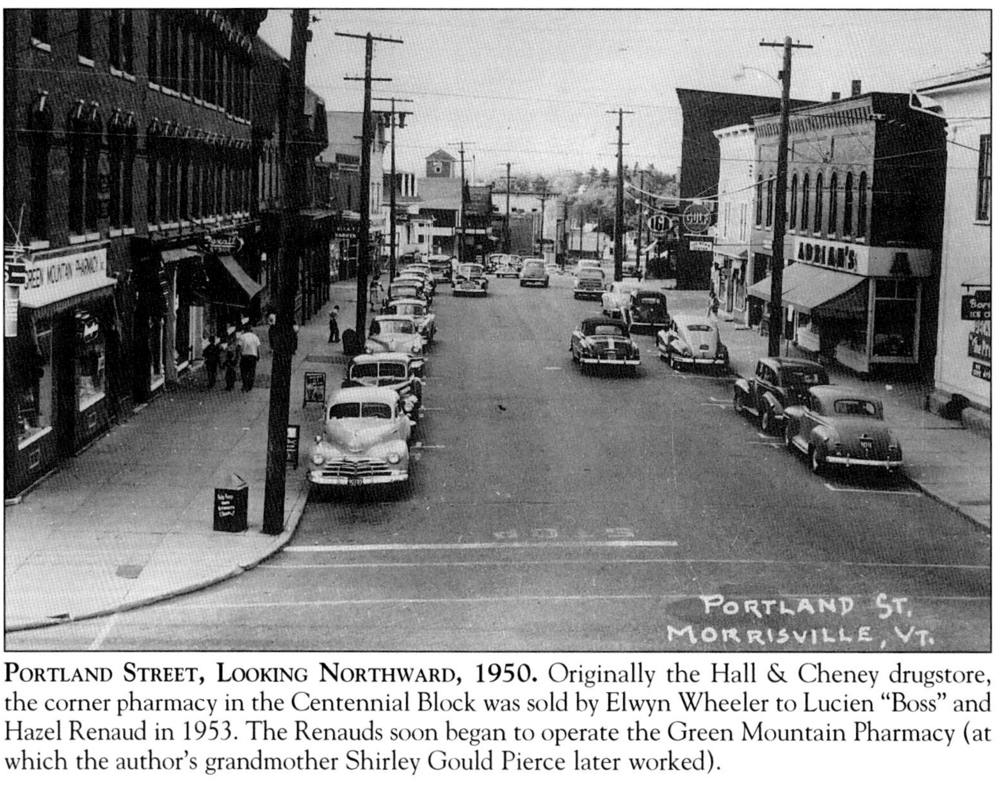

PORTLAND STREET, LOOKING NORTHWARD, 1950. Originally the Hall & Cheney drugstore, the corner pharmacy in the Centennial Block was sold by Elwyn Wheeler to Lucien "Boss" and Hazel Renaud in 1953. The Renauds soon began to operate the Green Mountain Pharmacy (at which the author's grandmother Shirley Gould Pierce later worked).

Three

The Neighbor to the North: Hyde Park

The town of Hyde's Park, or Wilkes (prior to the rewriting of the charter) was chartered on August 27, 1781, to residents of Norwich, Connecticut. The town was named after Capt. Jedidiah Hyde, who was one of the chief grantees and had surveyed the township. The "'s" was later dropped. Hyde Park was settled by John McDaniel, Esq., on July 4, 1787. Originally from Canterbury, New Hampshire, McDaniel had made his way along a footpath to Hyde Park from a settlement in Cabot. The original Hyde Park settlement was in Centerville; however, an absence of water in that area inhibited growth. Hyde Park's geography offered many mill possibilities to the early settlers in other areas, thanks to the Lamoille River, Green River, and Town Hill Brook.

Hyde Park's growth was helped by the building of a road from Waterbury, which was completed in 1834. In 1836, a courthouse and jail were built due to a committee's decision to give the county seat to Hyde Park. That decision gave the town a new sense of importance. Hyde Park was considered the geographical and political center of Lamoille County. Several attempts were made in the mid-1800s to remove its county seat status. Morristown residents made another attempt in 1910, after a devastating fire destroyed 20 main buildings. Every attempt failed, and Hyde Park has remained the shire town of Lamoille County.

"Hyde Park is our Town; We love her as we should."—Rev. John Nutting.

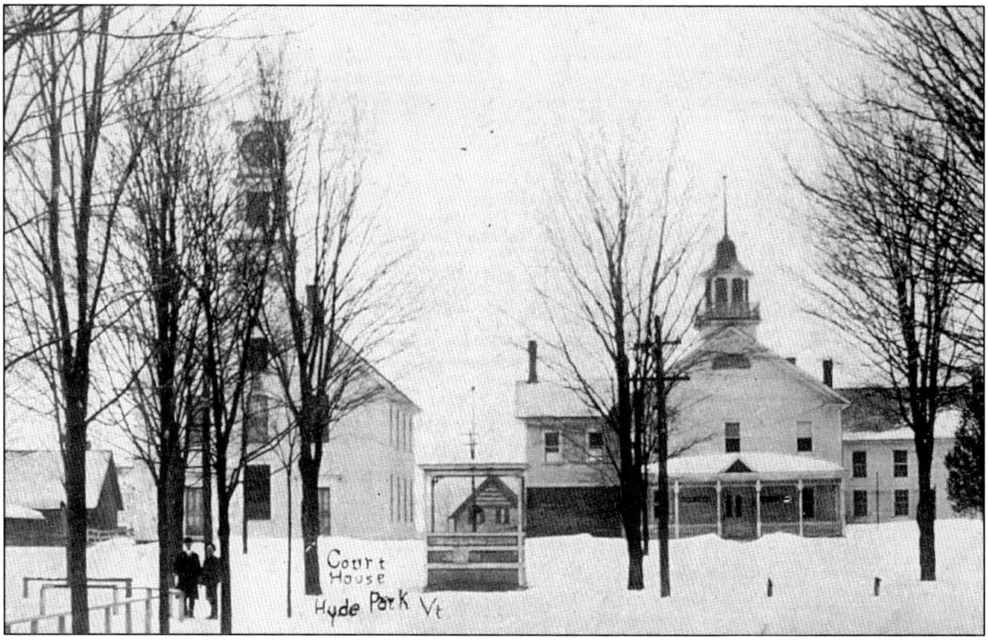

HYDE PARK COURTHOUSE AND JAIL, C. 1900. Hyde Park alone bore the expense of constructing the county buildings in 1836, after being given the county seat. A 25-foot addition was made to the courthouse in 1875. The terrible fire of April 17, 1910, began at the jail with flames spreading quickly to the courthouse. By the time the fire was extinguished, Hyde Park had suffered $125,000 in property loss. Hyde Park's future looked dark, but surrounding towns quickly rallied to help the shire town.

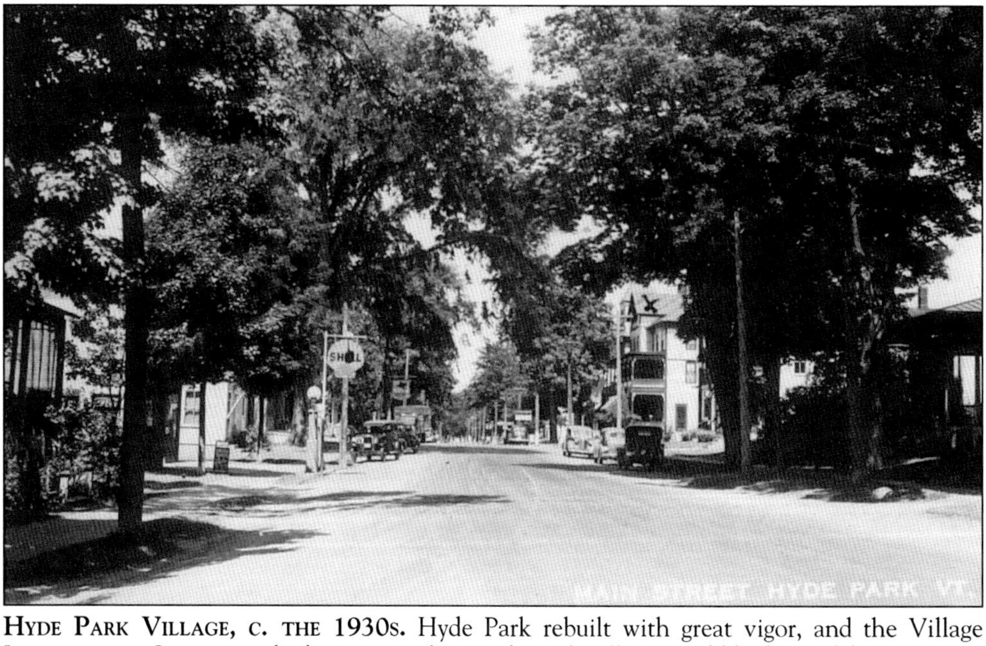

HYDE PARK VILLAGE, C. THE 1930S. Hyde Park rebuilt with great vigor, and the Village Improvement Society worked to ensure that Hyde Park village would be beautiful once again. This view shows Hyde Park's Main Street at some time during the 1930s. The large maple trees were a project of the Village Improvement Society.

Four

The Neighbor to the South: Stowe

The town of Stow (without the "e") was named after a town in England. It was chartered on June 8, 1763, to Joshua Simmon and 64 others. Stow's earliest settler, Oliver Luce, arrived from Hartland on April 16, 1794. Capt. Clement Moody arrived on the following day. Most of Stow's early settlers were from the town of Woodstock and the states of Connecticut and Massachusetts. "From this small beginning a frugal, hardworking, self-reliant, and resourceful people created a town that grew and prospered. Land was cleared, farms established, mills built, stores opened, schools were staffed, churches founded, and a thriving community was formed."

Like its neighbors, Stow was very prosperous in its early settlement days. Growth was slow but very steady. Unfortunately, in 1803 an eighth of Stow's population, 40 of whom were children, died when a dysentery epidemic struck. Stow's population soon rebounded.

The year 1838 brought the addition of an "e" to the town's name, making it Stowe. Stowe's area grew substantially in 1848 with the annexation of the town of Mansfield. Stowe gained more territory in 1855, when it received a part of the town of Sterling. In the early 1900s, Stowe's growth was rapid and began to differ from that of its Lamoille County neighbors. Stowe's population had grown to 1,926 people. "Inevitably, major social, economic and technological trends over two centuries brought change. The dominance of agriculture, in its various forms, gave way in the latter half of the 20th century to a burgeoning of recreation-oriented, year round-activities."

In 1912, several Swedish families brought utilitarian skiing to Stowe. It was the ingenuity of local enthusiasts that gave birth to the sport of recreational skiing and a major tourism industry. Ira Allen and his surveyors had once considered Mount Mansfield worthless, but soon it was the epicenter of what would become the Ski Capital of the East.

"In Stowe, community interest in the environment, conservation and stewardship, planning and historic preservation, is strong."—Quotations from Ned Lang.

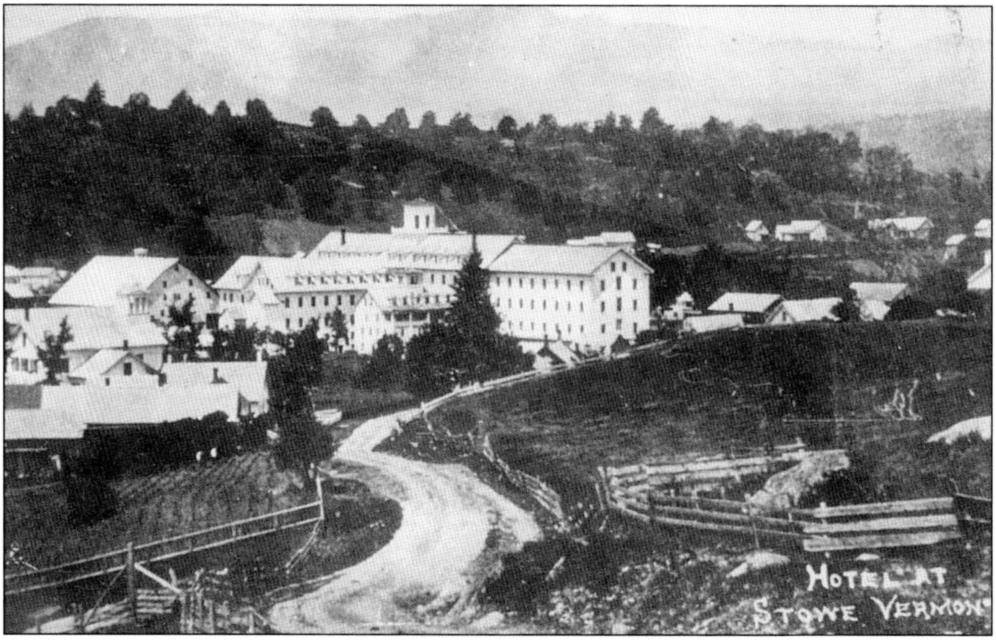

The Mount Mansfield Hotel, c. 1885. The Mount Mansfield Hotel was built in 1863 on the south side of Stowe's Main Street. It could accommodate 500 guests in 200 rooms and had a livery building with a capacity of 100. The large hotel burned to the ground in October 1889. School Street can be seen in the foreground.

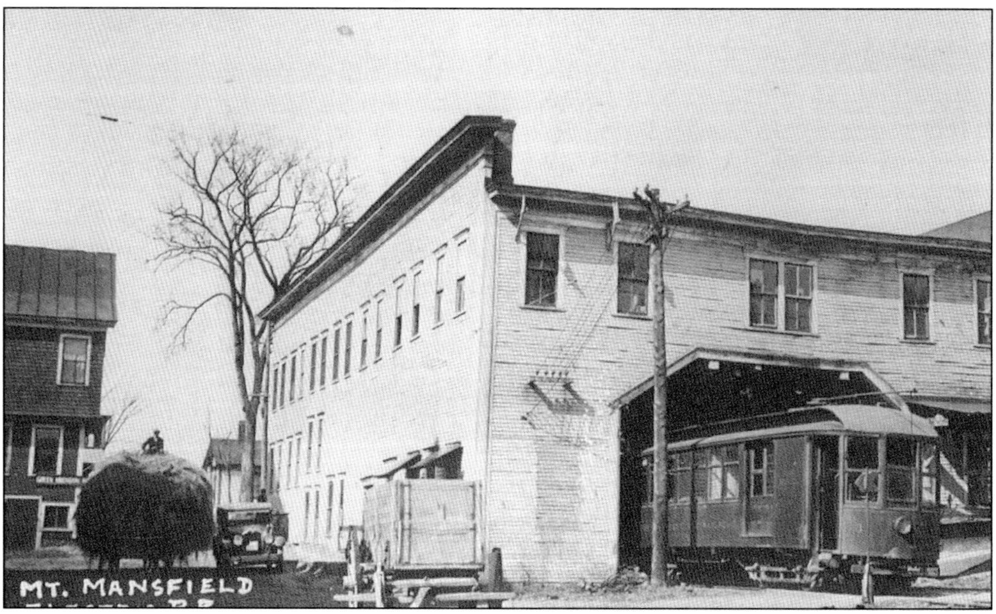

The Mount Mansfield Electric Railroad Depot, c. 1929. The Mount Mansfield Electric Railroad offered three or four daily round-trips between Stowe and Waterbury from 1897 to 1932. The railroad was never a financial success and, in 1932, Route 100 was built by the state along the railroad bed after its termination. The cement road allowed for easy travel between Wilmington and Newport. The railroad depot building still stands as part of the Green Mountain Inn.

Five

The Neighbor to the East: Elmore

The town of Elmore, location of the Elmore State Forest and Lake Elmore (formerly Elmore Pond), was chartered on August 21, 1781. The grant had been made to Samuel Elmore in 1780. Elmore's first settlers arrived in July 1790. Included among them were Martin and Jesse Elmore, James and Seth Olmstead, who later built the first hotel-tavern in town, and Aaron Keeler. The majority of the early settlers came from Sharon and Norwalk, Connecticut, and the surrounding area. By 1791, the census showed that Elmore's population was 12. Elmore's growth was very slow but steady; by 1900, Elmore's population had risen to 550, due mainly to the prospering settlement to the east.

Elmore was considered rich in farmland, but it also had many mountainous areas to the west that were described as "broken and unfit for farming." Elmore was also very heavily wooded and was one of many Vermont towns where the lumber trade thrived. A prospering settlement grew in the hamlet of East Elmore. Soon, East Elmore became a very busy place and was the location of a store, school, post office, many homes, and several mills. By the early 1900s, the lumber had nearly disappeared and, with it, the village of East Elmore, which today is a dense wilderness. Elmore is truly one of the best-kept secrets in Vermont; it is the lake, the mountain, and the vast wilderness that secure Elmore as the "beauty spot of Vermont."

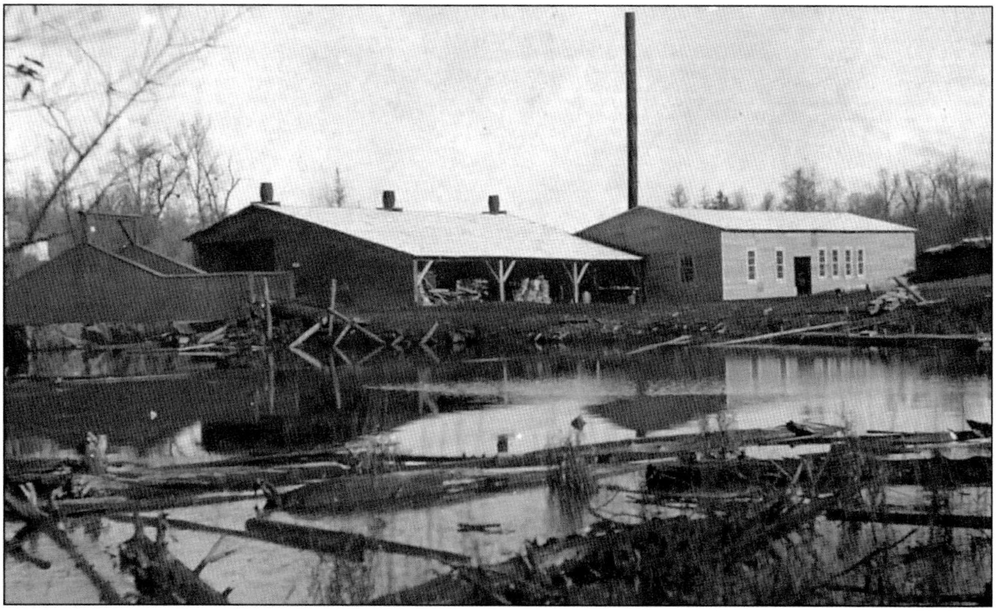

MORSE'S SAWMILL, C. 1890. James and Ira Youngs built one of several sawmills at East Elmore c. 1871. George A. Morse soon acquired the mill and manufactured one million feet of lumber per year. Within 30 years, lumbering on a large scale had virtually disappeared from East Elmore.

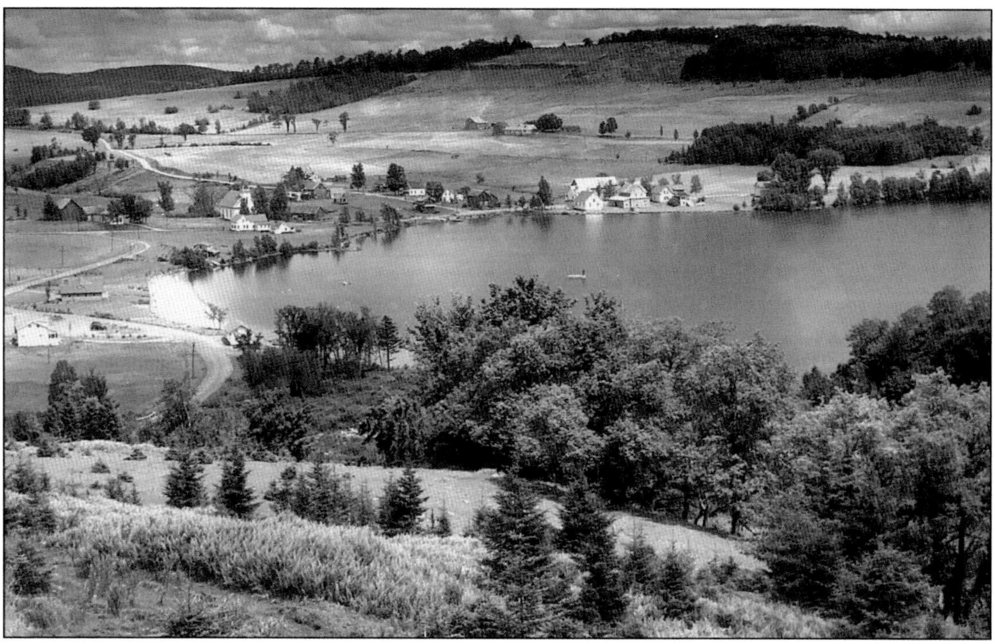

ELMORE VILLAGE, C. 1940. This photograph, believed to have been taken in the early 1940s, shows the tiny, charming village of Elmore, located on the shores of Elmore Pond. "Elmore was an ideal place to grow up," says Cynthia Bryer. "There is a lot of undeveloped land there, and the lake and mountain are so beautiful. I remember the Elmore Store's penny candy, the one-room school, and the very friendly people who lived there. Elmore was a really neat community to live in."

Six

The Neighbor to the Northeast: Wolcott

Named in honor of one of the original proprietors, Maj. Gen. Oliver Wolcott, the town of Wolcott was chartered on August 22, 1781. The first settlers, Thomas Taylor and Seth Hubbell, arrived in April 1789. These two and the other early settlers endured many hardships during their early days in Wolcott, of which Hubbell kept a very comprehensive record. Wolcott's first town meeting was held on March 31, 1791, and Robert W. Taylor was elected town clerk. Records show that in 1794, there were four voters in the town, all of whom held some public office.

Wolcott was another Lamoille County town that benefited from the arrival of the railroad. Wolcott soon became prosperous, with three general stores, two grocery stores, a furniture store, a drugstore, a shoe shop, a hotel, two millinery shops, and about 50 homes. One of the largest general stores in New England could be found in Wolcott. Charles E. Haskell, a man of honesty and integrity, owned and operated the C.E. Haskell general store, built shortly after he arrived in Wolcott in 1885.

Wolcott's population has fluctuated throughout the years and at times has declined steadily. The census of 1900 showed that Wolcott had 1,066 residents. The 2000 census reported Wolcott's population at 1, 456. These figures show a gain of 390 people in 100 years, 227 of whom came after 1990. "There aren't that many jobs in Wolcott," said Douglas Bryer; "that might be one factor that led to its slow growth, but the land is so beautiful, and Wolcott is perfectly situated in the heart of the Lamoille River Valley where fishing and hunting abound. I am surprised that more don't want to call Wolcott home."

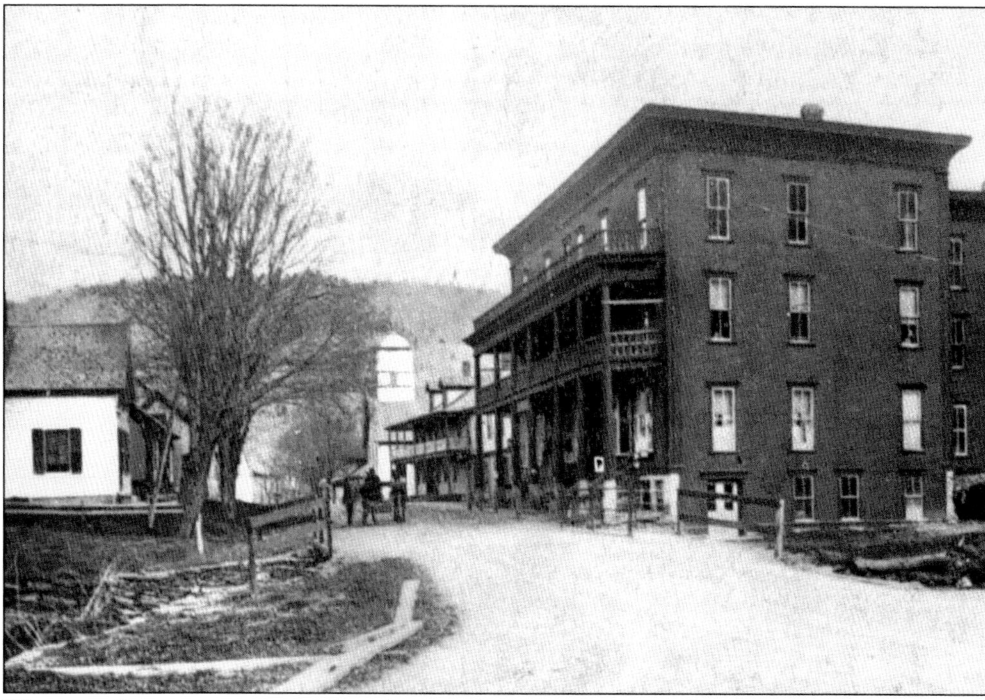

WOLCOTT VILLAGE, c. 1900. This photograph shows Wolcott village at the dawn of the 20th century. Wolcott village was very attractive and included a town hall, church, stores, and the Wolcott Hotel. Ira Woodbridge built the Wolcott Hotel (right) prior to 1874. It was known throughout the county as a "well-appointed hotel."

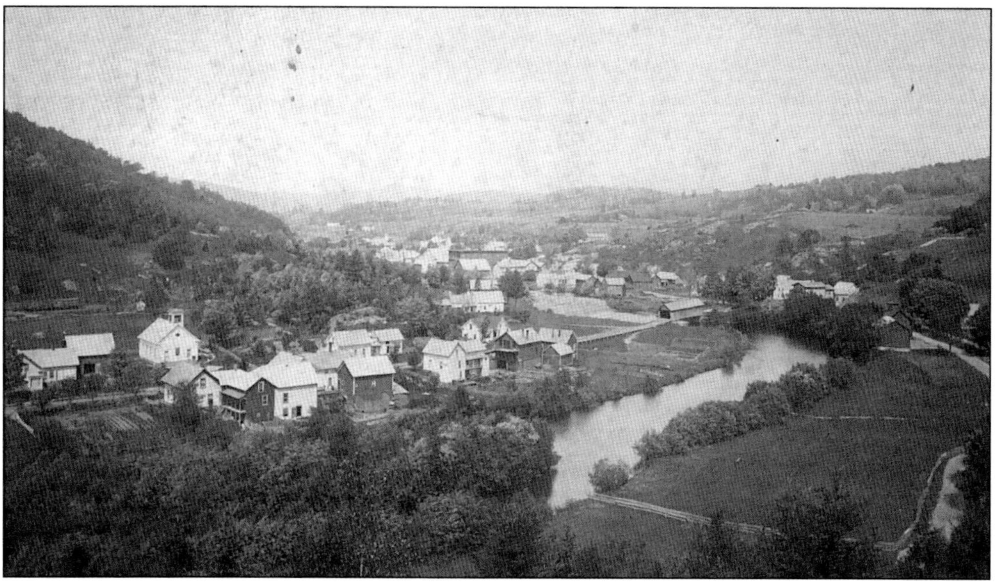

WOLCOTT VILLAGE, c. 1900. "Wolcott used to be a big place you know," according to Ruth Reed, a descendant of Thomas Taylor. A lifelong Wolcott resident, Ruth Reed said that Wolcott has been a wonderful town for her to call home. However, she misses the many nice houses that used to line the village streets. "It was once a very pretty village" in the days of the prospering Wolcott.

Seven

The Neighbor to the Northwest: Johnson

Although considered by many as a legend, it appears that Johnson's difficult beginnings began with a charter granted in 1780 to Joseph Brown of Jericho. Brown started an allotment called Brownington. Shortly thereafter, the Browns were captured by Indians, taken to Canada, and sold to the British. They remained in captivity for three years, during which time the charter fees went unpaid. Believing that Joseph Brown was dead, a grant was given to William Samuel Johnson on February 27, 1782. When Brown was released, there was an immediate dispute over rights and a compromise was made. Brown was granted the town of Brownington, and Johnson received an official charter for the town of Johnson on January 7, 1792.

Johnson's first settler, Samuel Eaton, arrived in 1784. Not long afterward, Johnson's settlement began to prosper. Luck was on Johnson's side in 1814, when British soldiers entered the town during the Battle of Plattsburg on a raid. Thanks to the settlers' hospitality, Johnson was spared and the raid never occurred. By 1880, Johnson residents were taking full advantage of the Lamoille River's waterpower. Several sawmills, the Johnson Woolen Mill, a butter tub, and a starch factory were built.

In 1828, the Lamoille County Grammar School—later the Johnson Normal School, the Johnson State Teachers College, and Johnson State College—was built. Next to religion, education was a priority for early Johnson early settlers. It was known that "the more you know, the further you'll go . . ."

"Johnson is a small town with many close circles and groups that come together to form a very fine community."—Phyllis Jewett.

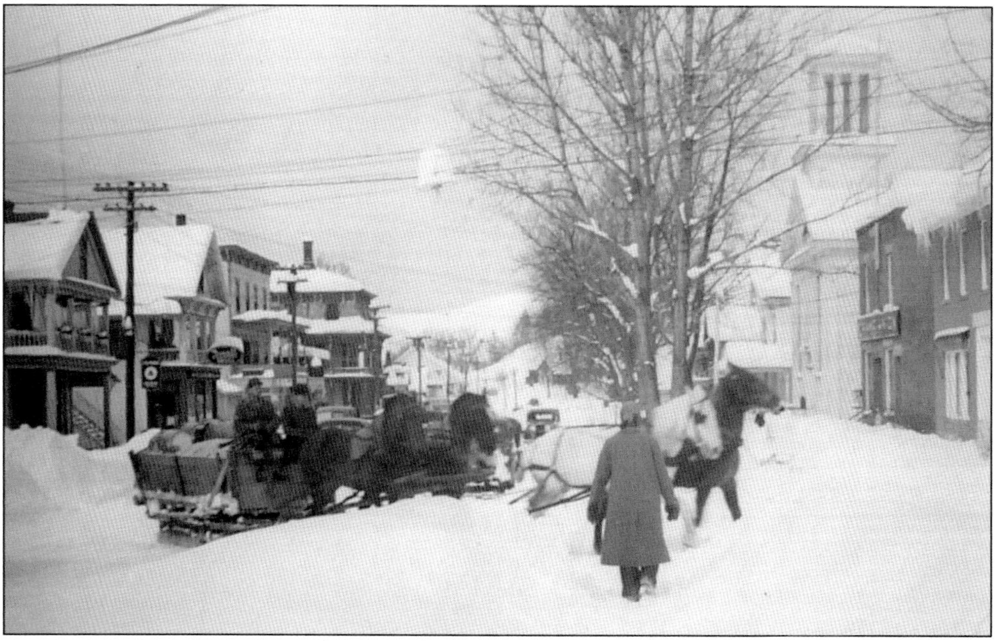

JOHNSON VILLAGE, C. 1937. The Nye Block store was built in 1868 by Leonard Knight. It was called one of the most elegant stores in the state, outside of the cities. The building's size was meant to accommodate Johnson's expected growth after the arrival of the railroad. It can be seen here on the left and toward the center.

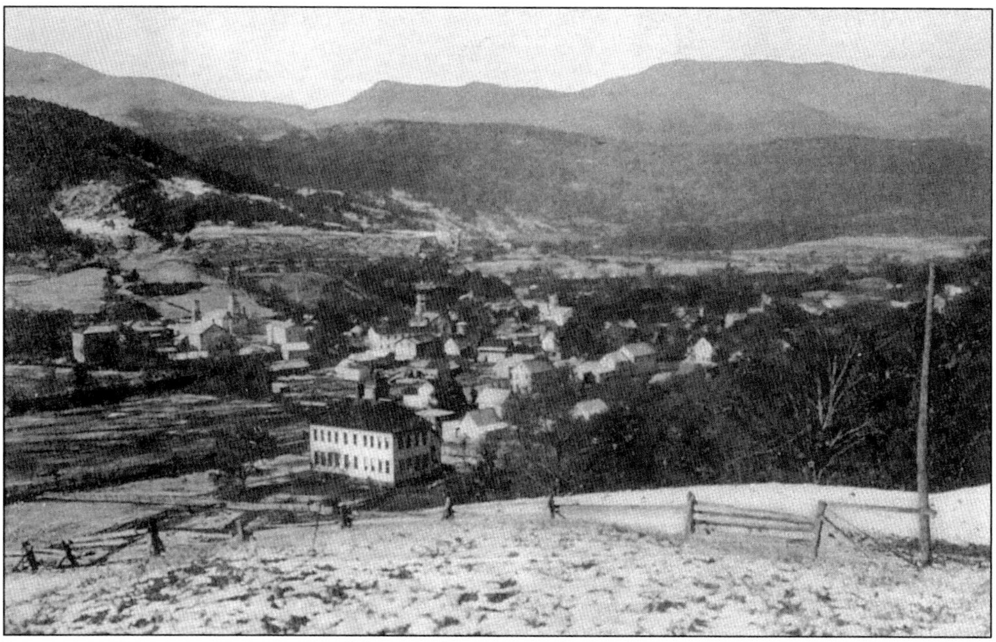

JOHNSON VILLAGE, C. 1900. Lifelong Johnson resident Phyllis Jewett was born in a Main Street building in 1918. She has watched Johnson grow and change over the years and points out that while Johnson was a railroad town, it never grew as people thought it would. The big population boom expected after the railroad's arrival never really came, and Johnson's growth has been gradual since the initial influx, as with the rest of Lamoille County.

Eight

A Town Photographed 1970–1980

Robert L. Hagerman was born on November 7, 1931, to Mr. and Mrs. Oliver Hagerman Sr. in Evanston, Illinois. He graduated from Yale University and never married. He worked often as a newspaper reporter and, in 1966, he came to Morristown where he became actively involved in several public service organizations. Hagerman authored *More About Morristown 1935–1980*, published in 1982 by the Morristown Historical Society as a supplement to Anna Mower's original work.

Hagerman also took more than 3,700 photographs of Morristown as a comprehensive photographic record. He felt that, with time, they would grow in historical value, saying, "Already some things I froze in time have changed." He presented the Morristown Photo Archive, 1976–1980, shortly after its completion for public viewing in the Morristown Centennial Library. He also presented a copy to the Vermont Historical Society. Hagerman's time here in Morristown was short, yet his contributions were enormous. He died on December 16, 1982, after a two-year struggle with advanced multiple myeloma and further complications from diabetes. Those who knew him loved him dearly, and those who did not know him, knew of him. As a tribute to the man who was taken before his time, I present to you the following photographs by Robert Hagerman.

"It is not length of life, but depth of life."—Ralph Waldo Emerson.

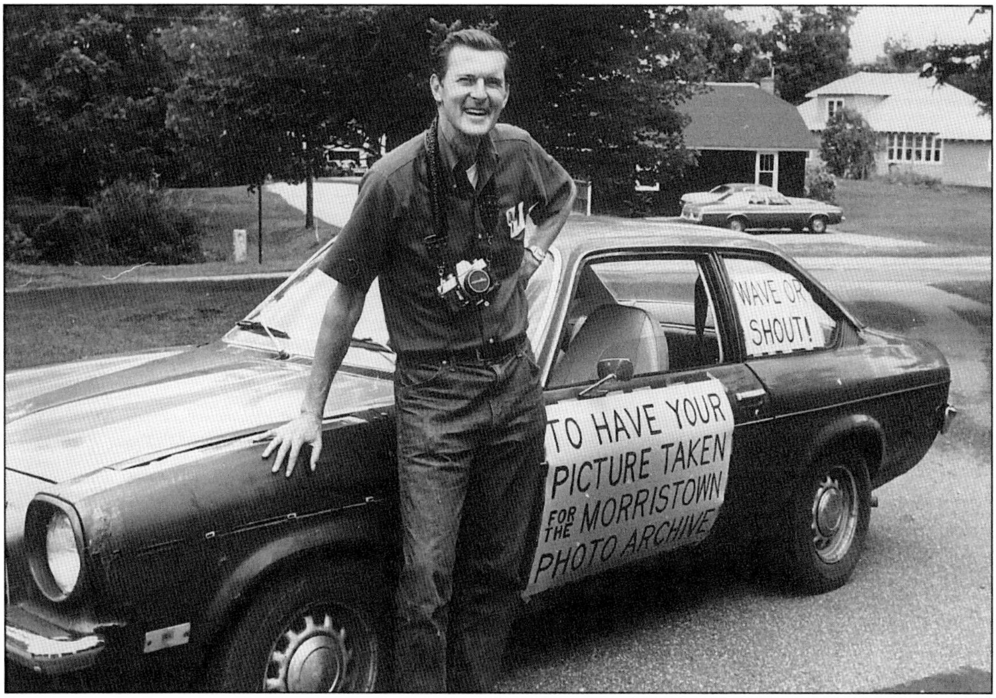

ROBERT L. HAGERMAN, 1978. The photographer himself took the time to have his picture taken on September 16, 1978. Anyone in Morrisville could simply wave or shout and Hagerman would be more than happy to take their photograph for the Morristown Photo Archive.

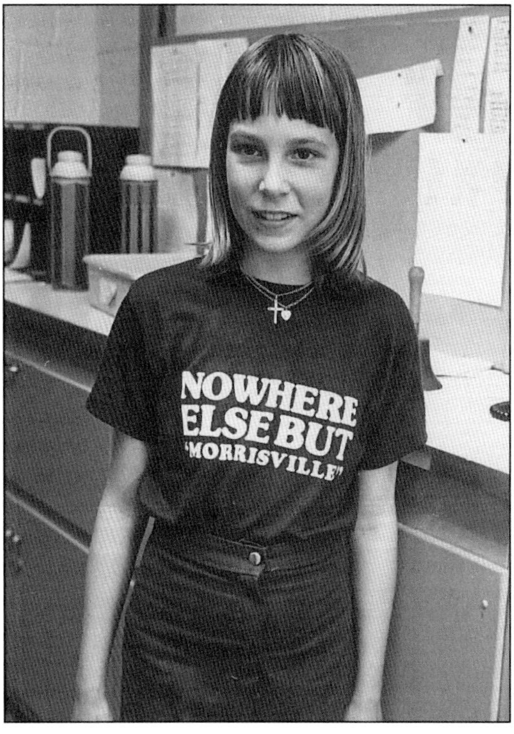

"NOWHERE ELSE," 1978. Morristown Elementary School sixth-grader Jean McCarthy summed up for photographer Robert Hagerman a common sentiment in Morrisville with her shirt reading, "Nowhere Else But Morrisville."

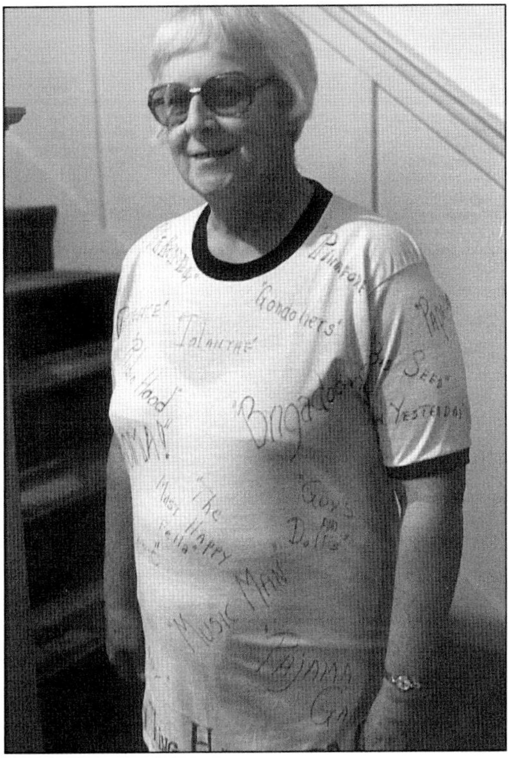

MARY SANDERS MITCHELL, C. 1978. Mary Mitchell was the first female member of the Morrisville Military Band in 1946, playing various instruments over the years. Her father, Don A. Sanders, her brother Willard K. Sanders, and her husband, Leslie Mitchell, were all band members who helped her cause. Soon, many other women were joining the band.

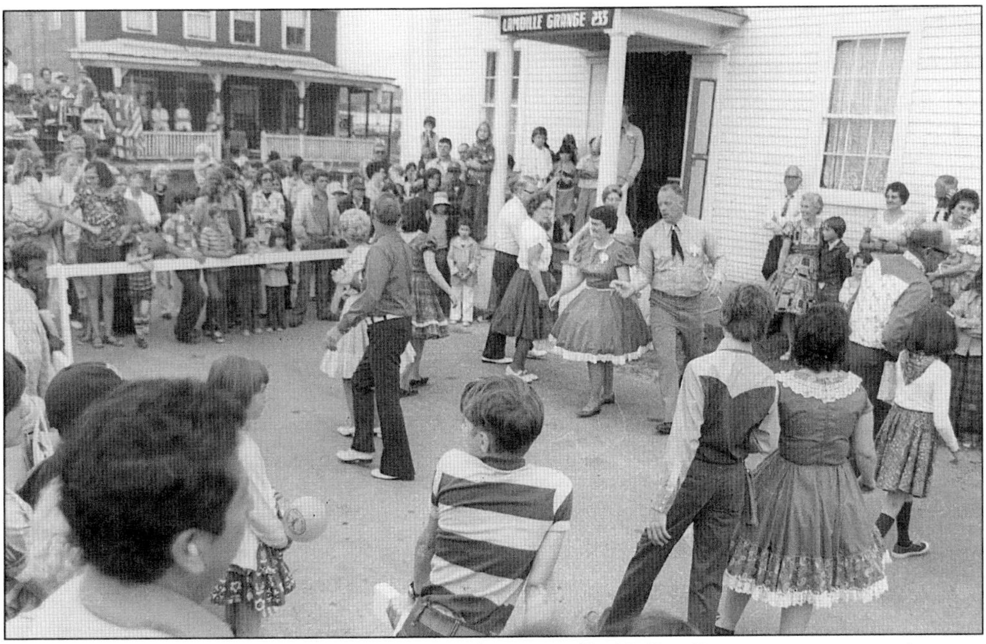

THE LAMOILLE VALLEY SWINGERS, 1977. The Lamoille Valley Swingers, a square dancing club formed in 1975, participates in the Independence Day celebration of 1977 in front of the Lamoille Grange Hall 233, on Pleasant Street. This building was the first Peoples Academy and, at the time of this photograph, had just undergone a major tower renovation. A replica of Peoples Academy's bell tower was constructed, and the original bell was placed in the tower.

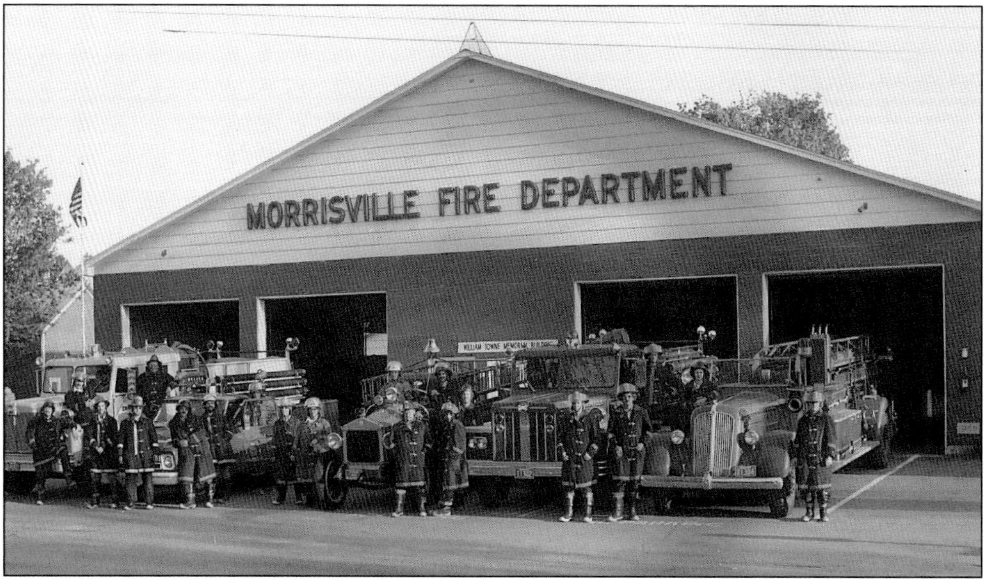

THE MORRISVILLE FIRE DEPARTMENT, 1978. Numerous fires plagued Morristown throughout the years. In 1968, Morrisville's own fire station, built in 1949, burned to the ground with much equipment being lost. A new station, the William Towne Memorial Building, was soon built in the same location. Another devastating fire struck Morrisville on February 24, 1927. Flames broke out in the third floor Centennial Block apartment of Albert Styles. The fire department responded quickly, but it was too late. Morrisville's great Centennial Block was gone.

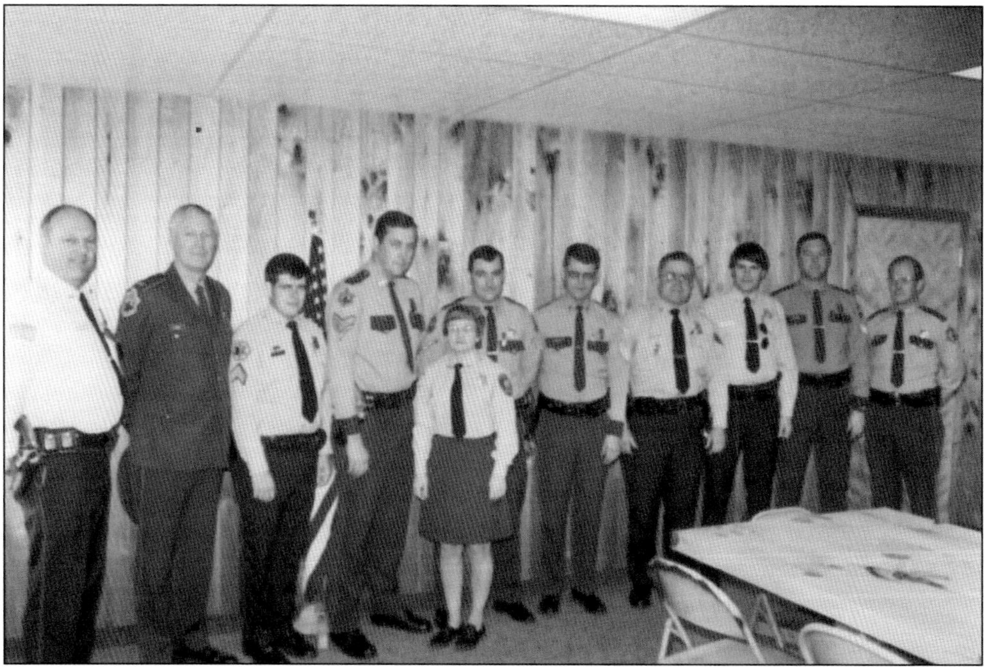

THE MORRISTOWN POLICE DEPARTMENT, 1978. Seen here shortly after the dedication of the new Morristown Public Safety-Ernest H. Clegg Building are officers of the Morristown Police Department and other law enforcement agencies. Lawrence "Bud" LaClair, longtime police chief, is at the far left.

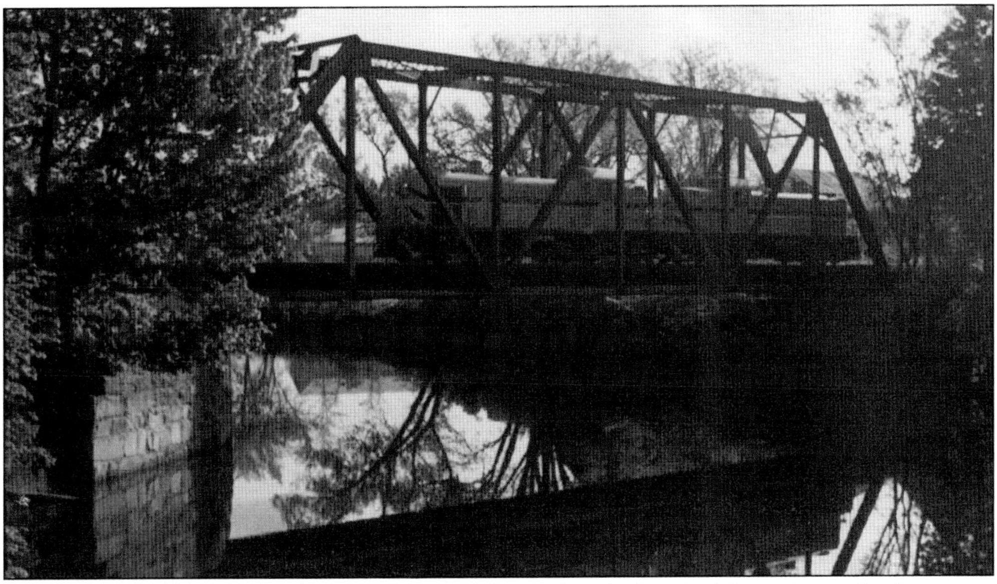

THE LAMOILLE VALLEY RAILROAD, 1978. The railroad that had brought such change to Morristown was, in the seventies, causing many headaches for Morristown and other towns along the line. St. Johnsbury & Lamoille County Railroad Inc. was established in 1945 and was followed by three decades of troubles. The railroad's operating speed had decreased from 25 mph to 8 mph, and the line was in desperate need of repair. A major rehabilitation was conducted in 1979, after the Lamoille Valley Railroad Company acquired the line.

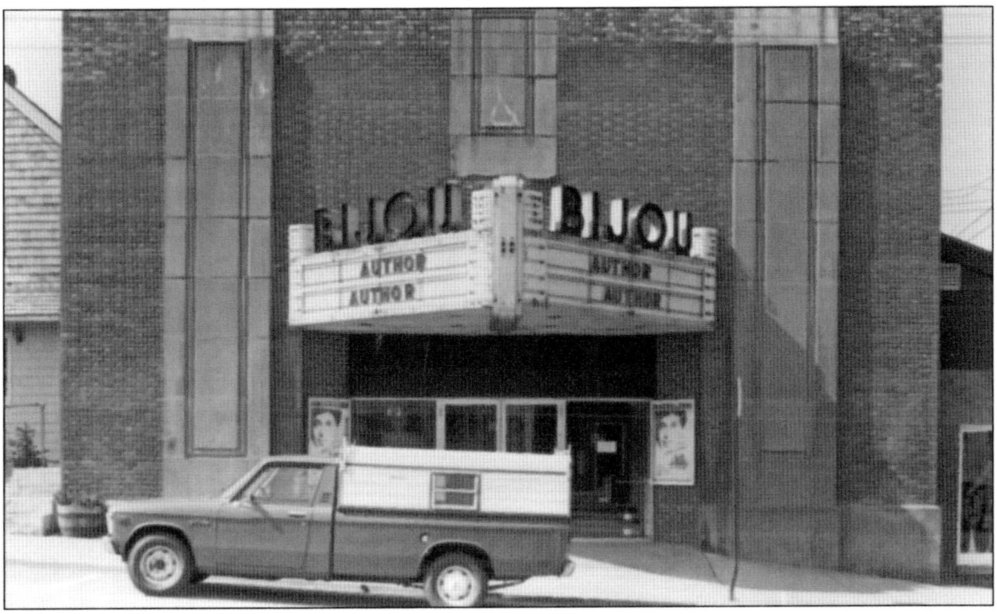

THE BIJOU THEATRE, C. 1978. Bijou Theatre founder Leon C. Emmons died in 1936, a year before the arrival of some major competition. His widow, Gussie Emmons, took over and commenced a major building program in 1937. The brick structure was constructed around the wooden one, the interior was then demolished and rebuilt, and the new and modern Bijou opened up four days before the Tegu Theatre, on September 6, 1937. The theatre stayed in the Emmons family until the 1980s, when it was purchased by J.B. McKinley.

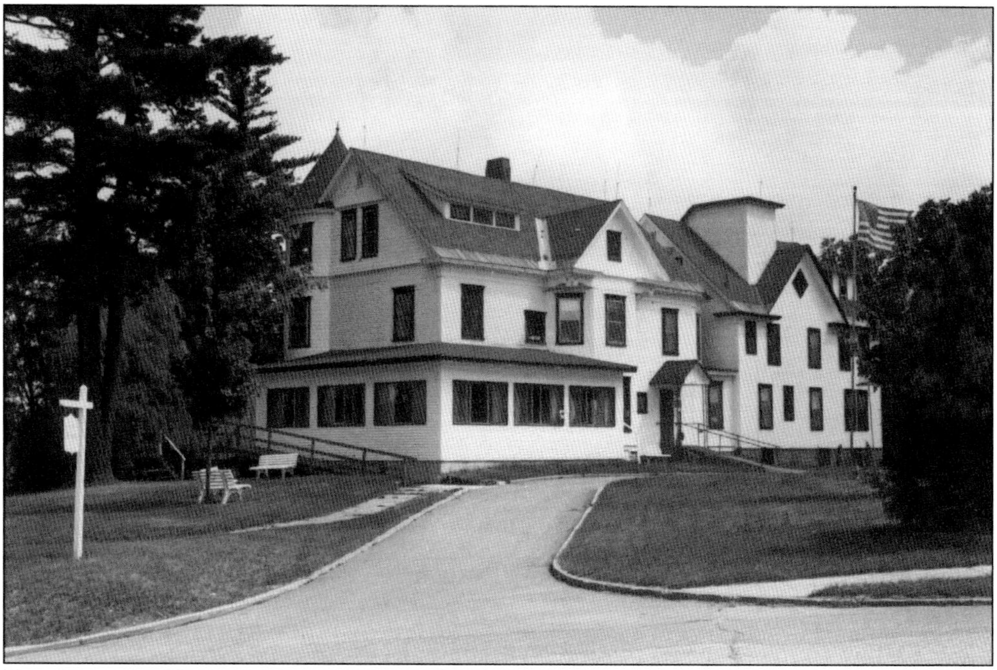

The Dumont Nursing Home, 1978. The former Copley Hospital opened as the Dumont Nursing Home in 1960. When the Dumont Nursing Home and Convalescent Center opened on Harrell Street in 1972, Herbert Kaufman from Massachusetts began Morrisville Nursing Home Inc. at the former Copley location. It was later renamed the Dumont Manor.

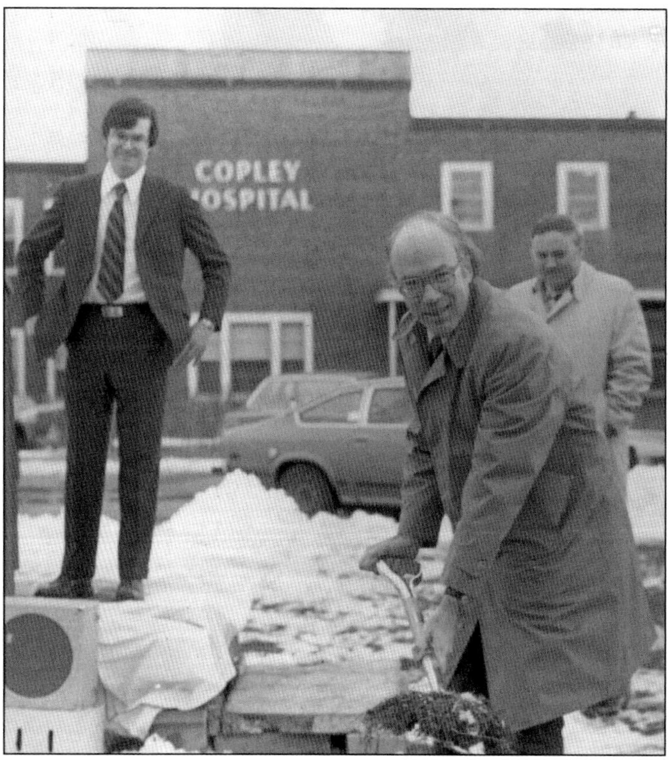

Copley Hospital, c. 1978. A modern brick structure was built in 1958 to house Copley Hospital. Throughout the years, the hospital conducted expansions to accommodate increasing numbers of patients and advances in the medical field. Following renovations in 1966, 1971, and 1975, there was a major modernization effort in 1978. Photographed here is the groundbreaking ceremony for the two-year building project.

THE LONG BRIDGE CONDEMNED, c. 1978. The Long Bridge over Lake Lamoille was one of the only bridges to survive the 1927 flood; however, time wore on the large bridge. Major repairs were made in 1969 and 1970. In 1977 the end came: Morristown's selectmen ordered the Long Bridge closed and barricaded due to its unsafe condition.

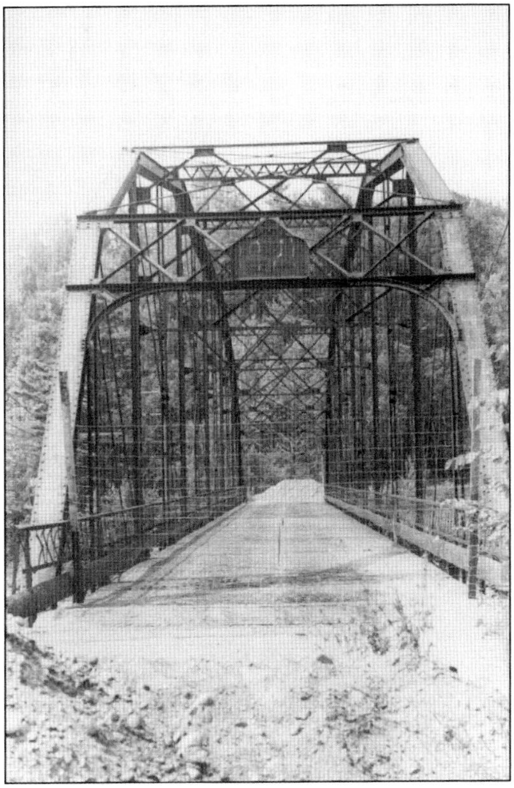

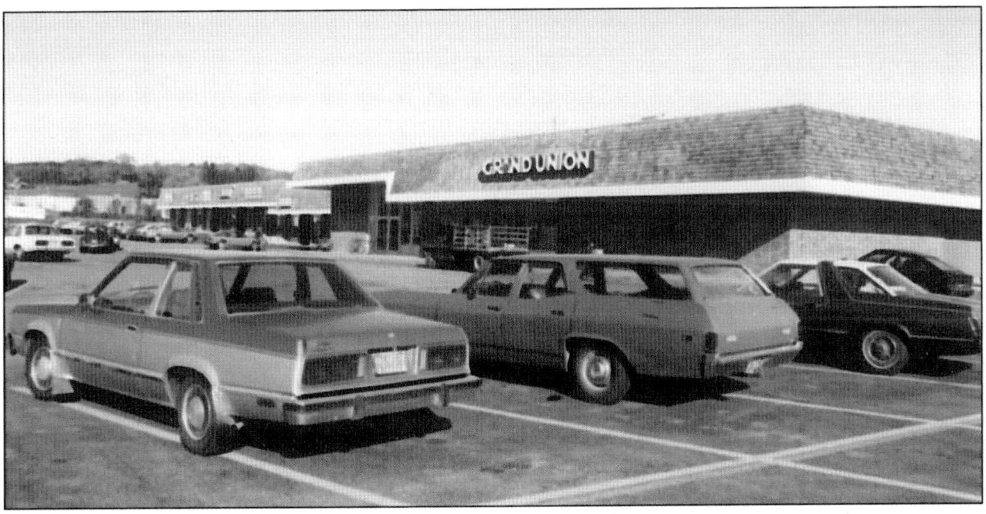

THE NORTH END, c. 1978. The sixties and seventies brought growing commercial activity into the Morrisville suburb, located to the north of the village. Much of the North End development occurred after 1965, as more and more businesses and industries began moving to the spacious lands off Brooklyn Street. Howard A. Manosh created the Northgate Plaza in 1971. This plaza soon became home to an expanded Grand Union Company store, as well as Fashions and Fabrics, Carwin Corporation, and Dot Discount Store.

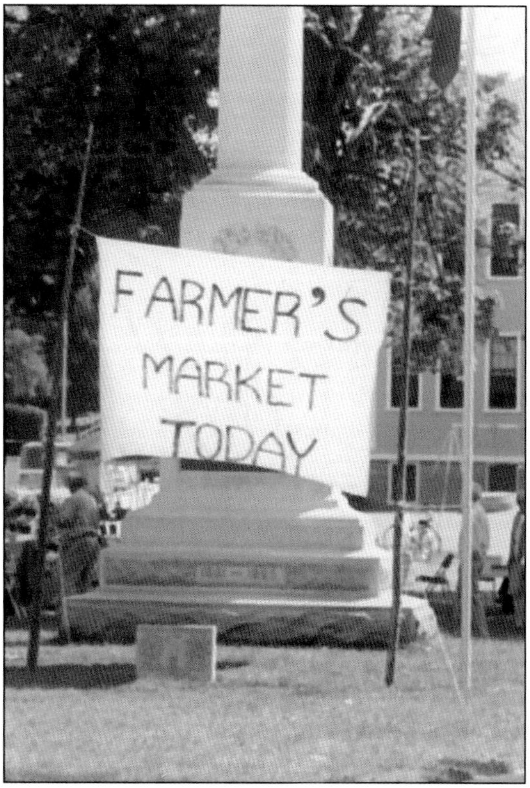

ACADEMY PARK, C. 1978. After an initial attempt by the Morrisville Food Co-op in 1975, the Lamoille Valley Farmers Market was restarted by the Lamoille Valley Growers Association Inc. in 1977. Pictured here is Academy Park in 1978, which was the home of the Farmers Market for more than a decade. Academy Park also remains the home of the still-used Morristown Graded Building, which was spared when the second Peoples Academy was demolished.

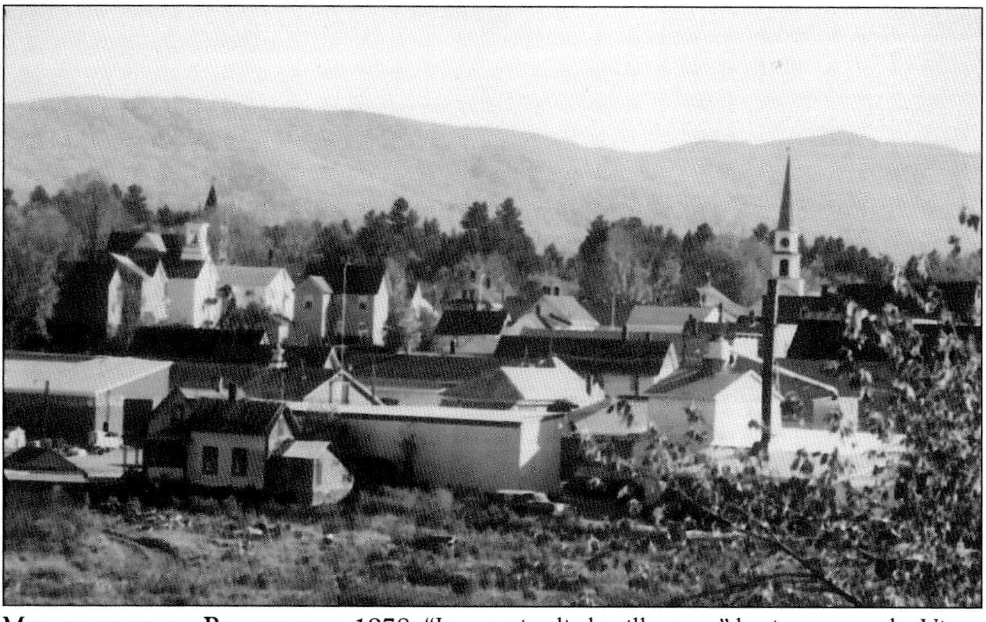

MORRISVILLE FROM BROOKLYN, C. 1978. "In a quaint little village . . ." begins a poem by Viany Ferland. Many would describe Morrisville as quaint or picturesque, and it seems certain that Robert Hagerman was one of those people. The photographs that he took during the 1970s show a town that is prospering, a town that is bustling, a town that is caring, a town that is friendly and, most importantly, a town that to so many is home sweet home.

Nine

TODAY, TOMORROW, AND BEYOND

The Morristown of 2001 is far different from that of 1901 or even 1991. To change is to transform and, as these very pages have shown, Morristown has gone through multiple transformations since its initial settlement. Someone once said, "the only thing that is permanent is change."

Today, Morristown continues to thrive and prosper; yet, like many towns, it is constantly under the pressures of further growth and development that could lead to unwanted change. The hope is that Morristown will remain a vibrant town and will maintain a strong sense of community far into the future.

"The future depends on what we do in the present," said Mahatma Gandhi. The decisions made today will impact the town that the next generation will inherit. The current generation can help shape the Morristown of tomorrow, ensuring that a strong community is sustained. It took the effort, determination, cooperation, and sensibility of previous generations to create what is all too often taken for granted today. Even greater efforts will be needed to maintain all that is treasured.

With this book's conclusion at hand, please think about the images that you have seen, the events, the places that are no more and never will be again, and the people whose very existence was frozen in time through them. Most importantly, think about the dreams that filled the minds of Morristown's past residents and led them to mold the community that they did. May our dreams, too, bring a bright future.

"The future belongs to those who believe in the beauty of their dreams." —Eleanor Roosevelt.

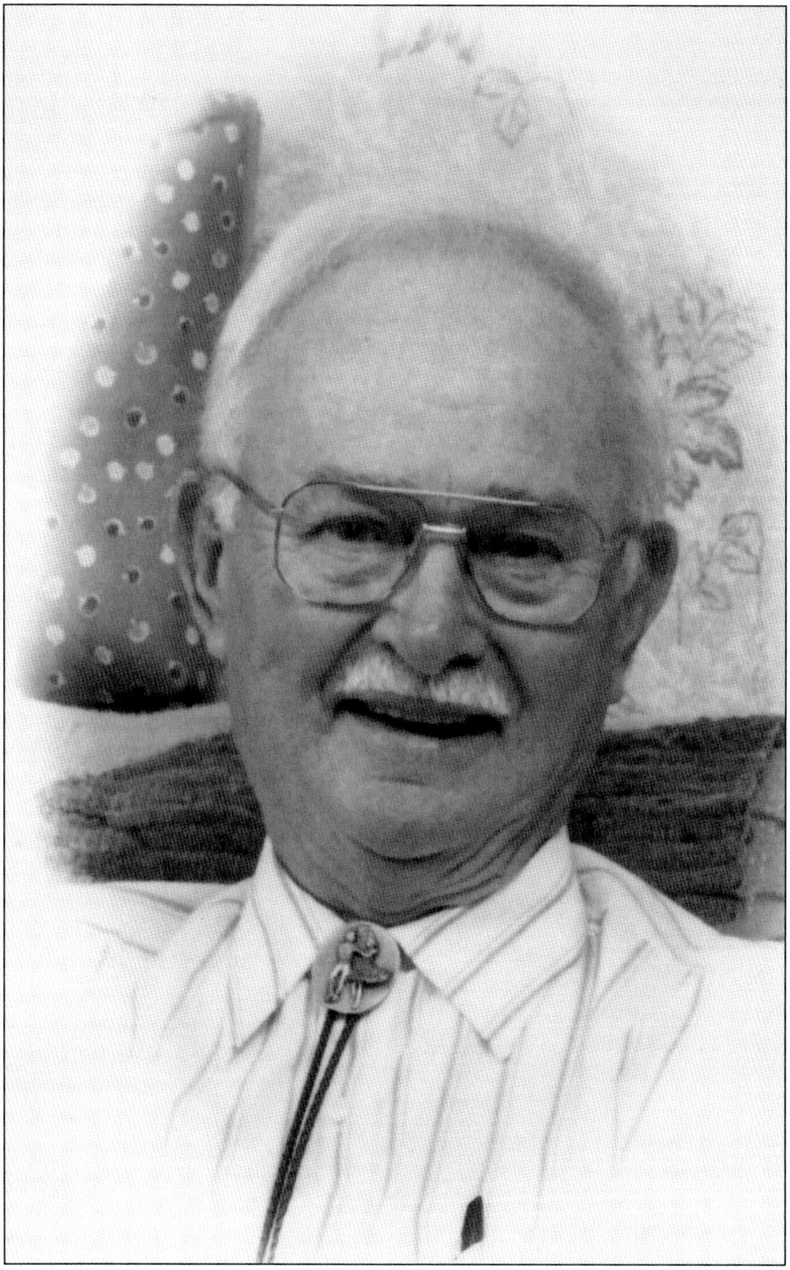

Sydney C. Mander, 1922–1998. Sydney Mander served as town clerk for 25 years and did much for the community in which he lived. He was well respected, loved by many, and he truly made a difference in Morristown. He and his wife, Ida Mander, were instrumental in Morristown's 1981 bicentennial celebration. Every year he emceed the Independence Day parades. As J.B. McKinley wrote after his death, " 'Syd' emceed a town not just parades . . . He knew what is important—family, community, country . . . He helped us to remember what it is to be an American . . ." Mary Ann Wilson, town clerk, said of Mander, "No one will ever epitomize Morrisville the way he did."

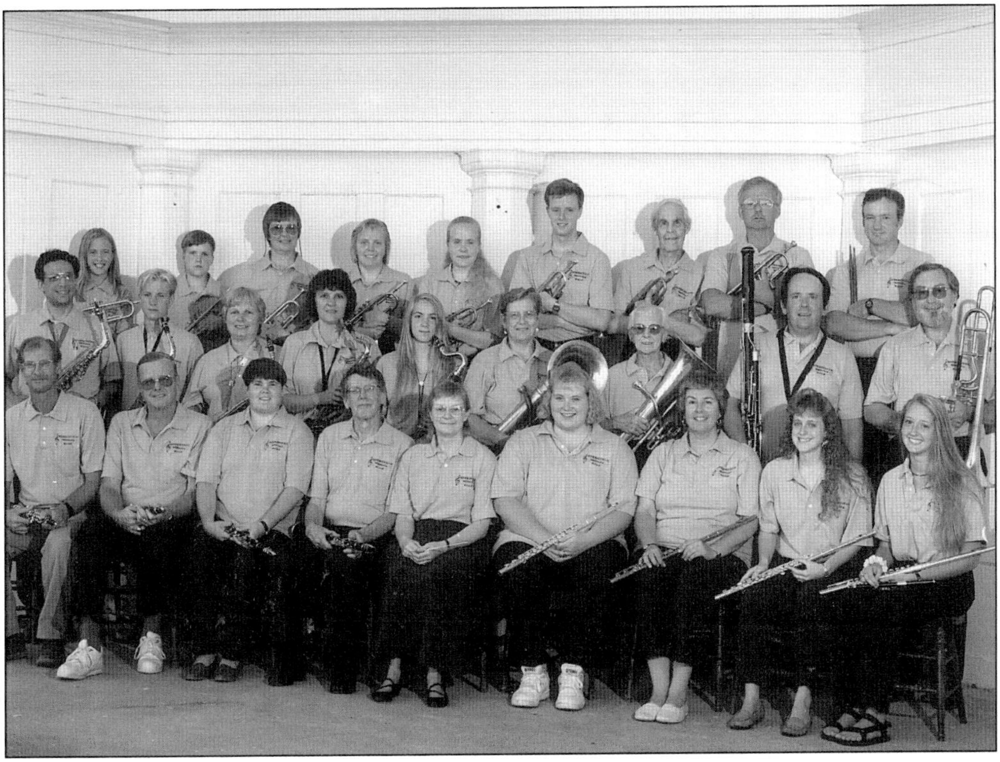

THE MORRISVILLE MILITARY BAND, 1995. On July 1, 1995, the Morrisville Military Band celebrated its centennial. Bands from Williston, Rutland, Fairfax, Fletcher, Westford, and Waterbury helped the Morrisville Military Band celebrate with a parade and daylong festival, which concluded with a massed band concert. Band member Mary Mitchell composed "The Centennial March" for the occasion. Enjoying the celebration is the author, who began playing in the band in 1994 and is pictured on the right with saxophonist Jessica Allen.

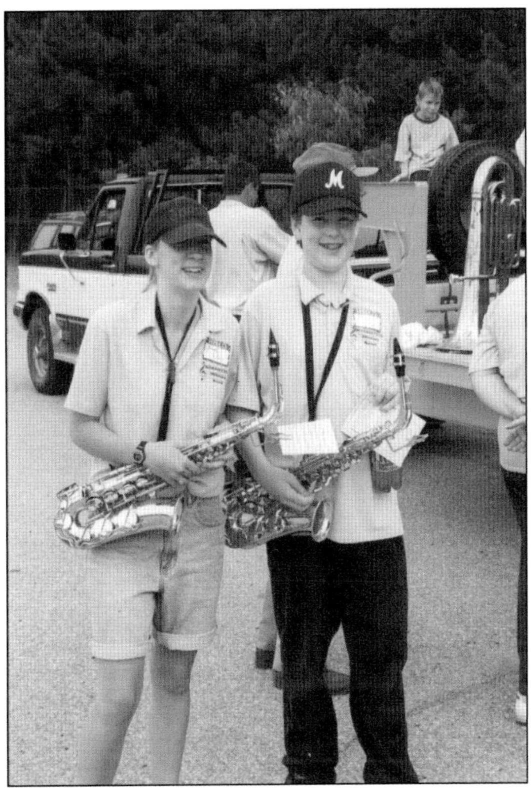

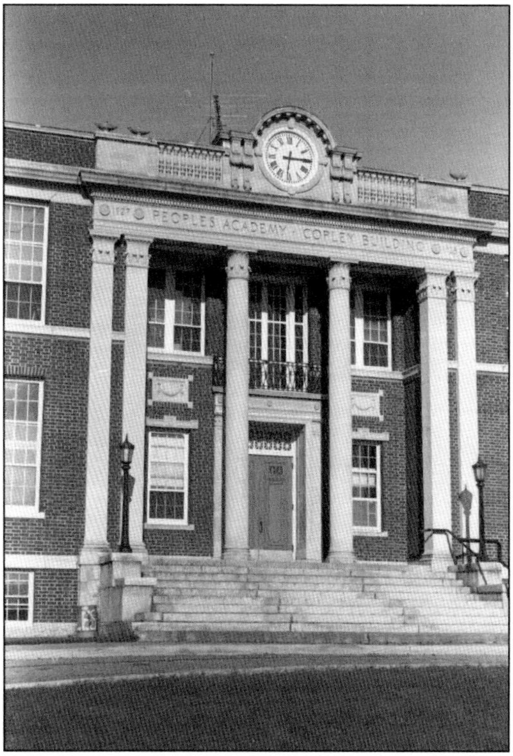

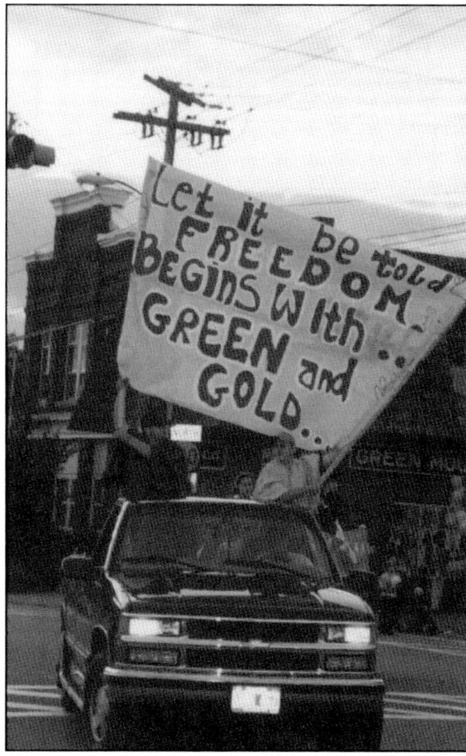

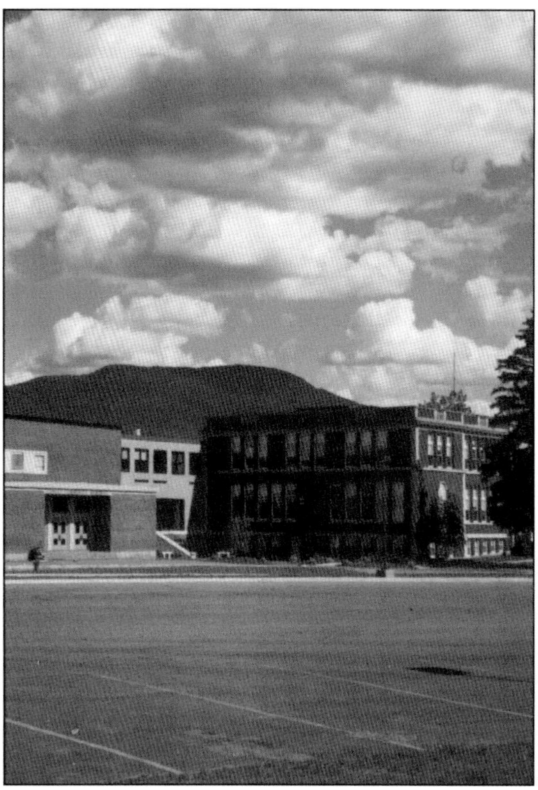

"LET IT BE TOLD," 1999. Peoples Academy has undergone many improvements throughout the years, and in 1998–1999, a major construction project commenced. The building's size was becoming inadequate, and several facilities, including laboratories, were in desperate need of upgrades. Although very costly, the end results were extraordinary. Much has changed at Peoples Academy since its original founding, but what has not changed is the commitment to educating and learning that is embodied in the faculty, staff, administration, and school board. Morristown is becoming known as one of the better school systems in the state, and Peoples Academy is on the leading edge of new advances in the field of education, whether technological or methodical. Peoples Academy alumni and students are proud of their school and share their sentiments with homecoming parade onlookers in 1999: "Let it be told, freedom begins with green and gold."

The Morrisville Post Office, 1999. In 1966, the Morrisville Post Office moved to its Main Street location, where it remained for 34 years. When it became evident that a larger post office was necessary, a great effort was made to keep it downtown. Many options were presented, and after the renovation of the Drowne Block (which had been the home of Adrian's Store and then Ben Franklin's) was completed in 1999, the post office moved into its former home of 61 years.

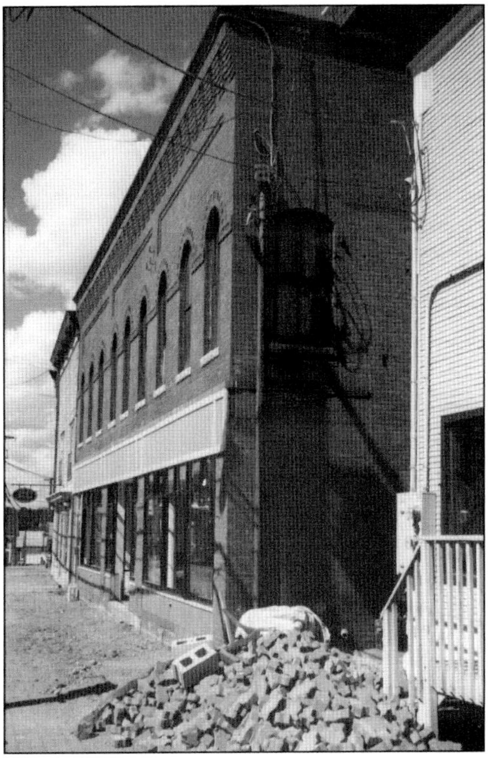

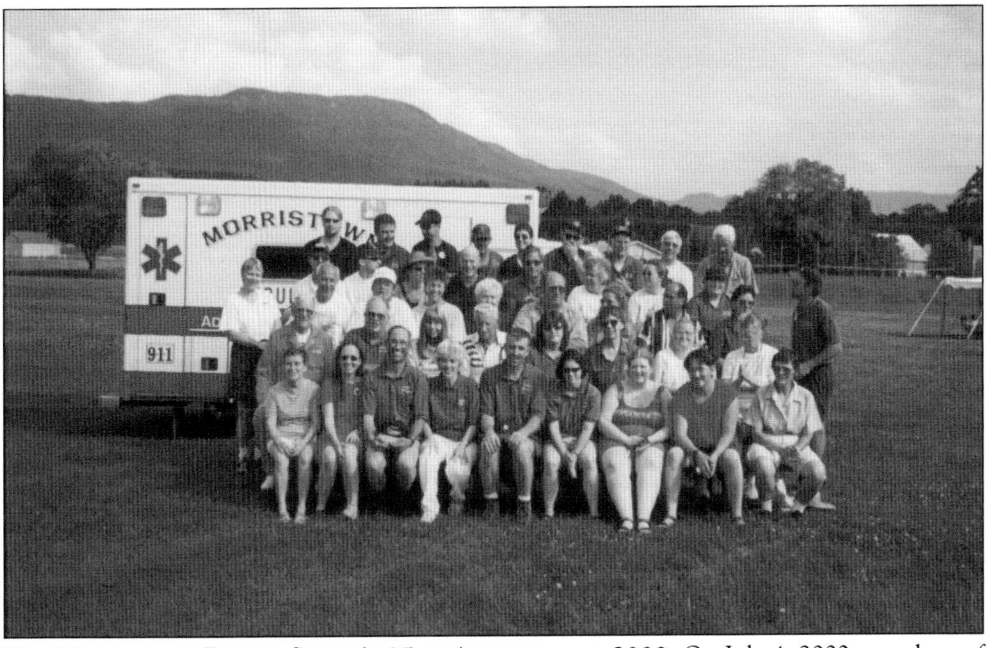

The Morristown Rescue Squad's 25th Anniversary, 2000. On July 4, 2000, members of the volunteer Morristown Rescue Squad celebrated their 25th anniversary in conjunction with Morristown's Independence Day celebration of the past, present, and future. Although often in need of more volunteers, the rescue squad is a dedicated and committed group—an invaluable segment of the community.

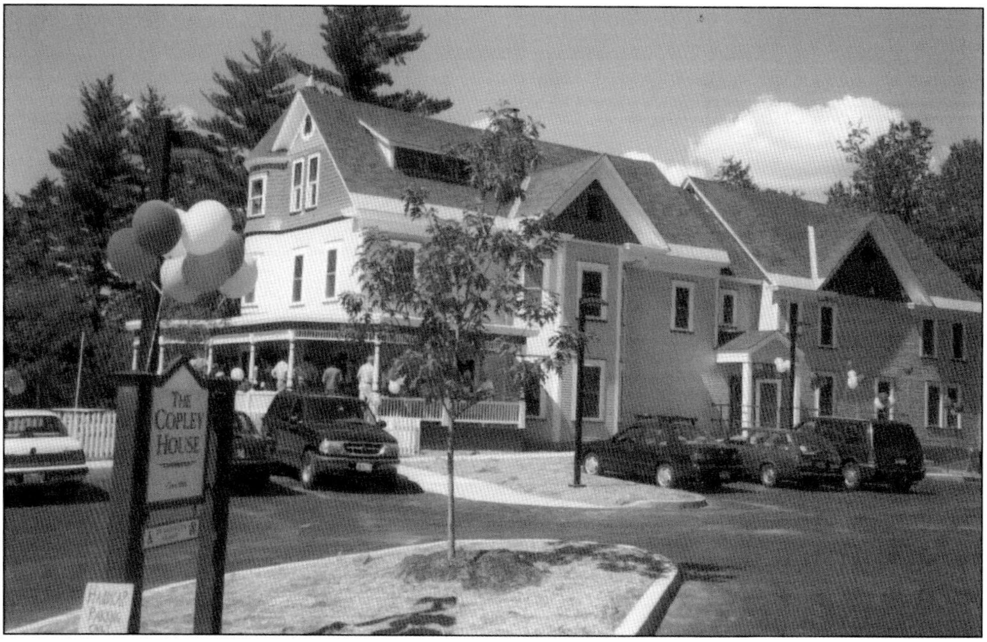

THE COPLEY HOUSE, 2001. On July 20, 2001, the former Copley Hospital and Dumont Manor was officially dedicated after a major renovation and restoration by the Lamoille Housing Partnership, which converted the 105-year-old building into low-income housing for persons with mental disabilities.

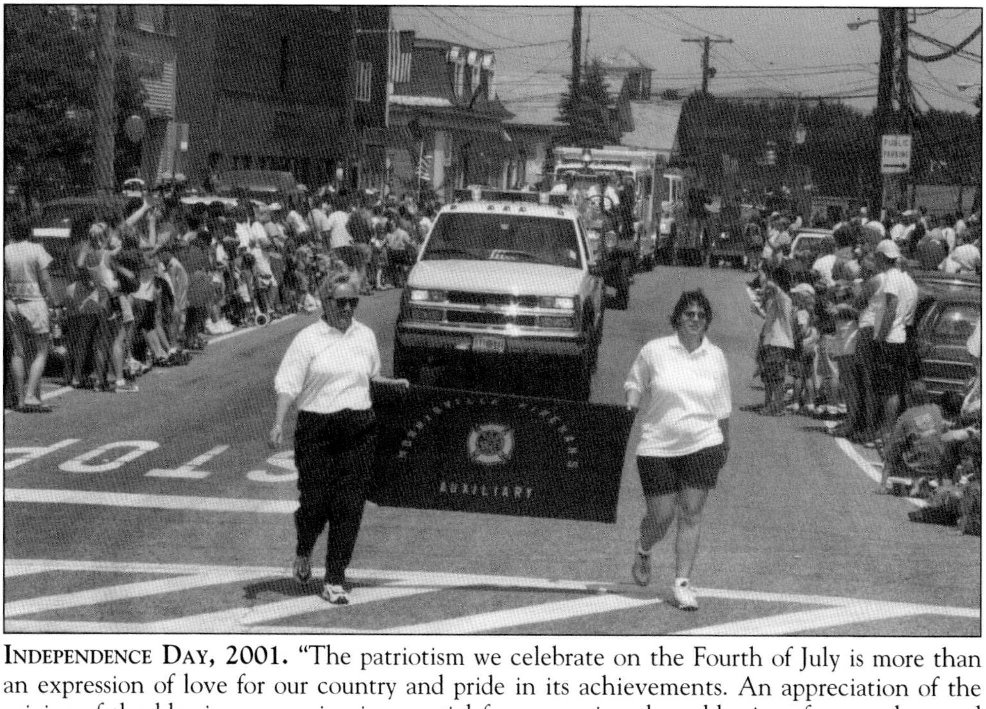

INDEPENDENCE DAY, 2001. "The patriotism we celebrate on the Fourth of July is more than an expression of love for our country and pride in its achievements. An appreciation of the origins of the blessings we enjoy is essential for preserving those blessings for ourselves and our children and grandchildren. . . . Patriotism is more than a sentiment. It is a necessity." —Thomas Sowell.

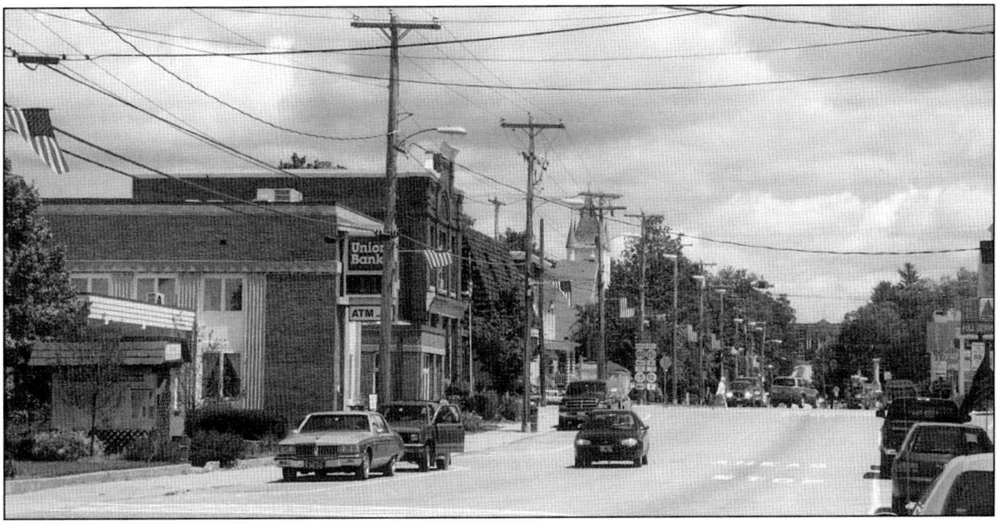

THE PRESENT. "This has always been my home. Even though I've lived in other places, Morristown has truly always been my home," said 91-year-old Marguerite Woods. "So much has changed . . . Morristown has been so good to me." Then, she smiled and said, "It's your turn . . . it's your generation." Her words brought to mind these of Pres. John F. Kennedy: "the torch has been passed to a new generation of Americans." Marguerite Woods continued, "It's a small world . . . and for goodness sake, we don't want anymore wars." The current generation has experienced far fewer hardships than those of yesteryear. There has been no Great Depression, no World War, no draft, no presidential assassination, no gas shortage, no food rationing, and no threat of impending annihilation. Many who lived through those experiences are beginning to depart; they are passing the torch, hoping that it will be carried on.

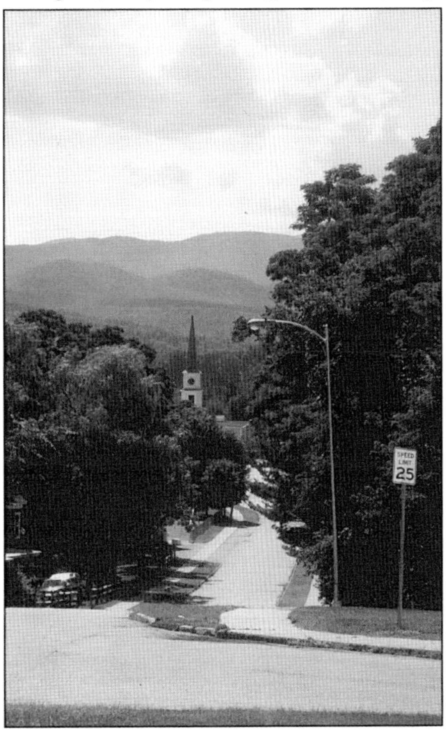

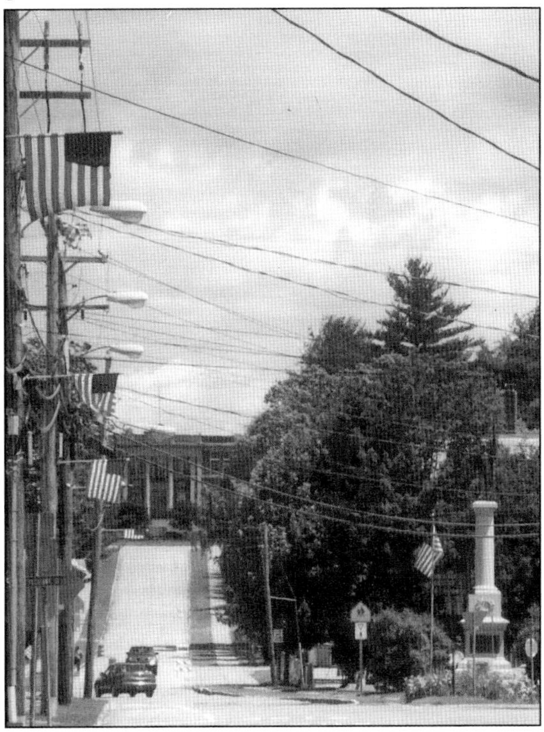

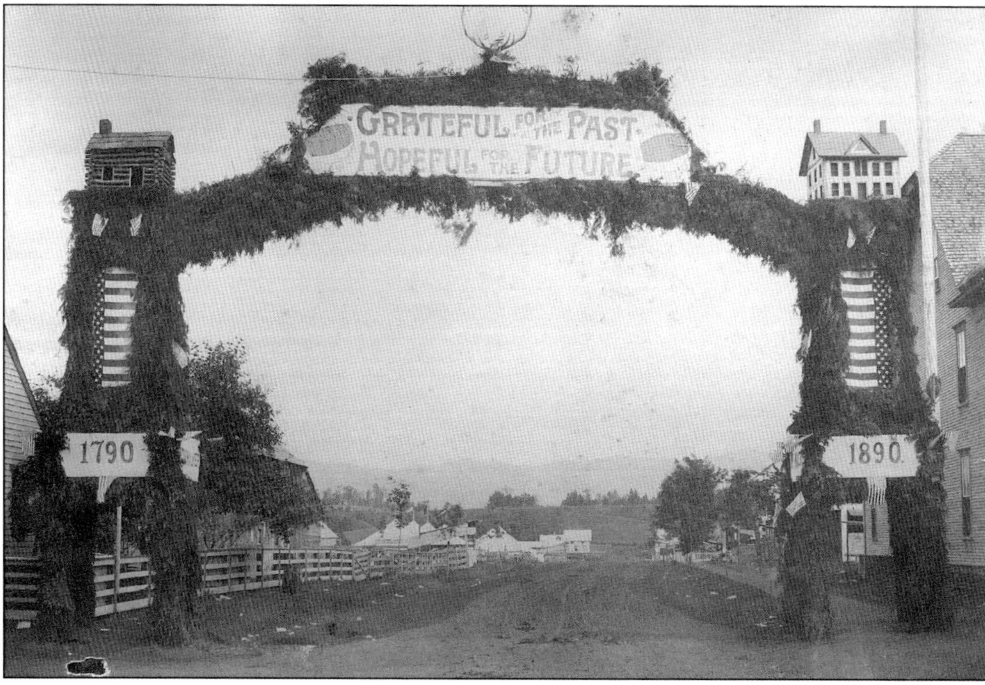

"GRATEFUL FOR THE PAST—HOPEFUL FOR THE FUTURE, 1890." The words painted on Morristown's Centennial Arch bring to light the spirit of those who lived in somewhat uncertain and often turbulent times. They were truly grateful for their past, and they were very hopeful for the future and what it would bring. To requote the sentiments of prominent Morristown citizens H. Henry Powers and Sydney Mander, "We have much to be proud of and more to be hopeful for" . . . much more.

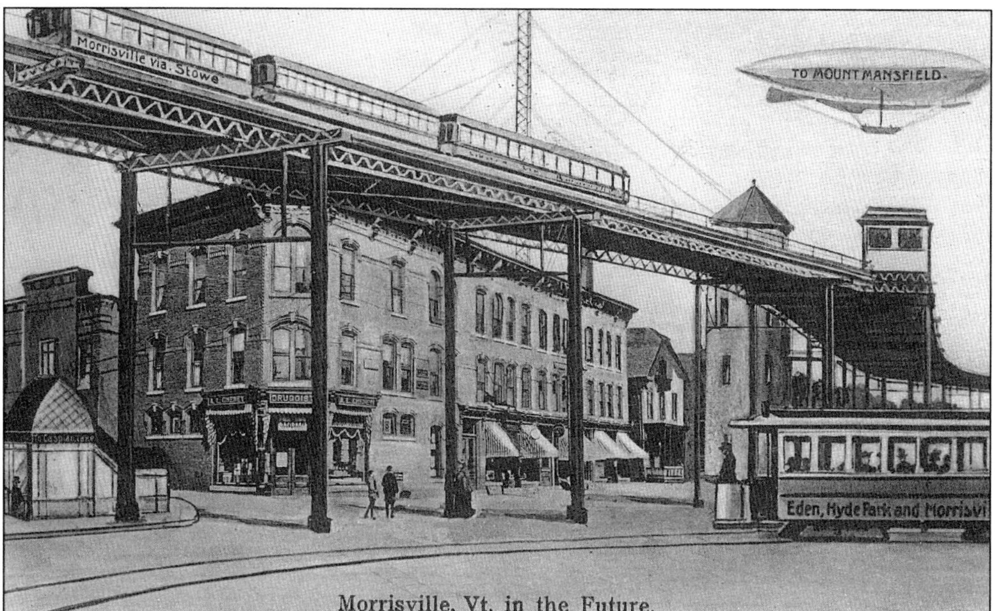

MORRISVILLE, THE FUTURE. "The future lies before you, like paths of pure white snow. Be careful how you treat it, for every step will show."—Unknown.